Paul Laxton

26 YEARS BEHIND BARS

THE RECOLLECTIONS OF A PRISON GOVERNOR

Limited Special Edition. No. 6 of 25 Paperbacks

Paul Laxton was born in Darwen, Lancashire in December 1952. He was educated at St Mary's College, Blackburn, which was then a Roman Catholic Direct Grant Grammar School for Boys. In 1979, the author graduated from Keele University with a Bachelor of Education degree (upper second class honours) in history and education. He taught at High Schools in King's Lynn and Newcastle-under-Lyme before joining the Prison Service as a uniformed officer in 1984. The author served at nine different jails, rising to hold posts as Deputy Governor at Dover, Ford and Lewes prisons, before retiring in 2010. An active trade unionist, he served on the National Executive Committee of the Prison Governors Association from 2007 and was awarded Distinguished Life Membership on retirement. After leaving the service, he moved to West Yorkshire with his wife, Leonore, where he keeps himself busy as Editor of the Retired Governors Newsletter, Chair of the West Yorkshire Civil Service Pensioners' Alliance, and as an active member of the Campaign for Real Ale. When he can find the time, few things make him happier than a day at the races. Paul Laxton is a lifelong Blackburn Rovers supporter and a member at Lancashire County Cricket Club.

This book is dedicated to my former colleagues in the Prison Service, who despite the massive spending and staffing cuts, and the indifference of politicians and public alike, keep on doing a superb job under the most trying working conditions in a generation.

Paul Laxton

26 YEARS BEHIND BARS

THE RECOLLECTIONS OF A PRISON GOVERNOR

AUSTIN MACAULEY PUBLISHERS™
LONDON • CAMBRIDGE • NEW YORK • SHARJAH

Copyright © Paul Laxton (2020)

The right of Paul Laxton to be identified as author of this work has been asserted by him in accordance with section 77 and 78 of the Copyright, Designs and Patents Act 1988.

All rights reserved. No part of this publication may be reproduced, stored in a retrieval system or transmitted in any form or by any means, electronic, mechanical, photocopying, recording or otherwise, without the prior permission of the publishers.

Any person who commits any unauthorised act in relation to this publication may be liable to criminal prosecution and civil claims for damages.

A CIP catalogue record for this title is available from the British Library.

ISBN 9781788788472 (Paperback)
ISBN 9781528956246 (ePub e-book)

www.austinmacauley.com

First Published (2020)
Austin Macauley Publishers Ltd
25 Canada Square
Canary Wharf
London
E14 5LQ

To my long-suffering wife, Leonore, for her unstinting support and quiet acceptance of frequent and lengthy retreats to my study.

Table of Contents

Chapter 1   11
Introduction

Chapter 2   14
Prisons and the Society They Serve

Chapter 3   30
Prisoners

Chapter 4   45
Prison Officers

Chapter 5   60
Prison Governors

Chapter 6   77
Prison Workers Miscellany

Chapter 7   92
Prisons and Politicians

Chapter 8   111
Prison Service Inspectors and Reformers

Chapter 9   125
Prison Service Employment Practices and the Headquarters Culture

Chapter 10   142
Prison Service Staff Corruption and Discipline

Chapter 11   160
Postscript: A Prison System in Crisis

Chapter 1
Introduction

I formally joined Her Majesty's Prison Service on 8 May 1984 having taken my entry test at Leicester on 1st October the previous year, and having been interviewed at Norwich on 22 December 1983. My recall does not extend to knowing when the letter of acceptance arrived, except that it was some weeks later, and neither can I recall the medical examination. As ever in the Civil Service the wheels ground slowly. The only criminal justice connection to my seniority date, as it was known, that I can find is that 8th May is Gary Glitter's birthday. Rather more pertinent and better known is that it is also the anniversary of VE day. My final day in the Prison Service was 14 October 2010, curiously enough the anniversary of the Battle of Hastings. On reflection, the coincidences seem very apt given the extent to which I felt embattled in the latter part of my service as my hopes of career advancement were met with a blank wall of senior civil servants and their acolytes of which more is said in Chapter 9.

I can recall certain events from the first day with almost as much clarity as the last. Walking up to the gates of HMP Stafford in the same lounge suit that I had worn for my wedding some two years earlier, I was filled with natural trepidation about whether or not I had done the right thing in abandoning the familiar world of school teaching for the alien world of prison. The Governor of Stafford at the time was the late Colin Heald, a formidable man who dominated a room and in front of whom we swore the oath of allegiance. Even though I am a confirmed unbeliever, I could not summon up the courage to ask to affirm, rather than swear. Later that morning, the four of us who had reported that day sat on a swivel chair to be photographed. We were told with great relish that this chair was perched on what had once been the trapdoor for the gallows at Stafford. Whether this was true or not, I cannot say with absolute confidence. The last execution at Stafford actually took place as far back as 1914. The prison was closed for civilian use in 1916 and did not re-open again until 1940. During World War II, it was used as an overspill local prison and so did not have a direct relationship with the courts that could hand out the death sentence. After the war, Stafford became a training prison, which it remains to this day. A working gallows was therefore not needed. However, the accommodation used to take photographs at HMP Bedford where I served from 1991 to 1993 was most certainly based in the old hanging shed last used for the execution of James Hanratty, the A6 murderer, in May 1962. The building was demolished in 1993 after a Category B prisoner who had broken out of his cell used the old hanging shed as a bridge to the perimeter wall and made good his escape. After the demolition, many staff obtained gate passes to take out bricks from the building as souvenirs.

For the record, I will list the establishments and HQ divisions where I served for over 26 years, but otherwise this book takes a thematic rather than a chronological approach and these will fit into the narrative to illustrate the theme under review. After completing an initial four weeks of induction to the service at Stafford, it was off to the Officer Training School at Wakefield for eight weeks before being posted to HM

Detention Centre Werrington House, close to my then home in Stoke-On-Trent. There I remained as a Prison Officer until October 1990. In that year, I had been accepted on to what was then the new Accelerated Promotion Scheme, and so I was off to Wakefield again; this time to the now defunct Staff College at Love Lane just by the prison, as a member of APS 1 for six months of management training before being posted to HMP Bedford as a Principal Officer; thus missing out the Senior Officer rank. The uniformed rank structure is explained in detail in Chapter 4. I served at Bedford from April 1991 to October 1993 and after leaving the Accelerated Promotion scheme transferred to Wakefield which still houses the largest concentration of sex offenders in Europe, many of them Category A. Having been promoted to the junior Governor grade, Governor 5, I transferred to HMP Woodhill, then a local prison, in May 1995. Two years later I was promoted in situ to Head of Operations and Security in what had just become a high security establishment. In November 1998, I moved on for a brief sojourn as Head of Security and Regimes Training at Prison Service College Newbold Revel near Rugby. I returned to the field in January 2000 as Deputy Governor of HM Young Offender Institution Dover and in April 2001 moved sideways to be Deputy Governor of Ford, an open prison in West Sussex that has had its fair share of negative publicity in recent years. During my tenure at Ford I was Acting Governor for three months pending the appointment of a new 'number one'. In January 2005, it was time for a stint at what was then Surrey and Sussex Area Office in Woking for what was euphemistically called development. Nevertheless in the same year I finally passed the Assessment Centre and was now eligible for promotion to in-charge Governor as a fully accredited Senior Operational Manager, to use the terminology employed by the Prison service. I would never be promoted substantively to in-charge Governor and had to content myself with a stint as Temporary 'Number One' at HMP Coldingley for three months in the summer of 2006. The following year I moved to Lewes for my third Deputy Governor post and remained there until May 2010. My final posting was to Headquarters in May of 2010, regarded by many of us as the equivalent of exile to a Siberian Power Station, the fate suffered by former Soviet Premier Georgy Malenkov (1902–88), for a low key role as a functionary in Population Management Unit. Five months later it was all over. I departed at the conclusion of the Annual Conference of the Prison Governors Association (PGA), of which I was a National Executive Committee member. I shall say more about the PGA in chapters 5, 9 and 10.

    Enoch Powell (1912–1998) is reputed to have said that all political careers end in failure. It may explain why so many former senior politicians feel a need to write their memoirs. Powell himself was a notable exception although he does have an admiring biographer in Simon Heffer. It is fair to say that the overriding purpose of most memoirs is to set the record straight and justify the author's actions at critical points in their career. Politicians believe that their reputations are unfairly traduced by the media, and by supposedly loyal colleagues who frequently provide the media with the stories that determine their reputation. The desire to set the record straight is therefore an understandable if rather egotistical response. This sort of memoir is strongly autobiographical often emphasising childhood and family influences. It is my view that with rare exceptions, (Denis Healey being the best example) political memoirs shed more heat than light, and do not enhance the reputation of the writer. Few emerge as more rounded individuals and even fewer appeal to the general reader. They are devoted followers of the 'Great Man' theory of history, unselfconsciously depicting themselves as the great men and women who for a time in their lives directed events and made and broke the careers of the lesser mortals who appear in the index. They most certainly do not subscribe to the notion that "Life is what happens to you while you are busy making other plans". (Allen Saunders 1957, more famously John Lennon 1980)

It is important to confess that my own Prison Service career ended in failure. I did not achieve my ambition to be a substantive in-charge Governor, a 'number one'. I make no apology for at times not avoiding the temptation to set the record straight despite knowing the pitfalls. However, only politicians can sell books on the back of frustrated ambition alone. The Strangeways riot of April 1990, a drama that was played out live television for 25 consecutive days thrust the prison system into the public eye like never before. Notorious prisoners had escaped, IRA prisoners had starved themselves to death and the Sunday papers in particular ensured that the crimes of Myra Hindley were never forgotten by the public. Prison disturbances were not new but the wholesale destruction of a mighty institution like HMP Manchester was without precedent. It shook the penal system to its foundations. Since 1990 prisons have become part of the staple diet of the press. I hope then to appeal to the general reader whose interest in the prison system has been ignited by the popular press but remains unsatisfied by sensational headlines and occasional exclusives about notorious prisoners such as Ian Huntley. However, I would hope that this book proves to be more than just extended light reading. My intention is that this book is also educational and shows the penal system in the context of social, organisational and political change; in particular, the impact of the decline of deference, the suffocating nature of public sector bureaucracy and the rise of political correctness. It is intended that explanation accompanies information. For this reason, I have rejected a chronological approach in favour of a thematic one. The book is written from the perspective of a participant observer. It is not an autobiography nor is it a history, although inevitably it contains elements of both as it would fail without them. As a Prison Governor, I undertook occasional speaking engagements to local professional or voluntary organisations. They were always interested in the opinions of the practitioners regarding a range of criminal justice matters. I was always careful to differentiate my personal opinion from what was required of me when representing the Prison Service in public. In retirement there is no such constraint and there will be no shortage of opinion based on intellectual rumination, the observation of human behaviour over a long period, and personal and professional experience.

Chapter 2
Prisons and the Society They Serve

There is no single blueprint for the design of a prison in Britain. Much will depend on the age of the buildings being used and also on the type of offender being held. We owe the Victorians a great debt for their public buildings and they also bequeathed to us the forbidding dark fortresses with high walls that sprang up as penal establishments in our towns and cities. In 1815, there were still 225 offences punishable by death. This was known as the 'bloody code'. By 1861, when sodomy ceased to be a capital offence this had been reduced to four: murder, piracy, treason and arson in a naval dockyard. Occurring alongside the reduction in capital offences was the demise of penal transportation to the colonies as an alternative penalty to a date with the hangman. Transportation was officially abolished in 1868, but in practice it had ceased a couple of decades earlier as a consequence of much increased voluntary migration to Australia. The Victorians were therefore in need of an alternative method of punishment in the face of the assault by penal reformers on the bloody code and the decline of penal transportation. The sentence of imprisonment therefore replaced the former draconian punishments. Prior to the 19th century prisons mainly held individuals awaiting trial at the Assizes (replaced by Crown Courts in 1972) or held individuals awaiting the carrying out of transportation, death sentences and other public punishments such as whipping or the pillory. They also held debtors and before the 'Glorious Revolution' of 1688, those who displeased the King. The Tower of London was best known as the place where such political prisoners were held.

There were precedents for custody being used as punishment as opposed to the reasons outlined above. Where it was used it was normally combined with hard labour. As early as Tudor times, there was provision for vagrants and the idle, able-bodied poor to be sent to local Houses of Correction. Prison hulks were in use from 1776 until their abolition in 1857. The 1799 Penitentiary Act however, signalled the sea of change that was coming with respect to the punishment of less serious crime, i.e. that which did not attract the death penalty or transportation. It provided for single cells, silence and continuous labour. The Victorians and their immediate predecessors therefore embarked on a building programme. In 1816, the first national prison, Millbank, in London was opened. From here on prisons would cease to be mainly centres holding those awaiting trial, one of the punishments described in the previous paragraph, or discharge of debts although debtors continued to be imprisoned until 1869. They would be places of punishment that criminals would dread almost as much as the hangman or the dangerous voyage to Australia. The Victorian ruling classes retained both the fear of and contempt for the common people, 'the mob,' the violent potential of which had so disturbed an earlier generation of aristocrats that successfully steered the UK through the French revolutionary and Napoleonic wars, which raged intermittently from 1792 to 1815. An uncompromising combination of deterrence and retribution was as much a feature of the new penal code as it was of the old. To emphasise the purpose of prison, the Victorians introduced the treadmill and the crank, and gave prisoners unpleasant tasks such as picking oakum, the teasing apart of heavily tarred old rope to extract fibres that could be used in ship's caulking. These tasks were not abolished as part of a prison sentence until 1898 when later Victorian reformers were starting to question whether a harsh unremitting regime simply hardened the criminal and made them even worse. Courts also had the option to impose hard labour as an integral part of the sentence, and this was not abolished in England until 1948. Scotland followed in 1950 and Northern Ireland in 1953. In the Irish Republic, hard labour remained on the statute book until 1997. Rather like medieval castles with their high walls and forbidding gates they were designed to overawe the population, intended as much to deter from without as from within. Indeed the medieval castles at Oxford and Lancaster became prisons during the English Civil War, ceasing to function as prisons as recently as 1996 and 2011 respectively.

The typical Victorian prison was built to a radial design with an administrative centre as the hub and the prison wings as spokes. The inspiration was probably the plans produced in 1791 by Jeremy Bentham (1748–1832), a celebrated pre-Victorian thinker and philosopher who envisaged not just prisons but also workhouses, lunatic asylums and other institutions being built on the panopticon (all seeing and constant surveillance) design, although no true panopticon prison was ever built. The closest to the Bentham blueprint was Pentonville, North London, opened in 1842. As a rule, the accommodation blocks would be four and occasionally five stories high and from a central point on every level on prison officer could see clearly down each corridor. In the days of the separate system when prisoners were forbidden to speak to each other, prison officers, then known as warders, were ideally placed to see and silence idle chatter. In terms of supervision and staff safety in the modern prison system, the radial design continues to prove its worth. I visited the private sector prison at Forest Bank (Salford) before it opened. The contractors there were using the radial design but with the addition of a solid soundproof floor, roof if you were underneath it, which split off the top two from the bottom two landings thus enhancing staff safety. As private sector prisons then operated with lower staffing levels than the public sector, this was a very necessary enhancement.

Subsequently, the design of prisons rather like house building has been subject to architectural fashion and like high-rise flats has been the subject of design disasters. HM Prison Risley and HM Prison Coldingley opened in 1964 and 1969 respectively are just two examples with spurs, short corridors and blind corners that were the complete antithesis of the traditional radial design. The biggest design disaster of the lot was the now closed HM Prison Holloway, Britain's largest female establishment in the heart of North London, which was completely rebuilt between 1971 and 1985. A much superior design is the one used for both HM Prison Woodhill and HM Young Offender Institution Lancaster Farms opened in 1992 and 1993 respectively. These were the last two new prisons built in the public sector until HMP Berwyn which opened in 2017. Since then the Home Office and from 2007 the Ministry of Justice which took over the responsibility for prisons from the Home Office has preferred to commission new prisons from the private sector and to add wings and house blocks to existing institutions in a piecemeal fashion. I did not work at Lancaster Farms but I did work at Woodhill from 1995 to 1998. The four original house blocks for the main prison were each split into two identical triangular shaped halves with 20 single cells on each landing with the two upper levels being galleried. A large association and communal dining space was available on the ground floor, known traditionally as 'the ones'. Between each half was a sterile central core on three levels housing offices, storerooms, tearooms and the like. Ingeniously the buildings were angled so that prisoners in the communal area could not see any of the other three house blocks and thus were unable to see incidents elsewhere in the establishment. Lancaster Farms differed in having only two landings. The custodial blocks were light and airy wholly unlike the stygian gloom that pertains in many traditional establishments even at the height of summer. Unfortunately, Woodhill cost around £120 million to build rather than the projected £72 million. As a consequence, future designs would be more utilitarian.

However, all new accommodation buildings after the Manchester riot were built with integral sanitation in the cells and with the exception of a small number of prisons that have call systems that allow prisoners to leave their cells and use the toilets, usually known as recesses, during lock up periods, all cellular accommodation now has toilet facilities. We cannot blame the original Victorian architects for the absence of in-cell sanitation as they were originally provided and seen as an integral part of the silent, separate, single cell system that allowed prisoners to contemplate the enormity of their offending. Apparently in cell sanitation was removed at Mountjoy Prison in the Irish Free State in 1939 on the orders of a civil servant who believed that prisoners were using too much water. In England, the reason was more prosaic, simply to make room for more prisoners. For those of mine and many earlier generations of prison officers, the smell is one of the abiding memories of time spent in harness, a heady mixture of shit, stale urine and sweaty socks. No prison officer ever forgets morning unlock when 'slop out' is called and prisoners emerged from their cells, pots in hand, heading towards the recesses to tip the contents down the sluice. We were taught always to unlock away from the recess thus avoiding having prisoners behind you carrying the contents of their pots and deterring them from throwing the contents over you, not that it was always a deterrent. Those who were not able or not minded to use the pot defecated into toilet paper or newspaper, and the contents were thrown out of the window and between the bars on to the yards below. These were known as shit parcels. Every morning an individual prisoner or a work party under the control of a prison officer collected them before prisoners used the affected area for exercise or movement to activities. Christmas Day was no exception. When I joined in 1984, most prisoners wore prison clothing and few things were more disgusting than prison underwear and socks after being worn for a week. Plastic prison issue shoes only heightened the problem of sweaty feet. There was no incentive to look after prison issue clothing and socks were ideal receptacles for turds as an alternative to toilet paper.

The lack of in cell sanitation did not just mean the absence of flush toilets. It applied also to fresh water for drinking and for washing. The prison bathhouse is one of my abiding early memories. The visit to the bathhouse was a weekly ritual and prisoners were allowed precisely 10 minutes in the bath. Unless they used the gym, there was no access to showers. Washing was therefore carried out on a daily basis stripped to the waist in the same recess where other prisoners were emptying their pots. This was the grim reality in much of the prison estate when I joined in May 1984 at HMP Stafford. Some years later when I was a Principal Officer at Bedford, one of my tasks as wing manager was to appoint staff to what were called fixed posts. An officer appointed to a fixed post could reliably expect to carry out this duty on his or her scheduled shifts in between the usual landing duties carried out at unlocks, lock ups and mealtimes. Any brief delight that a probationer may have felt at gaining a fixed post so quickly was swiftly extinguished on learning that the post was in the bathhouse. At Bedford, the job was universally known as 'willy watching'. Fortunate was the junior officer who escaped the rite of passage of six months in the bathhouse.

As has been said, the Victorians built their prisons for single cell occupation and solitary contemplation. The problem with single cell provision is that it invites the cheap and lazy alternative to spending money on new accommodation. It is called 'doubling up'. By 1984 when I joined the Prison Service, the prison estate was suffering from severe underinvestment and neglect of infrastructure. Wormwood Scrubs was appallingly damp and the Prison Hospital at Brixton was an affront to a civilised society. Overcrowding simply added to the problems. Local prisons became human warehouses. The establishments most hard hit by overcrowding were the 'local' prisons, i.e. those which received prisoners directly from court, both sentenced and on remand. Unlike the training prisons which received prisoners on transfer from the locals to serve their sentence, they could not declare that they were full. It is of course exceptionally difficult for anyone to predict how many prisoners will arrive from court on a given day. The inevitable outcome was not just doubling up, but also trebling up. Small local prisons such as Bedford and Shrewsbury frequently held more than two and half times the number of prisoners for which space was officially provided. Risley Remand Centre as it was then had some of the smallest cells I have ever seen house three men. Remember that there was no in cell sanitation and that prisoners would leave their cells only to collect their meals, (and return promptly to their cells), to 'slop out', as the degrading practice of emptying pots was known, three times daily, and finally for the statutory daily one hour in the open air, marching around the exercise yards. In excess of 22 hours daily confined to these overcrowded cells was the lot of most prisoners in local jails. The exceptions were the fortunate few who had a job in the prison or who had acquired a place at education, itself frequently cancelled because of staffing constraints. Only Category A prisoners and those on the Escape list could routinely expect a single cell. Such a squalid environment had a brutalising effect on both staff and prisoners and was the catalyst for the Manchester riot in April 1990.

Prison numbers rose in the 1980s as a consequence of the Conservative government's tough stance on law and order. Mrs Thatcher's Government had released funds for prison building, but inevitably there was a time lag between the approval of plans and the opening for business. The government was determined not to suffer a similar embarrassment to that which it suffered in 1985 when it was forced into early releases on parole to alleviate overcrowding. The explosion of anger from prisoners came before the programme was anything like complete. Post-riot there was an improvement in conditions. Numbers fell as the courts turned to non-custodial penalties as alternatives to short-term incarceration in establishments which were seen as making people worse rather than better. By 1993, the prison population had fallen back to 42,000. However, that year Michael Howard became Home Secretary. His Labour shadow was Tony Blair, future Prime Minister. Mr Howard was a firm believer that prison works. Mr Blair took the view that Labour had previously been weak on crime and needed to rebrand itself as a party of law and order. His slogan of "tough on crime, tough on the causes of crime" became even better known than Mr Howard's mantra 'prison works'. Once in office in 1997 Mr Blair appointed a series of hard-line Home Secretaries as the major parties competed with each other in a macho competition to see who could be toughest on criminals, exhorted regularly by a popular press that bayed for blood. By 2004, the population had almost doubled. The average Crown Court sentence had increased from 20 months to 27 months. The rate of imprisonment by magistrates climbed from 6% to 16% in the same period. Given that the maximum sentence permitted to magistrates in respect of a single offence is 6 months this increased significantly the throughput of petty offenders in local prisons. The inevitable result was a return to overcrowding and a new building programme lagging behind. These days the system is more sophisticated than simply trebling up or bedding prisoners down on gymnasium floors. Each prison still has its Certified Normal Accommodation (CNA) but also now has a fixed overcrowding limit, called its Operational Capacity. Overcrowding is therefore official policy. Thus on a daily basis Population Management Unit and the Youth Justice Board for juveniles monitors numbers, facilitates transfers and arranges for prisoners sentenced or remanded into custody by the courts to be re-directed to an alternative local prison. If this is inconvenient for relatives and legal advisors to visit, this is simply tough. On occasions, police cells have been used. As there are relatively few juvenile establishments, these most vulnerable offenders can be placed up to 200 miles away from their home.

All male adults who find themselves in custody will be incarcerated in either a local prison or a dedicated remand centre until they are either given bail, have charges dropped, are acquitted, given a non-custodial sentence or transferred to an allocated training establishment to complete their sentence. Obviously only the last of these applies to those who were on bail pending trial. The system is broadly replicated for women and for young adults (over 18 but under the age 21). Juvenile offenders do not come into contact with the adult system and are not allocated from local prisons. The High Security Estate does what it says on the tin and houses those prisoners in Category A, those considered most dangerous to the public, those for whom "escape must be made impossible". Some local prisons have a high security function to facilitate the pre-trial remand of such provisionally categorised prisoners. Since 1995 there has been no Category A escape from a closed prison, although a Category A prisoner was sprung from a prison escort vehicle en-route to court in January 2012. Category B prisoners are "those for whom escape must be made extremely difficult". A Category B prisoner would not routinely be serving less than seven years. Most prisoners are in Category C defined as "those lacking the resources to escape but cannot be trusted in open conditions". Category D prisoners are "those who can be trusted in open conditions" and apart from those waiting transfer, are found exclusively in open conditions. All prisoners have regular reviews of their security and have the opportunity, based on risk to move down (and sometimes up) the system. Amongst women and young persons, a Category A equivalent prisoner is described as having restricted status. Female sentenced offenders are classified as closed, semi-open or open and young adults as suitable for closed or open. As one would expect, all remand (untried) prisoners are held in closed conditions.

Open prisons are probably the least understood and most misrepresented part of the prison estate. Indeed the notion of an open prison is an oxymoron. There are no walls and no barbed wire. The purpose of the fence is to stop the public from looking in rather than prevent prisoners from getting out. If you can imagine your garden fence which simply screens you from your neighbour when both of you are at ground level, then you've got it. Prisoners can and do walk out of the main gate. HMP New Hall was England's first open prison for adults, opening in 1933. In my time New Hall became a closed prison for female offenders. HMP Ford, perhaps the best known of the open prisons where I was deputy governor 2001–05, is actually divided by a main road. Every weekday morning and afternoon large numbers of prisoners clad in regulation green tracksuits and overalls trek across the road to the workshops and the large prison horticultural operation. They trek back again as the kitchens, communal dining area and sleeping accommodation are on the other side of the road. It is a familiar sight to the locals in this sleepy rural paradise situated between Arundel and Littlehampton in West Sussex. Also on a daily basis, a selected number of prisoners dressed in their own clothes take the 15-minute walk to Ford Station to catch the train to outside work or community projects. In open conditions, prisoners have rooms rather than cells. They have their own room key. Some will be housed in dormitories. At Ford one house block looks like 1970s student accommodation. The remaining accommodation is in single storey huts that once housed national servicemen. Until 1960 Ford was Royal Naval Air Service Ford, part of the Fleet Air Arm. Ford is not the only establishment that was once a military base. Between the two types of accommodation is a cricket pitch where in summer prisoner teams face local cricket clubs in friendly fixtures. The cricket pitch has another tradition. On the stroke of midnight on New Year's Eve, prisoners emerge from their rooms to do a conga around the boundary. Sadly in 2010 this fairly harmless tradition degenerated into a riot of which more in Chapter 3.

Excluding satellites there are eight open establishments for male adults and they are an integral part of the system. Additionally there are two open establishments for women and one for young male offenders. HMP Ford where I was Deputy Governor for four years is perhaps the best known because of the attention it has attracted from the press, often as a consequence of tip offs from within. HMP Leyhill has also attracted adverse attention mainly because of its role as the only open establishment catering specifically for sex offenders. The popular press and thus the general public throw up their hands in horror at the thought of sex offenders, murderers and other violent offenders living in open conditions separated from the community by no more than a flimsy fence. I would contend that the risk to the public is far greater if such prisoners were released at the end of their sentences from conditions of high security wholly unprepared for an integrated return to the community. Open prisons are almost all in fairly remote locations with little or no public transport with towns of any size being at least three miles away. It is a complete myth that there are small communities in fear of their lives. In reality such communities as there are co-exist peacefully with their prisons. At Ford until the staff housing was sold off after 1987 most of the inhabitants of the hamlet of Ford were prison officers living in quarters barely 400 yards from the prison. North Sea Camp on the Lincolnshire coast is probably in the most remote location of all amongst the prisons that are part of the open estate. Leyhill open prison is deep in rural Gloucestershire, and Standford Hill is on the Isle of Sheppey being one of the three prisons that is part of the Sheppey Cluster. Spring Hill is deep in rural Buckinghamshire, next door to Grendon, the unique therapeutic prison. Only Kirkham open prison in Lancashire is particularly close to a town with good public transport links.

The most iconic image of a prison is Dartmoor. It is also the most remote with the nearest town being more than twelve miles away. The small village of Princeton existed only to serve the prison, although like everywhere else, staff accommodation was sold at a discount to the existing prison officer tenants, many of whom over 30 years have inevitably sold up to wealthy retirees and second home owners. The image of Dartmoor is that of the forbidding, mist shrouded fortress that held some of England's toughest convicts. It is indeed a stunning sight as the prison comes into view at the top of the moor. Dartmoor had a major prisoner mutiny in 1932 which was resolved within two hours. There were no staff injuries and one prisoner received a gunshot wound. Prison Officers at Dartmoor had access to firearms until as late as 1956. My esteemed former Bedford colleague, Dave Bone, was the last mounted officer in the service and it is his proud boast that he carried out the final mounted shift on Christmas Eve 1973. A photograph of him mounted can be found in the Dartmoor museum. Staff rode ponies to supervise prisoners at outside work on the moor. Absconding from work parties was the favoured mode of escape. However, getting off the moor was fraught with danger for the unwary. Frost that penetrated to the bone, fog that totally disorientated the escapee and bogs that could suck a man to his doom, were and still are significant hazards. Perhaps the most famous absconder was gangland enforcer Frank 'The Mad Axeman' Mitchell in 1967. However, it is much more likely that a car organised by the notorious Kray twins collected Mitchell at a convenient rendezvous, rather than him engaging in a yomp across the moors. Contrary to public perception Dartmoor has now been a Category C prison for more than 25 years. During World War I, after conscription was introduced in 1916, it housed conscientious objectors who were treated much more harshly than their counterparts in World War II. Eamon De Valera (1882–1975), future Premier and President of the Irish Republic was also incarcerated in Dartmoor for a period after the failed Easter Rising in Ireland in 1916. After the war, it resumed its role as the penal dustbin for the most incorrigible criminals. Now those roles are history. It no longer houses those who are legends amongst the criminal classes. The modern Dartmoor prisoner is much lower down the food chain, home to those simply deemed untrustworthy in open conditions but lacking the resources to escape.

A genuine purpose built fortress (other than a castle) that has been adapted for use as a prison can be found on the Western Heights at Dover where I was Deputy Governor 2000–2001. The site was originally used as part of coastal defences against invasion by the French Emperor, Napoleon Bonaparte, at the beginning of the 19th Century. The Prison Commissioners acquired the site in 1952, and in 1957, it opened as a Borstal. With the abolition of Borstal training in 1983, it became a Young Offender Institution until being re-rolled as an Immigration Removal Centre in 2002. Unlike most closed establishments that are protected by high walls and fences, apart from the gate lodge area, Dover is protected by a deep moat. Young Offenders who dropped themselves into the moat in a bid to find an escape route were disappointed, that is those fortunate enough not to fracture or break bones as a consequence of a twenty foot drop. They would have to be rescued by staff and face the inevitable extension to their sentence in the subsequent disciplinary procedure. One story has passed into legend and no doubt been improved with the telling. An immigration detainee succeeded in scaling the wall of the gate lodge from inside and jumped to freedom. Unfortunately, he broke his leg after jumping from a height of fifteen feet. Determined to make good his escape he dragged himself to the garden of a residential property a couple of hundred yards from the prison, into which he collapsed exhausted. Unfortunately, he chose the Governor's garden!

My first posting after prison officer training was HM Detention Centre Werrington House, on the edge of the Staffordshire Moorlands, close to Stoke-On-Trent. Werrington, as it is now known, still houses young offenders aged 15–18. In 1984, it was a Senior Detention Centre housing young men between the ages of 17 and 20 at the time of sentence with a tough regime that was abolished in 1988. Discipline was military in nature. Unlock was at 06.30 and bedtime was at 21.00 with lights out an hour later. Every morning after breakfast there was an outdoor parade which included military drill following which the trainees, as they were known, were marched to work. In fact they marched almost everywhere, including to the prison chapel for divine service, which at one time was compulsory. Roman Catholics attended Mass, but every other inmate was placed in the default category of Church of England. I can still recall the spectacle of around 60 trainees marking time outside the chapel whilst being sworn at both profusely and profanely by an escorting officer, all under the beaming gaze of the chaplain in full priestly garb awaiting the arrival of his flock. If, as an officer, you were detailed chapel, you accompanied your charges into the chapel. One Roman Catholic colleague regularly took Holy Communion when supervising Mass. It did not discourage him from swearing at trainees on the return march to the dining room.

On Saturday mornings, the living accommodation was cleaned from top to bottom. The highlight of Sunday morning was the Governor's inspection. Boots were bulled, bed linen made into rectangular packs, and shaving kit and cutlery were laid out on the bed. Trainees stood to attention when it was their turn to be inspected. The accommodation at Werrington in those days was not cellular, apart from a couple of punishment cells. Instead the inmates lived in large ward like dormitories. The dormitory officer was expected to ensure an immaculate turn out at Governor's inspection. The minority of officers who like me were not of a military background, had to learn speedily what was required. There was an hour's compulsory Physical Education daily and two hours at weekends, unless the trainee had a visit to which they were entitled once a fortnight. P.E. sessions were hard with a heavy emphasis on circuit training and general physical fitness. Organised games were largely for the weekend. With only two PE instructors on a small staff in a small establishment that held no more 120 trainees, prison officers particularly the younger ones assisted with sports and games at weekends. The object was to channel excess energy and testosterone. A quiet evening's association period was a sign of a job well done. Radio and TV were both heavily restricted. A normal week's pay in 1984 was the princely sum of 57p. This was enough to purchase an extra letter in addition to the free one that was issued and a couple of chocolate bars. Detention Centre trainees were not permitted to smoke. At the time they were the only sentenced prisoners not permitted the tobacco privilege. Hard physical worked filled the gaps between sleeping, eating and PE. Floors were scrubbed by young men on their hands and knees. In the prison gardens, there was the backbreaking work of weeding amongst the establishment's own vegetable patches. The meals were unexciting and unappetising but the trainees needed every calorie and there was little waste. Every day the Governor would come to the dining room and taste the meal in front of the trainees. Fortunately, he liked Cottage Pie with cabbage or swede (both grown in voluminous quantities at the prison) which was pretty much the staple diet. For those who reached the top privilege level, there was a chance to work outside the gate on the prison farm. There were no risk assessments and safe systems for milking cows in those far off days. As a regime it was tough and enforced with military inflexibility. Prison officers were on top and the trainees knew it. Despite the harsh regime and arbitrary discipline few kicked against it.

Detention Centres for the 14–21 age group split into Senior (17–21) and Junior (14–16) were provided for in the 1948 Criminal Justice Act. It was this act which abolished birching as a punishment available to the courts and Detention Centres giving a short, sharp shock to the recipient of the sentence were seen as filling the gap. However, unlike Approved Schools from which a good number of trainees would have graduated, corporal punishment was not available. Adult prisoners and Borstal trainees could still be birched for serious offences committed in custody such as mutiny, gross personal violence or gross insubordination by order of visiting magistrates. Birching in penal establishments was abolished in 1967 by reforming Home Secretary Roy Jenkins. The Detention Centre sentence was normally three or six months and exceptionally nine months where consecutive penalties were involved. The regime was intended to punish but more crucially by its harsh nature to deter. It was specifically not intended to be a stepping stone to Borstal training and adult imprisonment. The intention was to stop petty offending from escalating with a 'short, sharp shock'. As such the sentence was much shorter than the three years (later reduced to two years) Borstal training available for hardened young offenders. The Borstal system for young offenders was named after the first such prison at Borstal in Kent was opened in 1902. Part of the regime was based on the great public schools with a house system, housemasters, a matron and a heavy emphasis on competitive sport. Young men would be spared the baleful influence of adult recidivists and instead exposed to positive adult role models. Unlike staff in adult prisons (and Senior Detention Centres) prison officers wore civilian clothes. The Borstal system lasted 80 years until it was abolished by the 1982 Criminal Justice Act. The former Borstals became Youth Custody Centres and staff went into uniform. An indeterminate sentence of up to two years was replaced by determinate sentences of youth custody up to the maximum provided by statute for an adult. One by-product of this reform was that young men under the age of 21 serving custodial terms either less than or in excess of a Borstal sentence were no longer housed in adult prisons, other than on remand.

The 1982 Criminal Justice Act revived the notion of the 'short, sharp shock' and the Home Secretary at the time, William Whitelaw, was a great believer in the salutary experience. However, the available sentence was reduced to a minimum of 21 days and a maximum of 4 months as opposed to the previous 3, 6 and exceptionally 9 months sentence structure. The law of unintended consequences struck and the 'short, sharp shock' disappeared a mere six years later. With their abolition the last vestige of a deliberately punitive system disappeared from the custodial landscape. It is fair to say that the DCs as the establishments were known, were popular with the law-abiding public, not least because of the harsh retributive nature of the regime. The TV exposure of alleged brutality by prison officers at New Hall Detention Centre gave ready ammunition to penal liberals to whom young offenders were not anti-social thugs but instead were victims of social exclusion and discrimination. The new shorter sentence did not find favour with the courts which typically wanted to lock people up for longer but also were of the view that the Youth Custody Centres provided a more positive regime. Over the Christmas period in 1984 Werrington House incarcerated a mere 34 trainees, leaving 86 beds unoccupied, which in anyone's language was uneconomic. Less than three years previously it had been necessary to put mattresses on the gymnasium floor. The following year Werrington re-rolled as a Youth Custody Centre and it was not alone. The DC sentence was simply abandoned by the courts, seen as ineffective, irrelevant and increasingly out dated. My own view is that Detention Centres were effectively sabotaged by poor drafting of the law and poor sentencing decisions in the courts. To have any chance of succeeding DC trainees needed to be penal system virgins. Instead the Courts imposed repeat DC sentences, imposed DC sentences on previous Borstal trainees, and even imposed DC sentences on those who had done short periods on remand in adult jails. There was no fear factor for this class of trainee and they were free to contaminate those coming into contact with custody for the first time. As a sentence, it will never return any more than the Isle of Man could reinstate the birch as we now have the Human Rights Act to thwart the demands of many law abiding citizens for malefactors to be punished, and for that punishment to have a degree of unpleasantness that reflects community anger, rather than simply be calibrated in time served.

Werrington House had opened as a Detention Centre in 1957. It had been an industrial school from 1895 to 1955 when it was acquired by the Prison Commissioners. My impression some 27 years later was that very little money had been spent on it in the interim. Trainees were housed in large dormitories like hospital wards housing up to 24 inmates with a toilet and a couple of sinks at the end. In high summer on humid nights, there was the unmistakeable fetid smell of body odour and discarded socks that clung invisibly to the fabric of the place. Mercifully the trainees did not need to slop out. There was a communal dining area and large communal washing area where trainees queued to use one of the 30 or so wash basins arranged in a long line. It is inconceivable now that young offenders would be housed in dormitory conditions. It would be an invitation to murder and would see the worst facets of American medium security correctional facilities replicated here. There was little in the way of constructive work or training and the absence of such facilities was keenly felt when the establishment re-rolled as a Youth Custody Centre taking young offenders between the ages of 15 and 21. A motor cycle repair shop and a concrete shop was the limit of constructive work available for trainees who had not or never would graduate to the farm party or kitchen. For most, the work was internal cleaning or maintenance of the internal grounds which involved much litter picking, weeding and bin emptying. Much of it was about killing time. As a party officer, autumn was a delight as gathering up autumn leaves was a welcome diversion from the daily tedium of trying to appear busy. Werrington was not the only establishment with a sparse and unconstructive regime. Stoke Heath Youth custody Centre in rural Shropshire boasted a coal party which moved coal from one side of a bay to the other and back again on a daily basis. This was the penal equivalent of whitewashing coal undertaken by National Servicemen in the 1950s. If one looks at the films from that era where any of the scenes are set in prison, there will be the ubiquitous mailbag shop. Well I can tell you that prisoners at HMP Stafford were still sewing mailbags when I joined in 1984 and continued to do so until the end of the decade. The mid-1980s was the apogee of the era of despair in penal policy, often referred to as 'nothing works'. However, there were intellectual stirrings and in 1985 Ian Dunbar, a former Governor of Wakefield and Wormwood Scrubs and by then a Senior Civil Servant, published a seminal document, 'A Sense of Direction'. Dunbar coined a rather unfortunate acronym, IRA, which stood for Individuals, Relationships and Activities as the key components of the humane management of penal institutions. His work influenced the entire system for the better, but most particularly after the Strangeways riot and subsequent report by Lord Woolf jolted the government into long overdue reform. The Prison service adopted a Statement of Purpose: "HM Prison Service serves the public by keeping in custody those committed by the courts. Our duty is to look after them with humanity and help them lead law abiding and useful lives in custody and after release."

As a consequence of the dormitory accommodation and the paucity of the regime, Werrington only took trainees serving up to twelve months, which expanded to eighteen months when the gaol was threatened with closure. In those days, the maximum remission of sentence was one third, although parole (release on licence) was available for prisoners serving twelve months or more and could see them released as early as one-third of the way through the sentence, provided a minimum of six months had been served. With the abandonment of the Borstal system, Youth Custody, apart from the Detention Centres became simply a mirror image of the adult system. In 1988, the Detention Centres were rebranded and integrated into the Youth Custody system. Youth Custody Centres were renamed Young Offender Institutions and the new sentence was called Detention in a Young Offender Institution. In reality, the title was a bit of spin. For those over 18, the punitive Detention Centre regime was completely abolished. For those between 14 and 17 (14-year-olds were not taken out the system until 2000), two important features were retained: the smoking ban and compulsory PE on all weekdays. The other important changes were that 17-year-old offenders were now classed as juveniles and were tried and sentenced in juvenile courts. All juveniles were to be accommodated in separate discreet accommodation, though sometimes in the same establishment as older young offenders, i.e. those between 18 and 21 when sentenced. This rectified the anomalous situation whereby juveniles sentenced to a term in a detention centre were accommodated discreetly, but juveniles serving a term of youth custody shared accommodation and facilities with more sophisticated offenders who could be as much as six years older. Werrington (by now the house had been dropped from the title) duly became a juvenile YOI in 1988. A new Governor, Peter Salter, unilaterally reinstated the smoking privilege, something which would have seen him on the other end of a health lobby lynch mob, the press, and superiors who would have instantly banished him to the Prison Service equivalent of a Siberian power station had this exercise of long defunct gubernatorial discretion been exercised 15 years later. I shall say more about prison governors in Chapter 5. Leaving aside the smoking issue and the ban was swiftly reintroduced by the next Governor, the regime became more constructive.

There is a clear divide in the nation's press between those newspapers which believe that prisons have gone soft, usually tabloids, and those which believe that they are the colleges of crime with unacceptable and demeaning conditions, usually broadsheets. Largely the division is about the purpose of prison, whether they are for punishment and deterrence on the one hand, and reform and resettlement on the other. The Prison Service statement of purpose leans very definitely towards rehabilitation. The distinction is important. In practice, there is a degree of synthesis between the two positions on the purpose of prison, but there is an on-going tug of war between proponents of the philosophies to try and ensure that the system is more reflective of their point of view. So what has changed since 1984?

The most obvious physical change in closed prison conditions is the demise of 'slop out' as a direct consequence of the Strangeways riot in 1990. However, instead of one's cellmate defecating into a pot and perhaps putting the contents out of the window, he defecates into a flush toilet in the corner of a frequently shared cell. In most refurbished prison accommodation the toilet is not even screened. Thus prisoners eat their meals in a toilet, a fact pointed out repeatedly by Her Majesty's Inspectorate of Prisons, but unless there is a sudden release of the funds needed to create separate sanitation facilities in prison cells, only the most modern accommodation will have the privacy we take for granted at home. It is not just a question of funding. Creating separate toilet space in Victorian prisons involves the loss of every third cell. In a society where the prison population has more than doubled since 1993, loss of accommodation on this scale cannot be afforded given the competing priorities for public spending. There is no political will or public appetite to shift spending towards further improvements in prison conditions. The Strangeways riot has already had a number of mentions in this chapter. However, its most significant consequence was not the sometimes short-lived improvements that followed the riot, and more particularly, the report of the Wolfe inquiry into it. The biggest consequence of all was that the media developed an appetite for prisons as a newsworthy item, in particular influential tabloids such as *The Sun* and the *Daily Mail*. In 1994–5, a media firestorm accompanied the short-lived Category A escapees from Whitemoor and Parkhurst, and the suicide of Frederick West in Birmingham prison. The response was hysterical compared to a similar period August 1964 to October 1966 when two Great Train Robbers, Charles Wilson and Ronnie Biggs, and Russian master spy, George Blake escaped respectively from Wandsworth, Birmingham and Wormwood Scrubs prisons. These escapes were followed by the Mountbatten report, which gave us the system of categorisation referred to earlier in this chapter and what we now know as the High Security estate. The threat in 1995 to Home Secretary Michael Howard's job was real and he needed the Prime Minister's support to survive. The Director General, Derek Lewis, recruited by the previous Home Secretary Ken Clarke from outside industry was summarily dismissed. Derek Lewis would later successfully sue for both wrongful dismissal, (which is breach of contract) and unfair dismissal. It is almost fair to say that there are occasions when certain newspapers devote as much attention to prisoners to whom they normally refer as lags and convicts as they do to the latest antics of minor celebrities or the latest outfits worn by the Duchess of Sussex.

The prison system is in part a reflection of our society, in particular its criminal elements, and also the response not only of lawmakers to that criminality, but those who seek to influence those lawmakers. The second huge change to have affected the prison system during my service is the drug culture, which very much reflects what has occurred in wider society. I was a teenager in the 1960s when drug abuse started to become an issue for the police and first exercised newspaper editors. The two came together over the infamous 'drugs bust' at Rolling Stone Keith Richards' Sussex home in 1967. More high profile raids on the new rock and roll aristocracy followed and in 1971 Parliament passed the Misuse of Drugs Act which gave us the classifications that we are familiar with today and prescribed draconian penalties up to life imprisonment for the supplying of Class A narcotics such as heroin and cocaine. In that era, narcotics were largely the preserve of a well to do Bohemian elite and those who sought to be part of it. The main difference from the 1940s and 1950s was that it was out in the open. The drug culture was largely alien to working class youth which preferred to spend its wages on the traditional legal drugs, beer and tobacco. Indeed it is fair to argue that in the early 1970s there was still a rough class divide as far as the use of illegal drugs were concerned. The rock and roll culture gradually democratised the use of illegal substances. This democratisation coincided unhappily with the decline of heavy industry which took the work out of traditional working class communities, emasculating the men and slowly reducing once proud communities to despair. Fathers who did not or could not work because the work disappeared struggled to be role models to their sons and indeed struggled to have a role in the family beyond being the source of conception. It would be wrong to blame deindustrialisation for all the social ills in what we used to call working class communities but are now underclass ghettos. The educated classes must also take their share of the blame. Feminism has taught that families do not need fathers. Uneducated males have fought back, when not in prison for petty crime by being feckless serial baby fathers impregnating ill-educated young women exploiting the generosity of a welfare state that has exalted single motherhood. Male underclass criminality and casual violence towards their women and other men's children in the home is as much a legacy of feminism as the proliferation of women in senior positions in our professions. Drugs such as cannabis (much stronger than in the 60s) and heroin are an integral part of that underclass culture. As these young men do not work, their drug habits are funded by crime. The addict has no conscience and no moral compass. All that matters is the next fix which as far as the unemployed and often unemployable underclass is concerned can only be funded by criminality. Thus the elderly who have just collected their meagre pension and their respectable neighbours who are out all day at work are the obvious soft targets for the acquisition of immediate funds. The really desperate and indebted will hire out their girlfriends for sexual services to dealers in return for the narcotics they crave. And then the cycle begins again tomorrow. This behaviour is replicated in prison.

It would be inaccurate to say that there were no illegal narcotics in British prisons when I joined in 1984. However, it was still only a peripheral problem. Within 10 years the service had found it necessary to introduce random testing by taking urine samples. There was also provision for target testing based on intelligence and the frequent testing of certain individual prisoners. Failure to provide a sample would be treated in the same way as the failure to provide a sample of breath to a police officer who suspects a driver of driving under the influence of alcohol in that it would be an offence. The general public and sometimes disingenuously sections of the press, expresses its astonishment that drug dealing and drug taking are rife within the nation's prisons. Members of Parliament including those with prisons in their constituencies struggle to resist the temptation to join the hue and cry against the system and those who work within it. If I am honest, were I a member of the general public with no experience of the system, I would probably be equally astonished. However, prisons are not institutions like schools and hospitals, which are an experience common to virtually every citizen. Rather they are the preserve of a hard core of offenders who populate the system for greater or lesser lengths of time, the staff who work within them and others by virtue of their office such as Inspectors, Members of Parliament and members of the Independent Monitoring Boards that each prison is required to have by statute. In total including recidivists currently in the community, rehabilitated offenders and retired staff, the number of citizens with direct experience of our prison system probably numbers little more than half a million, that is something a little less than 1% of the population. That is a huge knowledge gap and sadly not one that our media and the worst sort of populist politician make much effort to bridge.

Well, how do drugs get into prison? Remember many of our prisons are in urban areas. It is not difficult to throw packages over a 15-foot wall to be picked up by prisoner work parties who know exactly where and what to look for. Packages can also be hooked up to lines dangled from cell windows. As one might expect, packages of cannabis or harder drugs are small and can be stored up the back passage to be regurgitated and divided up later. Some of the most unfortunate establishments are those with only one exercise yard. A handful of supervising staff have no chance of beating prisoners to the contraband thrown over the wall. Most visits are held in open conditions and this is an obvious conduit. Drugs can be passed mouth to mouth during French kisses which are not permitted but difficult to prevent in a room that may contain as many as 150 people. Failing that the shared packet of crisps bought from the shop or vending machine in the visits facility is excellent cover for a pass. From there the prisoner can either take the risk of it being found on a search at the end of visits, or stick it up his arse. So how do visitors get the drugs through the front gate? When I first joined the service, I wondered aloud whether the short skirts and bare legs even in the depths of winter were a visible symbol of poverty. An experienced officer quickly put me right. The absence of irritating garments such as tights or trousers made a little under the table activity that much easier plus it was easier to give the old man a flash of what was waiting for him on release. Since those days we have moved on. Concealing drugs in the vagina, known as 'crotching', is a tried and tested method of smuggling, and without the encumbrance of leggings or tights, they are easy to retrieve. However, female visitors don't have to be this obvious. Goods can be retrieved on a visit to the ladies, and then passed as indicated above. When all else fails, there is the option to corrupt staff. Finally there is the option to admit your addiction, go legal and join the methadone queue, rather like the one you may see in your local chemist in your local community.

This is not to say that the service stands idly by. All prisons have a searching programme that includes intelligence led searching. Informants are cultivated. Drug dogs are a regular sight and are even used occasionally in open prisons. Netting is placed over exercise yards. CCTV is strategically placed. Operations are conducted by the police to catch the 'bowlers' who throw packages over outer walls and fences from property or pavements outside the prison. Prison grounds are searched before work parties are allowed out. Visitors caught with narcotics are prosecuted and serving prisoners disciplined. They are also placed on closed visits for a period. As recent high profile cases indicated, the service pursues corrupt staff vigorously where solid evidence is available. Yet despite all this activity, the detection rate hits only the tip of the iceberg. Prisoners running large scale smuggling operations from within prison, or those merely looking after their own needs have a major weapon that has only become widely available during the last twenty years or so; the mobile phone. It is a perfect size for fitting up the backside. It is undetectable by dogs although there is now technology to detect concealed cell phones. For those with reason to fear that they might be scanned or would simply prefer not have the function of their back passage impaired then there is the option of paying or pressuring other prisoners to hold the phone on their behalf. And if one is detected the major players will have no difficulty obtaining a replacement. The methods are similar to those for drug smuggling; bowling, crotching for handover on visits and corrupting staff. Mobile phones are plentiful, disposable and, for those with resources, easily replaced. The drug dealing business can easily be run from behind a cell door. At the first sign of staff, it can be quickly shoved up the backside. Because of the availability of mobile phones, the amount and quality of intelligence available from monitoring the official phones available to prisoners has dropped dramatically.

The general public would no doubt still be appalled and demand action. This is where our politicians come in, or rather they don't. It is possible to stem the tide but it requires draconian and expensive measures. It requires public spending and at its most extreme a repeal of the Human Rights Act, with the consequent withdrawal from the European Convention on Human Rights. The strongest measure would be the closure, or alternatively the fencing, of open prisons. Large amounts of money could be spent on netting to cover walkways on the inner side of prison walls. If open prisons were to be retained, then control rooms staffed round the clock monitoring CCTV could be deployed along with snatch squads equipped with German shepherd dogs to detect and apprehend offenders retrieving drugs, alcohol and/or mobile phone packages. All staff and all visitors subject to searching in all prisons (i.e. not just the high security estate) would be the norm along with the deployment of drug dogs on a daily basis. All staff entering the prison could also be scanned for mobile phones. (Experiments to block mobile phone signals have been conducted successfully but unfortunately the technology affects surrounding residential areas). All visits could take place in closed conditions, i.e. visitors separated from the prisoner in booths divided by a glass or other material through which people can see and talk to each other, but not have physical contact. I would imagine you get the picture. So next time you hear a politician berating prisons and by implication their management and staff for being infested with drugs, ask them what measures might work, what they might cost, and in the case of a minister, whether he is prepared to resign if the Chancellor will not provide the resources. Cheap solutions are almost invariably useless. All we got at Ford open prison was a pyracantha hedge on the outside of the perimeter that would make it difficult for prisoners returning from Tesco or from the neighbouring churchyard to recover contraband to get back into the jail over the fence, on the basis that they would have to negotiate an extremely sharp thicket first. I visited Ford for the last time in the summer of 2009 and the hedge still hadn't grown sufficiently, some six years on from when it was planted. Measures such as the abolition of open visits (which would be extremely expensive because of the construction costs involved) would almost certainly be viewed by the courts as a breach of the human rights of both the prisoner and his or her visitors. It is the very same Human Rights Act that led to a judgement that prisoners must not be forced to endure 'cold turkey', but instead be given the heroin substitute, methadone, which can be prescribed perfectly legally. It isn't only pond life politicians who demonstrate inconsistency and sometimes hypocrisy in their quest for a sound bite that might save their seat. Her Majesty's Inspectorate of Prisons has the same contradictory approach. Prison management teams are excoriated for the scale of their drug problem, but at the same time the Inspectorate consistently makes recommendations to water down the kind of intrusive searching that detects and deters those seeking to, or pressured into bringing in narcotics. In a letter to the *Daily Mail* published in 2011, Bryan Pailing, former West Midlands Area Manager in the Prison Service, criticised the doublespeak of the Inspectorate from the unassailable vantage point of retirement. No doubt when in service he made his views known privately, but then going public in attacking hypocrisy is not compatible with a career. In the public sector, the ability to articulate should never be confused with the right.

As I have said earlier, prisons in part reflect our society, and they also reflect the work of legislators and those who seek to influence them. There is no war on drugs in our society. If there was such a war and it was being won, there would be no queue of heroin addicts outside your chemist, there would be much less acquisitive crime from individuals in the grip of their addiction and no lawful means to pay for it, and the penalties imposed by law for drug offences would be toughened and imposed with their full rigour. It follows logically that if such a war was being won in wider society it would also be in the process of being won in prisons with much less need for the kind of overbearing and enormously expensive preventive security described earlier. Such a war would also require the determination to tackle endemic fatherlessness, poverty of aspiration and a culture of dependency. It also requires jobs to be available and our young people skilled to fill them.

The third major influence on the system and the one most responsible for change since 1997 is the rise of identity politics, often referred to colloquially as 'political correctness'. This philosophy does not merely hold that society is unequal (which is obvious) but that those who suffer from inequalities are by definition, victims. There are a whole range of victims. Ethnic minorities, immigrants, women, gays and the disabled are all held to be victims of a white patriarchal system that institutionalises discrimination, social exclusion and denies people their human rights. To these groups can be added prisoners. To the politically correct prisoners are victims of an unequal society that condemned them to a life of crime and then incarcerated them as a punishment for something not their fault. Acquisitive crime such as that committed during the riots of August 2011 is therefore the inevitable consequence of a society that deprives its underclass of decent jobs, decent housing and opportunities in general to advance socially. The status and esteem that human beings need is therefore derived from criminality. The penal system simply reinforces inequalities and indeed magnifies racial inequality as the percentage of ethnic minorities in prison is double their representation in the community as a whole. As a philosophy, it is deeply flawed not least because it denies that human beings have free will. It also has no respect for property earned by hard work. Principally it neglects the fact that the main victims of crime are the law abiding poor forced to live cheek by jowl with the feral underclass on Britain's worst estates. Most poor people do not offend. Their most earnest wish is that their children graduate to the nation's middle class, but without losing contact with their roots. I have noted earlier the baleful influence of fatherlessness, one of feminism's bastard offspring, itself a manifestation of rampant political correctness.

Identity politics has a profound influence on the prison system and tilts the balance very much in favour of those who argue that prison is the punishment, and not a place where punishment is inflicted. They have had a number of significant victories. Prisoners can no longer be forced to endure 'cold turkey' as a means of weaning them off drugs, thanks to the Human Rights Act which in the final analysis allows the European Court of Human Rights (ECHR) sitting in Strasbourg to overrule the British courts and the wishes of the House of Commons. Prison Governors can no longer award added days, formally known as loss of remission; instead this power now lies with a District Judge. ECHR deprived Governors of this power in 2002. The first breach in this dyke was self-inflicted in 1998 when penal reformers succeeded in depriving the Governor of the authority to take remission when Detention and Training Orders replaced the previous sentence of Detention in a Young Offender Institution for juvenile offenders. Also from this point on, juveniles would be referred to as children. No one likes the thought of children being in jail. Changing the language was all important in changing public perception (hard) and winning the support of the political class (easy). The number of children in custody has fallen by 40% over the last ten years, a civilised development that has passed almost unnoticed by the general public.

More recently prisoners have won three further significant victories. In another attack on the authority of staff, a life sentence prisoner in Belmarsh used human rights legislation to compel prison officers to call him 'Mr'. ECHR has ruled that indeterminate sentences for public protection (IPP'S), introduced in 2003 breached Human Rights on the basis that the courses prisoners needed to demonstrate that they were safe to be released by the parole board were not available. The Coalition government has scrapped the sentence but there are still some 6,000 prisoners still serving these terms, 3,500 of whom are past tariff, the punishment part of the sentence. Speaking personally, I do not like indeterminate sentences. They concentrate absolute power into a small number of people who are in effect judge, jury and executioner when it comes to release, adding enormous uncertainty to the lives of prisoners, and as a consequence making the prison environment more volatile than it needs to be. Finally, in the summer of 2013 ECHR ruled that 'whole life' tariffs for murderers are a breach of their human rights. Thus those who espouse a hard line about the purpose of prison have had to content themselves with victories expressed in a prison population double what it was in 1993, an upward trend in sentencing, and a parliament that for once is refusing to obey ECHR and allow convicted prisoners the right to vote. They have won no victories against what they perceive as soft, drug-ridden prisons run by politically correct reformers handing out undeserved privileges funded by the taxpayer, other than to starve them of funds and turn them into hellholes.

Unlike gays, women, ethnic minorities and the disabled, all of whom are represented in prison, prisoners do not enjoy specific legislative protection. The focus has been the use and abuse of the Human Rights Act. Prisoners have long litigated, but until the Human Rights Act came into force in 2000, legal aid ceased at the point at which the appeal against conviction was dismissed. After this point, prisoners were forced to use their own resources or persuade a campaigning solicitor to take up the case at the expense of the firm. From that point until the reforms introduced in April 2013 by Justice Secretary, Chris Grayling, prisoners could apply for legal aid for challenges under the Human Rights Act in the secure knowledge that as a victim group they would have had a good claim on a budget that ministers could only reduce by denying legal aid to the deserving. Firms of solicitors specialising in Prisoners' Rights mushroomed, all paid for by you and me. By 2012, legal aid provision for serving prisoners had grown from £1 million annually to £25 million. This figure excludes compensation won, all of course shelled out by the hapless taxpayer.

The world I knew when I joined in 1984 has gone. As I have said, there has been real change for the better, but there has also been significant change for the worse, much of it I fear irreversible because of a political philosophy that elevates the rights of individuals and minority groups above those of the mainstream law abiding community. The remaining chapters will have more to say about those changes. Political correctness attacks the legitimacy of institutions that historically have protected the citizen from malefactors: the police, the courts and the prison service. It does so by a combination of erosion of confidence and infiltration of the ranks of the institution so that it can permanently and perversely change its culture. If you do not believe me, stop and consider the recent history of the Metropolitan Police.

Chapter 3
Prisoners

When people are put on the spot and asked what they know about prisons and the people who live and work in them, they will usually cite TV programmes such as the still repeated 1970s sitcom, *Porridge*, starring the late Ronnie Barker, and *Bad Girls*, a rather overheated drama series set in a women's jail in the 1990s. A few will remember the imported Australian drama series, *Prisoner Cell Block H*, which ran from 1979 to 1986, and fewer still the Lynda La Plante written series, *The Governor*, (1995–96) despite it being rather more recent. After that it is a struggle apart from the film *Scum*, (original version 1979) and its less well-known female counterpart, *Scrubbers*, (1983) both set in Borstals. Outside of the service, no one seems to remember the Strangeways (HMP Manchester) documentary series from 1980, and the BBC2 Timewatch programme, *Strangeways Revisited*, screened in 2001. Since I retired in 2010, a new documentary about Strangeways has been screened. More recently, there has been a warts and all documentary about HMYOI Aylesbury which houses some of our most hardened and dangerous young men between the ages of 18 and 21. Prisons have not historically appealed to TV producers in the same way as the Police and to a lesser extent our schools. Of course we have all been to school and most of us will have had some dealing with the police, with only a small proportion of that contact being as a result of being reported for or suspected of committing an offence. As I have said in the previous chapter, perhaps only around 1% of the population have experience of our prisons as an inmate, staff member or visitor. It is a closed world behind the walls, and therefore a permanently closed book to most of the population. Therefore it is not surprising that the general public labours under the sort of misconceptions that it would not have about other public service such as schools, policing and the NHS.

It would be wrong to say that *Porridge* does not contain more than a grain of truth. However it is now many years out of date, there are no drugs in *Porridge*, and it is a sitcom not a drama. Its job is to get laughs and it succeeds brilliantly. *Bad Girls* was equally compelling television, and I have to confess that my favourite episode was the recapture of an escaped female life sentence prisoner in an Amsterdam brothel by off duty prison officers enjoying a boys' weekend away in the city's red-light district. The drama specialised in farfetched plots that involved staff being involved in corrupt monetary and/or sexual relationships with a motley crew of equally unbelievable female prisoners almost on a daily basis. Despite this being the mid-nineties, the issue of illegal drugs was largely ignored. No one can deny that there is corruption and sexual abuse, but it is not endemic, institutionalised and condoned, which is how it was portrayed in *Bad Girls*. Scum was very different and so violent that Mary Whitehouse sought to bring a private prosecution against Channel 4 when the remade film was eventually screened in 1983. The film depicted gang rape, suicide and racism as well as endemic violence amongst the prisoners and brutal repression by staff. At the time the Borstal system was very much on its last legs, but again the viewer would have formed the impression that such events occurred on a daily basis, and that the staff cadre were as morally delinquent as those they incarcerated. However, in one sense Scum anticipated the future. Young Offender establishments are much more violent than when I joined in 1984, and gang warfare is now a major problem.

It has to be said that the press do not help to educate the public. They use terms like 'warder' and 'lag' on a daily basis. Prison officers have not been known as warders since 1921. Warders are in fact a museum grade, found in the Tower of London in a gaudy uniform. Amongst the staff working in prisons there are a number of collective nouns to describe prisoners, cons being the common slang expression amongst prison officers. No one I knew ever used the term 'lags'.

So what are prisoners like? I remember clearly my first encounter with serving prisoners. On my first day at Stafford, our small group of new recruits was taken to the mailbag shop to see for ourselves a selection of Stafford's finest. We were of course instantly recognisable to the fifty or so prisoners in the workshop as the latest raw recruits not least because we were in suits not uniform and were very obviously not governors. Our initiation consisted of loud jeering, audible insults and sexual innuendo. It was a ritual that we had to undergo and a test of nerve that was scrutinised by the beady eye of the Training Principal Officer. Stafford prison had a proud reputation in the service in that it was one of two dustbins for Category C prisoners, the other being HMP Camp Hill on the Isle of Wight. It took the worst behaved and the least motivated. It was an unpopular allocation, not least because for many it was far from home. Stafford was also a punishment transfer for those failed open conditions. We had been told that prisoners did not have horns or two heads, but some of them looked like Cyclops. They were truly an ugly bunch, the bottom of the heap, deemed fit only for sewing mailbags. However, further on in our training we had a different encounter with prisoners when the Training Principal Officer cancelled our day off on the Spring Bank holiday and entered us as a team in the 5-a-side football tournament, in which yours truly was the goalkeeper. As I recall, we finished unbeaten in the tournament. It was another test of nerve, mental strength and the ability to deal with a measure of physical intimidation. Clearly we all passed as the following week we moved on to Officer Training School in Wakefield.

Eight weeks without sight of a prisoner followed. Our section Principal Officer, Bill Wright, an affable and imperturbable character, told us simply, "don't worry about the cons… cons are just cons". In simple terms, he was saying that sooner you normalise the prison situation in your minds, the sooner you will normalise relationships. As I have said, my first posting was HM Detention Centre Werrington House, catering for young men aged 17–21. With few exceptions most of the trainees were poorly educated, had few social skills and even less self-esteem. Few had any experience of employment which was no surprise given the record of truancy and the absence of exam passes. Their homes were on the tough council estates of Wrexham, Stoke and Liverpool. When the change to youth custody came the following year, we would add Manchester to our catchment area. Families were often fractured. There were relatively few fathers in the visits room at weekend, and some mothers had the unenviable task of rotating weekend visits around two or more jails to see errant sons and husbands. On discharge, they would put back on the poor quality clothing in which they had sat in the dock, go home by train, and for those not scared or scarred by the DC experience, begin the cycle all over again. The prison virgins sadly enduring the company of more hardened inmates would learn new skills like how to hot wire a car or pick pockets at Aintree racecourse. They would also learn from those who had previously been imprisoned, that custody could not only be survived, but become a way of life.

On the outside, many of them affected to be hard men. Low intelligence worked in tandem with aggression. After lunch, it was a common sight for large numbers of trainees to be engaged in arm wrestling across the tables, baiting and challenging each other in the one permitted form of fighting as the testosterone flowed. It was rare to spot someone reading a book. There were, of course, genuine hard cases who would go on to be feared on their home estates and prisons, but for many it was a brittle facade of toughness disguising the self-loathing and the fear of being a target of the more predatory trainees. For this reason, fights almost always broke out in the presence of staff who intervened swiftly before anyone got seriously hurt. Face was further saved by putting up some resistance to staff, thus requiring force to be used. The use of Control and Restraint techniques, as they are known in these situations, has never been understood by the Inspectorate, a body which constantly deplores the frequency and alleged ferocity with which force is used, without understanding the context and without understanding adolescent psychology. Given the growth of the gang culture and its inevitable influence on prison life, it is hard to see how the use of force can be reduced without drastic reductions in the time young men spend in each other's company outside of the cells. Needless to say the Inspectorate also deplores any reduction in time out of cell.

As I have indicated, intelligence is found in reverse proportion to aggression in the average offender. This is not to say that overt violence is endemic throughout the system. Prison officers are not armed although they do carry batons which are very rarely used. Prison officers are much less numerous than the prisoners yet remain for the most part firmly in charge, or at least they did until Chris Grayling took an axe to staffing in 2013. The truth is that our prisons have always run with the consent of those incarcerated, a consent which now appears to have been withdrawn. Some prison officers are actually popular, a good number are respected and the majority are at worst tolerated. Most adult prisoners accept the legitimate authority of staff. As one would expect, young offenders are more challenging, partly because of the nature of adolescence and partly because of the pervasive gang culture. Taken as a whole, prisoners are remarkably acquiescent. The general public hears only of the exceptional times when major disturbances take place such as the Strangeways riot of 1990, and the Ford riot of New Year's Eve at the end of 2010. Other lesser disturbances involving smaller numbers of prisoners climbing on roofs or damaging a wing are more likely to found in local papers and possibly the middle pages of one of the nationals. The public does not then understand why concerted indiscipline is not put down with extreme force. I can only say that this not America or South Africa and our traditions are different. The aim is to restore rule by consent as swiftly as possible and this is done by treating a major incident as an aberration rather than expected normative behaviour which needs to be deterred by a harsh institutionalised punitive regime.

Practitioners will tell you, not necessarily in more PC language, that our prisons hold the sad, the mad and the bad. We work on the basis that very few are irredeemably bad. We work on the basis that there are degrees of badness and that most of the bad have it within them to change, particularly so amongst young offenders whose characters are not yet fully formed. We work on the basis that most offenders including murderers are capable of remorse and therefore capable of being released from a life sentence. We work on the basis that programmes designed to confront offending behaviour combined with incentives such as transfer to an open prison and/or early release can positively affect motivation to change. It is a fact that 97% of prisoners held in open conditions do not abscond. Often, however, it can seem to be the triumph of hope over experience when the same old faces return time after time until eventually they tire of offending. Nevertheless, I take issue with those ministers who see this as the fault of Prison

Governors and their staff. Firstly, there is strong evidence that longer sentences for serious offending coupled with the right sort of interventions have reduced reoffending rates. It is the serial petty offender returning at regular intervals for a few weeks porridge for which prison does not work, as there simply isn't time to do meaningful work with this type of offender. Secondly we must remember the type of communities to which prisoners return on release. Relatively few go back to leafy middle class suburbs. Most return to estates where working people are in a minority, pit bull terriers are the most popular breed of dog, and drug dealers lurk on every corner only too eager to lure newly released prisoners into their web. For many released prisoners, home on these estates will be a friend's sofa, as they will have frequently lost their tenancies because of anti-social behaviour or non-payment of rent.

These are not characters which readily attract sympathy. Nevertheless, serial petty offenders often have mental health problems which are compounded when combined with low intelligence. I am firmly of the view that we have free will and therefore a choice whether or not to break the law. It is not a stricture easily applied to the mentally ill. A generation ago a decision was taken to close the mental hospitals that were easily recognisable by their high walls which were often characterised as 'loony bins'. Apart from institutions such as Broadmoor and Ashworth hospitals which cater for the criminally insane, former mental hospital inmates would receive care in the community. A more accurate description would be couldn't care less in the community. This decision was taken almost contemporaneously with the spread of the drug culture that would destroy minds as well as moral compasses. The policy was supported by the left on the basis of social inclusion and supported on the right of British politics by those who sought to cut public expenditure. When any measure is supported across the political spectrum, it is time to be very afraid. High profile murders by schizophrenics make the headlines but are mercifully rare. What does not attract the headlines is the fact that our prisons have now taken over the role once carried out by mental hospitals. The fact is that residential mental health beds have fallen from 150,000 places in the 1950s to less than 20,000 today.

According to the Prison Reform Trust (PRT), 10% of prisoners have serious mental health issues. Given that the total population is around 83,000 that equates to over 8,000 inmates who are in the wrong institution at any one time. 10% of men and terrifyingly 30% of women coming into prison will have had a previous admission to a psychiatric institution. Given the paucity of mental health facilities in the community, those figures almost certainly understate the numbers entering prison with mental health problems. Indeed the PRT goes further and suggests that around 90% of prisoners have a least one mental health problem. As a conservative estimate, at least two thirds of prisoners have been using narcotics within 30 days of committal to prison and this comes as no surprise to criminal justice practitioners. An accurate figure is difficult to obtain as testing in prison reception areas cannot detect Class A drugs taken more than 4 days previously whereas cannabis can be detected up to 30 days. Reception testing typically produces a figure of around 60% which inevitably understates the problem. It certainly tells us a great deal about the part played by illegal drugs amongst the criminal community. Another study published in the International Journal of Law and Psychiatry came up with a broadly similar figure of around 8,000 prisoners suffering from Schizophrenia and other Psychoses. Alcohol abuse is the other massive contributor to mental health problems amongst the prison population. A survey conducted by Alcohol Concern in 2007 found that 35% of prisoners accepted that they had an alcohol problem. It is worth noting that some members of this group admitted consumption of an average 187 units per week which is roughly the equivalent of a 700ml bottle of spirits per day. Even if it is argued that present government guidelines of 14 units per week maximum for men is over cautious, it is clear that many other people in custody must have been drinking at hazardous levels well in excess of 50 units per week. An MOJ survey in 2013 found that 63% of prisoners were binge drinkers. These are staggering statistics. The cost of the habit is also staggering even allowing for the fact that the spirit of choice will be the cheapest 'paint stripper' coming in at around £8–£10 per bottle.

It would be ridiculous to argue that no one with a mental health issue should go to prison, as it would completely destroy any remaining concept of personal responsibility. It is evident that most prisoners are managed successfully within a prison environment without recourse to medication. There is much that can be achieved by counselling and support, education, diet, physical fitness and of course abstinence from alcohol and illegal drugs all of which measures have a significant impact on individual wellbeing. The argument essentially is that there is a hard core of individuals, not all of them located in hard-pressed prison hospitals, which should not be in penal custody. These individuals are a danger to staff and other prisoners as well as themselves and the immorality of their offending is outweighed by the immorality of dealing with them simply by imprisonment.

Prison staff will curse the courts for sending them the feeble minded, the self-harming and the schizophrenic, but as I have said judges and magistrates frequently have no choice. Care in the community, to the extent that it exists at all, has been superseded by care in custody, but even then only for a minority. It is exceptionally difficult to get a prisoner transferred to a psychiatric unit, (a process known colloquially with no concessions to political correctness as 'nutting off') as places are so few, but exceptionally easy for him to be returned to prison if his behaviour is unmanageable! I can also recall from my stint at Wakefield high security prison 1993–95 men being returned to jail from places like Broadmoor and Ashworth on the grounds that they were untreatable psychopaths. The word oxymoron does not begin to cover these situations and it is small wonder that some staff feel that they are running penal dustbins. On another occasion back in 2007, I was visiting HMP Birmingham prior to a job interview. The Governor's staff officer, a fast track graduate entrant, was proudly showing me the new modern house blocks which she informed me with no sense of irony were built on the site of the old Birmingham mental hospital. I wasn't convinced that she got my point when I responded 'So what's changed?' Suicide and self-harming in prison, at least in male establishments was not a significant problem when I joined. I cannot recall coming across any prisoner who habitually cut himself until the early 1990s. By then the drug culture had bit deep and the loss of mental health facilities had impacted on the section of the population most likely to need them. Prison officers have had to adapt to a population afflicted by sadness, melancholia and depression and they have worked wonders to keep down the suicide rate despite the lack of recognition by headline grabbing local MPs for whom self-publicity is all. It is only a question of time before corporate manslaughter legislation is used against the Prison Service over self-inflicted death when in reality prison establishments are reflecting social problems and the inability of our political leaders to grapple effectively with them.

I have said much about prisoners as a group and the remarkable level of homogeneity that pertains. Nevertheless each incarcerated individual has to make his own way through the system and each landing officer has to deal with a large number of individuals and not simply a collective. Prisoners can be every bit as fascinating as they can be both ordinary and terrifying. Each has their own survival strategy in prison. Papillon (Henri Charriere who was imprisoned on Devil's Island) and in England Charles Bronson had their exercise regimes. Other survival strategies are amusing and some rather less edifying. I have mentioned earlier the shit parcels being thrown from cell windows and can remember clearly a young offender by the name of Dewhurst who would happily collect and dispose of the shit parcels in return for half an ounce of tobacco. This relieved him of the problem of having to borrow at the normal prison interest rate of 100%. Failure to pay debts could lead to a severe beating. There was, and still is, the option for a prisoner to sell his arse in order to discharge a debt, inevitably without a condom. In the age of the mobile phone, relatives can be and are called upon to discharge debts. Other prisoners I can remember regarded being a member of what was called the Admin Cleaners party at Werrington as a perk. These were the days when prisoners cleaned offices under supervision and were the days before the smoking ban. Consequently, the ashtrays were lucrative sources of dog ends that could be recycled into slim roll ups. I can also recall supervising an outside working party clearing a path up to the main road when a dog joined us. As we could not take it back into the establishment, I deemed it wise to knock on a few doors and see if we could locate the owner of a pedigree Doberman. We succeeded and the work party were delighted with the small reward of a king size cigarette each. Jobs in the kitchen and prison reception are always valued, for the obvious reasons of access to food and clothing respectively. Prison reception areas are also sources of information. It is here that sharp-eared prisoners can identify sex offenders and others who might have reason to fear reprisals. Like every other commodity, information is valuable. The sharpest of prisoners collate information about staff; who gambles, who has had the bailiffs round, who is emotionally vulnerable, for these are potential opportunities to corrupt.

Prisons are tough places where it does not pay to be sensitive. Part of survival is also about winning small victories against the system. Those who watch the re-runs of *Porridge* will see the theme explored every episode as Fletcher and his fellow prisoners seek to get one over the ever-vigilant Principal Officer, Mr Mackay, so admirably played by the late Fulton Mackay. This brings me neatly to the tale of Piss Bed Smith. I never knew whether this young man genuinely had an incontinence problem or whether his bedwetting and the consequent need for a plastic sheet were his way of making war on the system. I tend to believe it was the latter if only because the other trainees left him alone, which would be unusual for such an obvious target. Smith actually acquired the nickname from a member of staff who was calling out trainees to receive their mail after the lunchtime meal had been served. When the officer called, "Smith," there was a chorus of "Which one, sir?" to which the officer responded, "Piss Bed Smith." A stony-faced Smith came to collect his post. The ritual was repeated with the next two letters on the pile and on two further occasions an expressionless Smith came to collect his mail. In fact he did not react at all. One up to him, I believe. Times have changed and these days an officer could expect to be fired for abusing a prisoner. 30 years ago prisoners did not complain about such treatment. They expected nothing and were not surprised when half of that was taken away.

In more recent years, Her Majesty's Inspectorate of Prisons have introduced the extent to which prisoners are treated with respect as one of their tests of a healthy prison. As such they expect that prisoners are no longer addressed by an unadorned surname. The way in which people were addressed and the way they addressed those above and below them in the social system was an integral part of the class system, which was often much more complex than a simple division between upper, middle and working. Back in the 1950s the *Daily Telegraph* discussed whether it should refer to a clerk as 'Mr'; it decided not. Certainly at that time and probably until the late 60s a junior male civil service clerk would have been addressed by surname and would have addressed his immediate superior as 'Sir'. It would have been a continuation of school. The use of surnames at school continued into adult life amongst public school alumni, even amongst close friends. When I joined the Prison Service in 1984, the social distinctions were simple; Governors were addressed as Sir or Governor, you and your uniformed colleagues were Mister, and prisoners simply had surnames. At this point surnames were probably only used routinely for schoolboys, prisoners and private soldiers. As a form of address, in adult civilian society it had become disrespectful. By the millennium, schoolboys had vacated this list. We have now seen a remarkable inversion as the linguistic codes of the old class system broke down. Newspapers and *The Guardian* in particular routinely refer to respectable public officials including ministers by surname alone. Yet it is the same *Guardian* reading classes who have insisted that male prisoners are addressed formally, (the mandatory use of unadorned surnames for women prisoners had been abolished by Roy Jenkins in 1966). In the light of the Belmarsh case, where a life sentence prisoner used Human Rights legislation to attempt to force prison officers to call him Mister, it is likely to become a disciplinary offence not to address a prisoner in this way. When I joined the service, the reverse was true and over familiarity was a disciplinary offence. There is something troubling about a society in which prisoners are required to be addressed formally, yet private soldiers who may be required to die for their country are still addressed by surname. The politically correct creed demands that the victim classes, which now include prisoners, are accorded extra privileges.

It is unarguably true that prisoners have become more litigious and more conscious of the rights they believe they should have. Until 2000 the rule of thumb was that a prisoner's legal aid expired with the failure of his appeal. Thus any further appeals had to be undertaken on a pro bono basis by campaigning legal firms who could recover their costs from the state in the event of success. Prisoners faced the same issue with civil claims against the Home Office (Ministry of Justice from 2007). In 1990, a significant change in the law allowed solicitors to take on cases on a contingency fee basis. Colloquially this has become known as 'no win, no fee' and no explanation is needed. Moreover, solicitors had to take their fee from the damages received, with the obvious risk to the solicitor if a great deal of legal work was undertaken for little reward. However in 2000 came a very significant change. Solicitors were now allowed to charge a success fee of up to 100% of the damages, payable by the losing side. In the case of successful prisoners versus the Prison Service, the losing side is the state, which of course means you and me, the taxpayer. In the same year, The Human Rights Act of 1998 was enacted. The third ingredient of this witch's brew is political correctness. As a victim group prisoners now found that the Legal Aid was prepared to be more generous. The upshot was an exponential growth in firms of solicitors specialising in prisoners' rights, all funded by the taxpayer at zero risk to the individual prisoner. We live in an era where the rights of an individual who is a member of a group labelled as disadvantaged trump those of the law abiding taxpaying community, using and abusing the Human Rights Act and Equality legislation. Thus a disabled paedophile serving in Lewes Prison was able to obtain £47,000 plus costs, a figure which does not include the costs of defending the action, because the Prison Service was held to be in breach of its obligations under the Disability Discrimination Act. Take it from me it is virtually impossible to defend a case under this act since the disabled person calls tune as to what are reasonable adjustments. On his return to prison in 2008, he commenced new litigation having obtained legal aid. This is the climate in which we now live and it is small wonder that prisoners are taking advantage. Hopefully Mr Grayling's legal aid reforms of 2013 will have gone some way to putting the genie back in the bottle.

It is tempting to believe that when not suing the Ministry, prison life is about SKY TV, substance abuse, (and in the case of open prisons) smuggled in strumpets. For the record, prisoners have had in-cell television as a standard privilege since 1997. Prior to that television was only available in communal areas during association periods. For the further record, prisoners do not have in-cell SKY TV and never have had in public sector prisons. I cannot speak for the private sector. It is true that many prisoners will have around 50 channels to choose from. This is because all new sets are equipped with Free View and have been for the last few years. Substance abuse is a major problem inside as I discussed in the previous chapter. As for smuggling in prostitutes to open prisons I can only say that I have heard the stories, which I suspect improve with telling, but have no evidence for such events and would be reasonably confident that none such occurred in my four years as Deputy Governor at Ford. Illicit alcohol was always a far bigger worry as it was not difficult to smuggle in and to avoid detection it was consumed as quickly as possible with the inevitable effect of severe intoxication where spirits were concerned. It is a matter of public record that the Ford riot of New Year's Eve 2010–11 was caused by alcohol and that only two prison officers and four support grades were on duty that night. No one should expect prisoners not to take advantage of such a situation. The only wonder is that alcohol fuelled disorder was not more frequent given that staffing levels were never adjusted and improved physical security refused in the face of a more challenging population. However, inmates in open prisons do have one obvious extra much prized privilege in addition to their own room keys and outside working opportunities. Much prized are town visits with relatives subject to satisfactory risk assessment. Hotels in Bognor Regis did a good trade and probably still do in weekend afternoon bookings catering for sex starved prisoners and their long-suffering partners. Rather less amusingly there were occasions when prisoners were caught in flagrante with their visitor in a visits room toilet, the sexual imperative being so pressing that no thought was given to the fact that rutting like animals could be observed by children. In closed prisons, prisoners are not able to leave their table so full intercourse is not possible, but it does not necessarily prevent furtive under the table activity.

Prisons are communities and therefore have rules: formal and informal, written and unwritten. In terms of the way in which prisoners' lives are regulated by the state, most of it is now written down. Prisons have always been among the most rule bound institutions and that has become even more so over the last years as discretion and individuality have been filtered out. By contrast, the self-regulation of the prisoner community is carried out by wholly unwritten rules. It is an oral tradition handed down by each generation. Amongst prisoners there is a distinct pecking order, dominated by the physically strong, and amongst adults it includes those with the ability to command external resources. As with any gang in the community, there is an acknowledged leader and known henchmen. Life sentences and long determinate sentences confer status where these prisoners are held in local prisons or have moved down the system to lower security establishments, except of course for sex offenders who are loathed as 'beasts'. Just as in the community, there will be rival gangs, and on occasion there will be confrontations. With young offenders they are more likely to occur spontaneously and in front of staff. At the foot of the pecking order are the inadequate, the debtors and other unfortunates who for whatever reason attract the attention of the dominant group. As one would expect also at the foot of the pecking order are sex offenders. However, this of little consolation to the other criminals in the dominated group as in most prisons the sex offenders are in their own segregated accommodation, and the few that are not are those that have managed to go undetected by their peers. Even amongst sex offenders, there is a pecking order; rapists outrank paedophiles.

In the middle, there is a group of prisoners simply trying to do their time as anonymously as they can. In Young Offender Institutions, the middle has been distinctly squeezed. I can remember Paul Whitehouse, Governor of Deerbolt 1984–92, pointing this out to me as an emerging trend as far back as 1991. Sentencing policy in the context of social change is at the heart of the matter. Courts have been encouraged to ensure that only those for whom prison is essential actually receive a custodial sentence, as the received wisdom is that prison can do more harm than good for young people and seriously blight their life chances as a term of imprisonment closes so many doors for the rest of their lives. The upshot of this is that basically honest young men who find themselves involved in a town centre punch up will not go to prison unless there are significant aggravating factors such as the use of weapons, serious criminal damage, or a history of multiple offences of violence. Other than in the wholly exceptional cases such as the riots of 2011, exemplary sentencing is sparingly used. This has the effect of keeping all but the most serious first offenders out of prison. It therefore has the effect of significantly reducing the numbers of hitherto respectable young people of reasonable intelligence sentenced to terms in custody. In terms of the makeup of the prison population, it takes out a mainly pro-social group who are a riskier target for bullies than the drug dependent, the sexually abused and the highly suggestible who inhabit the lower echelons of the inmate sub culture. The buffer zone amongst the young offender population that acted as a natural check on the excesses of the worst elements has gone. Thus those young offenders who would not choose gang membership are in the same difficult position as those denied it.

As a consequence, Young Offender Institutions have ceased to be the colleges of crime (if indeed they ever were) violently excoriated by penal reformers as places that corrupt unfortunate and vulnerable young people unfortunate enough to encounter the criminal justice system. Almost invariably a juvenile in custody has an offending history as long as your arm, has appeared regularly before the courts since he was ten (the minimum age of criminal responsibility) and will have had numerous non-custodial disposals, none of which involve punishment, before finally receiving a custodial sentence. They are already hardened, often feral criminals for whom the sink estates of our great cities are the real colleges of crime. Dog has already learned to eat dog. Custody is simply the postgraduate stage that further cements the pecking order of the streets. For those of you who remain unconvinced then the ITV two-part documentary on HMYOI Aylesbury is an eye opener. As I have said previously, prison reflects that which is happening in wider society. Gangs are not new but the extent to which they have transferred themselves from the street to the prison landing with no fall off in the level of aggression and animosity is significant. There has always been a degree of tribalism in much the same way as there is tribalism amongst football supporters which is now largely put aside when supporting England. In prison, the trend is the reverse of that with football hooliganism. Young men are clinging to the gang for identity, status and protection. Membership of a high status group protects your possessions, your backside and your relatives on the outside from intimidation. Thus the mean streets of South and West London are readily translated to the landings of the Young Offender Institutions that serve those areas.

The new kid on the block in prison gang warfare is the Muslim gang. In the community, Muslims who comprise around 5% of the population typically live in their own part of town which both protects and segregates. Muslims do not use public houses and few attend football matches both of which are very much the province of the host community. In prison the picture can be very different. In the decade 2004–14, the Muslim prison population almost doubled to around 15% of the total population. The largest concentration of Muslims can be found at Whitemoor prison in Cambridgeshire reaching a staggering 50% in 2017. Whitemoor is a high security establishment so it is inevitable that all those serving will have committed very serious offences including those connected with terrorism and therefore will be a highly radicalised population with dominant characteristics. The upshot is that those prisoners wishing to do their time quietly have another set of problems to confront which include attempts to impose Sharia law and forced conversion to Islam. The traditional balance of power has been upset in prisons like Belmarsh, Feltham and Whitemoor where regular gangsters have been forced to make their accommodation with the 'Muslim Boys'. It should be noted that Islam in prison is not exclusively Asian. Afro-Caribbean prisoners have been attracted in numbers and there is a sprinkling of white adherents to the Muslim faith.

There are, of course, written rules to counter intimidation, drug dealing and sexual abuse. The reason they are not more effective is the code of Omerta. 'Grassing', as it is known, is a cardinal sin and the reprisals for being suspected or caught can be brutal. Grasses are ranked on a par with sex offenders, known colloquially as nonces, and in rhyming slang as 'bacons'. Nevertheless, grassing does go on for a variety of reasons. The non-drug using minority and those prisoners trying to break their habit are not averse to tipping off staff, the anonymous note in the post box being a favoured method of giving information. However, intelligence often owes little to the moral minority. Established dealers take a dim view of rivals and are happy to de-rail their operations. Similarly those in debt have a vested interest in getting dealers and their henchman transferred, or alternatively getting themselves transferred. However safety is not guaranteed as it often easy to find out where an inmate has been moved to either within the establishment or to another prison. Debts being sold on or attached to a cell regardless of the occupant are other hazards for the unwary to negotiate. It is fair to say that the 'no grassing' rule is frequently observed in breach.

Another feature of the informal prison culture has been the greater tolerance of homosexuality than might be expected of a population that is largely ill-educated, more prone to prejudice and only too keen to ensure that someone is always below them in the pecking order as a potential scapegoat. The reason is fairly simple. Homosexuality provides an outlet for the sexual frustrations of otherwise heterosexual men. They become 'heteroflexible'. However, although it is impossible to quantify, it cannot be denied that a significant percentage of sexual activity in men's prison is undertaken under duress. The rapist enjoys protection not just from the prison code of omerta but also from the understandable reluctance of men to report traumatising sexual assaults which have wrecked their masculine self-esteem. In truth the real hidden rape problem in this country is to be found in our prisons. Duress is not simply about violent buggery. As I have said earlier, selling one's arse in order to obtain drugs, discharge debts or purchase protection is not uncommon. Buggery is even used as a form of discipline and is not always inflicted by those whose first preference is men. In 2008, 119 sexual assaults were reported by prisoners. In the same year, the US Justice Department calculated that there had been 216,000 sexual assaults in American prisons, a figure marginally higher than recorded in the community. Given that the USA incarcerates around 2.3 million people and there were another 312 million people living in the community this is a truly staggering figure. On this basis, American prisons are the rape capital of the world. Not all sexual assaults involve penetration but they all involve defilement and violation. There is no suggestion that the UK has anything approaching what is an institutionalised problem in the USA but it is difficult to believe that there is not serious underreporting of sexual duress.

However, consenting adults in prison are in a privileged position. If your orientation is firmly gay, then your lot is very much improved. Prison Governors no longer have the power to prevent the issue of condoms to prisoners. They are now handed out on request. When the Senior Medical Officer was an employee and therefore subordinate to the in-charge Governor, there the matter rested. However, since Prison Healthcare was contracted out to Primary Care Trusts, Prison Governors have had no say in the matter. In custody, homosexuality has therefore been medicalised. Although the reason for issuing of condoms is to prevent the spread of HIV, a prison cell or for that matter a prison shower facility, are not private places as defined by the 1967 Act. Indeed the 2003 Sexual Offences Act, while it abolished the strictly gay offence of gross indecency, continued to forbid sexual relations in public, a proscription applying to both gay and straight people. PCTs are therefore accessories to unlawful activity.

The general public may be surprised to learn that there is actually no means of charging a prisoner under Rule 51, the prison disciplinary code. This is because the disciplinary offence 'is Indecent in Act, Language or Gesture' is no longer provided for under rule 51. The reason for this is that the specifically gay male criminal offence of gross indecency was abolished in 2003. The only offences against the code which offer the potential of disciplinary action is paragraph 23 'disobeys any rule or regulation' or more usually paragraph 20 'uses any threatening, abusive or insulting behaviour'. However, for the former to succeed, the Governor must publish a specific Governor's Order forbidding homosexual acts. In our politically correct times, no Prison Governor could expect to survive above a further 48 hours in office, if he or she did so. Yet on the other side of the coin, quite properly Prison Governors enact local rules against sexual touching in the visits room, and therefore charges under rule 51 can be laid. There is, of course, the option to refer the matter to the police. It goes without saying that no police officer would risk his career any more than would a Prison Governor. Instead the prison service has moved in the opposite direction. In its guidance to staff on the disciplinary code, it recommends the use of paragraph 20 thus defining public sexual acts as insulting behaviour, but says that disciplinary charges should not be laid if prisoners are in bed together during the night as they are entitled to a degree of privacy! I stress this is not confidential official information. I found it without difficulty on the internet. Interestingly, there is potential for the dice to be loaded even further. The previous Director General, Phil Wheatley, won an argument with Ministers in that a prisoner's cell was to be treated as his/her home, which allowed prisoners to retain the privilege of smoking in their cells when smoking prohibitions were radically extended in 2006, an issue to which I shall return. This leaves clear wriggle room for Stonewall and a smart lawyer, although the de facto legalisation that I have described above is likely to be left undisturbed in the current climate. The other danger in a cell being treated as a private place is that searching would require a warrant.

Although homosexuality in prisons is under the radar, privileges enjoyed by prisoners are not. The newspapers get very excited about television, outside work placements at open prisons and cells decked out to look like three star hotel bedrooms. I have dealt with television earlier and outside work placements are available only after stringent risk assessments and several years of not just good behaviour, but active participation in offending behaviour courses. As for prison cells, you will not find a hotel bedroom where the water closet is in a corner by the table, nor will you find one where one occupant is forced to defecate in front of another. Yes prisoners can personalise their cells and those on the highest level of privileges can have their own bedding, but many cells in old local prisons are damp, covered in graffiti, the paint peeling and the toilets stained. They are Spartan environments and remain so even when a new occupant gives them a thorough clean. I have always believed that the sty makes the pig rather than vice-versa. It should not be assumed that accommodation in open prisons is always better. During my time at Ford (2001–05), there was still some dormitory accommodation and the funds to refurbish it came through pitifully slowly. The jail's Independent Monitoring

Board and the Inspectorate both quite rightly criticised the squalid and dehumanising conditions that prevailed in the induction dormitory. Cushy this was not.

Oddly enough tobacco smoking has not particularly exercised the press. The number of smokers amongst the male population in the UK has now dropped to around 21%, a massive drop from just over 50% at its peak in 1974. However amongst UK prisoners the percentage of smokers is around 80%. This is a compelling statistic and when added to the narcotic and alcohol problems already referred to, it can readily be seen that the prison population plus those recidivists temporarily in the community make up what can confidently be said to be the least healthy section of the population as a whole. As has been said, the smoking privilege survived because the prison cell was treated as a personal residential area and was therefore unaffected by the 2006 smoking ban in public buildings. By 2016, this position had become untenable and a phased smoke free programme was rolled out, of which more in Chapter 11. The Prison Officers Association supported a total ban citing the exposure of its members to passive smoking and the increased fire risk that comes with prisoner possession of matches and cigarette lighters. In America, the Federal Bureau of Prisons banned smoking and the possession of tobacco by prisoners in 2014. As recently as 1986, more than half of US prisoners received free tobacco. New Zealand introduced a smoking ban in 2010, and a new prison in the Isle of Man opened in 2011 is also totally smoke free. Juvenile prisoners have officially been denied the tobacco privilege since 1988 although enforcement was not total immediately. Only in 2007 did two juvenile establishments become completely smoke free in that staff and visitors were also prohibited from smoking anywhere on establishment property.

Although adult prisoners were now only allowed to smoke in their cells and therefore not in communal areas a change to administrative procedures consequent on the introduction of the Incentive and Earned privileges scheme in 1996 actually had the effect of giving convicted prisoners greater access to tobacco, allowing them to purchase tobacco from private cash which was administratively amalgamated with earnings to produce a total spend. Previously only un-convicted prisoners could purchase tobacco out of resources other than prison earnings. It was also noticeable that in the latter years of my service adjudicating Governors were discouraged from taking away in possession tobacco from prisoners serving periods of cellular confinement. The official line had got softer and the probable explanation is the fear of prisoner reaction. We live in a culture of entitlement fuelled both by consumerism and political correctness and in prison this means that prisoners who by nature are not conditioned to fear consequences, have significant potential to riot despite the fact that conditions broadly are much improved, prison administration is more responsive and the prison disciplinary code is much less draconian. In the first decade of the 21st Century, the drive for decency, defined as conditions which you would find acceptable for an incarcerated close relative, made great strides under the leadership of former Director Generals, Martin Narey and Phil Wheatley.

I was fortunate in my service that I never had to face rioting prisoners but I can recall having to retreat to a safe distance until reinforcements could be summoned to deal with unrest one night in the dormitories at Werrington. The most fractious nights were always a night or two before canteen, when tobacco was running low and trainees were suffering withdrawal symptoms. However, I can remember the impact of the Strangeways (Manchester) riot in April 1990; the 25 days it took to clear the jail of prisoners and its almost total destruction. Strangeways had to be wholly rebuilt and was not opened until 1994. The system held (just) in 1990 but there were other significant disturbances and one other prison, Pucklechurch, a male Young Offender Institution, was lost. Somehow we kept the lid on, but it was draining and nerve racking. The previous year there had been a very serious but much less reported disturbance at Risley. At one point a group of prison officers were trapped in a cell to which they had fled for safety as inmates rampaged. Gradually prisoners battered their way through a series of cell walls in a bid to reach the trapped staff. Only by using a cherry picker was it possible to remove the window bars and rescue the staff in the nick of time. In 1986, HMP Northeye in East Sussex was burned down. In September 1992, there was a major riot at Wymott, the second within the space of a few years in accommodation that was wholly unsuitable for the population it held. The most recent riot to seriously impact on public consciousness was that at HMP Ford on New Year's Eve 2010, the first ever significant disturbance in open conditions, this one being alcohol fuelled. As you can imagine, it was a constant battle to prevent alcohol getting past the very limited physical security. Given the risk of discovery bottles of spirits are consumed like pop with the inevitable effect on those with already aggressive tendencies. Ford had long ceased to be the gentlemen's prison dominated by bent solicitors, sophisticated fraudsters and other sundry middle class felons. Reflecting the system it served the dominant group was now younger men with established drug and alcohol habits who found themselves in Ford because the closed estate was overcrowded and the main criterion applied was their trustworthiness not to abscond. Indeed the absconding rate fell as the clientele of Ford deteriorated. Given that this class of prisoner could replicate their lives on sink estates with only the irritation of having to do a few hours' work on the prison farm or a little light litter picking getting in the way, it is no wonder that walking out of the gate held little attraction. If it was necessary to collect a package from a pre-arranged drop off point, a prisoner did not need to report sick, he could self-certificate. Honest!

The point I am making is that all policy changes potentially have consequences and have also to be seen against the social backdrop if disaster is not to happen. The impact of the smoking ban is discussed in full in Chapter 11.

One prisoner on his own can put out of action a number of cells if he is determined enough as being confined to the 'strongbox' is permitted only as a temporary measure. The thought of large groups of prisoners co-ordinating violence throughout the estate and taking large amounts of accommodation out of action almost simultaneously is not be contemplated lightly. Beyond that there is the unseen lasting trauma suffered by terrified staff and uninvolved prisoners. The kind of copycat rioting seen on the streets in August 2011 being replicated in our prisons over something as trivial as cigarettes was a wholly undesirable outcome, despite the irrefutable arguments against smoking. The understandable lack of public sympathy for prisoners, now much more prevalent than in 1990, could even be seen as a potentially exacerbating factor. It is fair to argue that experience of other countries has not been a total loss of control. However prison guards in the USA are armed. I can also recall the abolition of the largely forgotten alcohol privilege for un-convicted prisoners in 1987. Up to that point assuming they had a visit which they were permitted every day except Sunday, relatives could bring in one pint of canned beer for consumption in cell on a daily basis. The expected prisoner reaction to the withdrawal of the privilege did not materialise, much to everyone's relief. However, there is a difference between hitting 15% of the population and 80%.

One of the concerns of HMIP is that the distinction between the un-convicted, i.e. those in custody despite the absence of a guilty verdict, and the convicted has been so watered down in our local prisons as to be meaningless. Indeed HMIP go further and argue that they suffer worse conditions. The creation of wholly separate remand facilities is superficially attractive but given that the available prison estate which varies immensely in size, security, facilities and convenience of travel from sentencing courts, such a change would pose a huge logistical problem. As a solution, it has too many flaws which only adds to the allure of the do nothing solution.

I referred earlier to the Incentives and Earned Privileges Scheme (I&EP) piloted in 1995 and rolled out across the estate in 1996. It envisaged three levels of regime privileges; basic, standard and enhanced. In some prisons, there are super enhanced levels. Un-convicted prisoners would also be covered by the system, but differentials between them and the convicted would remain. It was made clear fairly swiftly that all prisoners were to enter the system at standard level. Thus only enhanced privileges would be earned. Mere compliance and avoiding the prison disciplinary system were not sufficient to merit promotion. Prisoners would be expected to co-operate with offending behaviour courses, challenge their addictions and take on responsibility. Standard privileges could be lost and would be regained by behaving in line with normal expectations, a term not always easily defined. Enhanced privileges varied a little from establishment to establishment reflecting local circumstances but typically included higher spending allowances at the prison canteen, longer visits and eligibility for extended family visits, and access to better-paid employment within the prison. However, the wearing of own clothes as a standard level privilege in some local prisons diluted it as a long established privilege for the un-convicted in the same way as the administrative amalgamation of prisoners' moneys. Privileges such as extra access to the gym were perceived by some to cut across the health needs of the rest of the population. Extra association was soon abandoned as it was staff intensive and was an early casualty of efficiency savings.

Despite reservations the scheme has broadly been a success, particularly in what were known as the dispersal prisons, these days better known as the High Security estate, although that success is now under pressure from radicalised Muslim prisoners who have replaced IRA men as those for whom co-operation with the system is an anathema on principle. For external critics, the principal weakness has always been what they perceive as the generosity of an unearned standard level. Internally prison officers have tended to the view that far too few prisoners are subject to basic regime, with fewer shorter visits, less spending power and less time out of cell. The problem is that it co-exists uncomfortably with the disciplinary system. Basic regime is supposed to be at a level higher than in segregation. However even prisoners segregated as a punishment must have exercise, are still entitled to visits and are not automatically denied access to the prison canteen. The most obvious and most meaningful loss of privilege will be television, which applies also to basic regime. On the crowded landings, a prisoner on standard regime may not be denied TV simply because his cellmate has been reduced to basic regime. It sounds easily solvable, until you have an odd number. Separate basic regime units (BRUs) are an option that has been tried but they suffer inevitably from being de facto segregation units but without the safeguards provided for in Prison Service Orders. At the risk of being out of step with those who would prefer to lock prisoners up and throw away the key, I would abolish basic regime thus leaving bad behaviour to the disciplinary system, of which more in Chapter 5, thus making I&EP an entirely positive tool. It then leaves open the possibility of reviewing standard level privileges and making for greater differentiation between the two remaining regime levels.

Ultimately, the corrections system seeks to reintegrate all but a small number of lifers for whom release is not an option back into society as fully-fledged, non-offending citizens. Crucial to that process is the restoration of self-esteem. Within establishments prisoners are trained by the Samaritans as Listeners who devote hours of their time to the acutely distressed and suicidal. They do it selflessly and save lives. They develop empathy, a quality that will help immensely in avoiding reoffending. As such, they deserve enhanced privileges. Almost as far below the radar is the charity work done by prisoners in many establishments including donating money from their meagre weekly prison earnings which often average less than £10. Finally I should add that one of my greatest pleasures was presenting certificates to prisoners completing offending behaviour courses. Beneath the bravado, the tattoos and the macho posturing often lurk shame and contrition, and a good citizen waiting to get out if only they can collectively stick to new peer group norms and individually find the courage and determination to put into practice on the landing and on the council estate what they have learned in the classroom. The challenge for our prison system, our probation services and our society is to support to their endeavours.

Chapter 4
Prison Officers

I sometimes think that prison officers are the most misunderstood workforce in the country, and not just by the newspapers which insist on referring to them as warders or guards. For the record, prison officers have not been known as warders and wardresses since 1921. Warders are in fact a museum grade found in a traditional uniform at the Tower of London. On the odd occasion that prison officers feature in a newspaper cartoon, they are always shown as burly individuals wearing a 1970s style uniform comprised of tunic, cap with slashed peak pulled down almost over the eyes, and of course extremely shiny size 12 boots, all this being complemented by the ubiquitous calf length key chain. It is *Porridge* preserved in aspic. The unmistakeably military Mr Mackay, the gimlet eyed strutting martinet still influences the perception of prison officers by the general public, despite the fact that much has changed over the decades since that iconic series was made. In 1985, tunics ceased to be worn on the landings when they were replaced by sweaters. After that, tunics were worn only in court as best dress. In 1995, court duties were contracted out to the private sector, apart from the escort of Category A prisoners. The upshot of these changes is that tunics are rarely worn other than for funerals. The wearing of peaked caps was also abolished in the mid-90s and they are no longer issued. The modern prison officer can order a baseball cap to keep his head dry and a fleece lined jacket instead of the traditional military style greatcoat for inclement weather. The changes have also affected female officers with hats and skirts no longer issued as uniform items. In Juvenile establishments, formal uniforms have been dumbed down to polo shirts and tracksuit bottoms. During Martin Narey's term as Director General (1998–2004), marching and drilling were removed from the training manual and replaced by more classes on race relations. Prison officers have effectively been demilitarised except when in riot gear, where like the police they resemble the French CRS. However, despite the overt civilianisation of the service and the dismantling of the seniority culture, it remains an organisation where traditions of formality not merely persist but are actively maintained.

I have to confess that some colleagues were initially a mystery to me. The main reason for that was the Armed Forces experience that I lacked. Male prison officers born between 1927 and 1939 had experienced peacetime conscription before its abolition in 1960. Among the younger men, the majority had served as regulars. Some two thirds of the men on my initial training course in 1984 had military backgrounds, despite the fact that the service was by then trying to recruit outside of its normal catchment area. Female prison officers, who until 1988 were restricted to working in female establishments, were less obviously dominated by former military personnel, but they still formed a significant and influential minority. Military slang was something I found incomprehensible but their overt values of loyalty and solidarity were ones I understood. Bonding over a few pints was another tradition that played well with me. Prison officers also preferred the tried and tested to the new-fangled and fashionable. These values were shared by another group of recruits whose numbers would grow as traditional industries declined, with former miners to the forefront as the Prison Service offered one of the few escape routes available from depressed and run down pit villages. The Prison Service had long been unionised, and working class former soldiers had no difficulty in rediscovering their roots in organised trade unionism. This should not surprise us, as historically the armed forces were class-based institutions divided into commissioned officers and enlisted men, a division in 1984 still replicated in the Prison Service. The highly disciplined characteristics of good soldiers co-existed readily with the innately suspicious view of authority held by trade unionists. It is this confluence that has made the Prison Officers Association a formidable trade union.

It was the downsides to the military mind-set that puzzled me. Firstly, many of my colleagues in the 1980s were vocal supporters of Mrs Thatcher, Conservative Prime Minister and hero of the Falklands, notwithstanding her known animosity to trade unions (apart from Solidarity in Poland). The Labour party represented everything that they loathed: crudely unilateral nuclear disarmament, appeasement of the IRA and gay rights, the last of which was very much an anathema amongst armed servicemen of that era. There was a very distinct canteen culture. I should be clear that a canteen culture is not innately unhealthy. Managerial condemnation of canteen cultures is often far more about imposing a barely hidden agenda of politically correct change than it is about rooting out poor behaviour for which sanctions have always been available. However, I found that a minority of ex-servicemen could be very rigid in their attitudes and on occasions some were downright intolerant. Their world was easily divided into black and white, good and bad, deserving and undeserving, and most importantly, the strong and the weak. The meek were most certainly not blessed, apart from the Prison Chaplain. Conformity to shared values was paramount. Amongst male prison officers heterosexuality was an assumed common factor. Like the armed forces there was no room for and no tolerance of male homosexuality amongst colleagues, (the women's service was very different) although attitudes to gay prisoners were somewhat more accommodating. The word gay was not part of the lexicon. The culture was explicitly macho. They were suspicious of outsiders and of academic qualifications. At its worst, these attitudes could manifest themselves in some very negative handling of people which bordered on bullying. In the aftermath of a series of suicides by young private soldiers at Deepcut barracks in Surrey, the Army has sought to clean up its act in this regard in more recent years. Ex-servicemen often expected the prison service to be an extension of the armed services with uniform, a rank structure based on class and education, and quasi-military discipline imposed on colleagues and prisoners alike. Additionally in 1984, there will still estates of prison service quarters which replicated the close and incestuous communities that lived around military barracks. This allowed prison officers from a military background to make minimal accommodation with civilian life. Other grades apart from governors were referred to as 'civvies', sometimes with a degree of contempt. Problem establishments and problem work areas within them flourished when a powerful minority dominated effectively encouraged by weak management. In establishments where freemasonry had a hold this was a toxic culture.

After training, my first posting was to Werrington House Detention Centre. As I have explained in the first chapter, these establishments for young offenders were very different than the rest of the system. Prisoners marched everywhere, there were daily parades and inspections, and there was compulsory PE in which young prisoners could expect to be 'beasted' on a daily basis with tough circuit training. It was an environment perfect for ex-servicemen, the bulk of whom had been NCOs. The regime pretty much allowed them to treat the young offenders as though they were raw recruits entering basic training with a daily diet of bollockings delivered in ferocious industrial language. It is fair to say that the rules which forbade the verbal abuse of prisoners did not apply in Detention Centres. Some of it was fairly mild, for example telling a forgetful prisoner it was a good job his balls were in a bag. However some of the other stuff was straight off the parade ground. A trainee whose boots were not gleaming might find himself told that the best part of him had run down his mother's leg at conception. The tongue-lashings were not moderated in front of the Chaplain. However by 1984, attendance at divine service was no longer compulsory, which did not go down well with a number of the ex-servicemen. I should explain that the word parade was in common use and that staff meetings including those where the Governor addressed the entire staff were referred to and advertised as staff parades which it was a potential disciplinary offence to miss without permission if you were on duty. A number of my colleagues felt that the same stricture should to trainees and chapel attendance. Indeed Reception officers of that era often refused to enter 'nil' in the space reserved for religion and told prisoners very firmly that those who professed no religion would be recorded as Church of England. One particular colleague would not record Rastafarianism as a religion on the basis that it was a criminal cult. These days that attitude would see the officer dismissed from the service.

Rank and seniority were hugely important in the lives of prison officers. Distinctions of rank were of course imported from the military and distinctions of seniority were still a feature of working class life. My father was a train driver and British Rail, as it then was, had a rigid seniority culture. Only in his mid-fifties did he graduate to driving inter city services which had lucrative mileage payments. Time in was the key criterion for prestige or sought after jobs. So it was with the Prison Service. The post of library officer was the almost exclusive preserve of officers with in excess of 20 years of service. Long serving officers did not demean themselves supervising prisoners at chapel. In local prisons, junior officers began their working lives on the top landing: the 'fours', and in some prisons such as Wandsworth and Lancaster Castle the 'fives'. Only the most senior men worked at ground level. It was the same in the censors office (back in 1984 all prisoner mail without exception was read). At Werrington I soon discovered that you supervised outside parties in winter and internal cleaning parties in summer. Taking the sun was another privilege for the long serving. As a junior officer, except when on escort duties, you could expect on a scheduled shift to be detailed a work party. Although part of the seniority system this was in fact a good thing because this was how you developed your prisoner handling skills. Apart from scheduled meal breaks a junior officer could expect to be facing prisoners all day at Werrington House as a consequence of the dormitory conditions. At weekends junior officers were detailed Sports and Games in the afternoon. Senior men were allowed the warmth of the visits room. Again it was an excellent system where you honed your skills. The downside of the weekend sport detail was that some of your long serving colleagues were reluctant to relieve you and supervise the showers which could mean having your own shower during your meal break. For some people, seniority was the closest substitute for the privileges of rank. At HMP Holloway, the women's jail, the number of an officer's key bunch reflected seniority, probably the most extreme example of the principle that I came across.

At the time, only two things cut across seniority: freemasonry and the 'cab rank' principle for the allocation of overtime. If it was your turn, then it was unequivocally your turn. This was important in establishments such as mine, where, unlike local or dispersal (high security) prisons, overtime was not always available. You could even land a good number on occasion. Freemasonry was not a service wide culture, but it is fair to say that it had a strong hold in certain establishments and cut across the rank structure. Thus, someone could be senior to their boss at work in the local lodge. It could and did affect access to career opportunities and continued to have influence in certain establishments even when merit had partly displaced the seniority culture. Wormwood Scrubs was reputed to have its own lodge. At Wakefield in my time there 1993–95, it was clear that there was a meshing of a group of senior managers with the POA Committee with freemasonry the common factor. Freemasonry was also hugely influential at Ford, a fact I discovered only after I had left when I was given a list of members of the brotherhood in that establishment. Let's just say that it explained a great deal. At its most corrupt it protected staff from disciplinary proceedings. In women's prisons, lesbianism was the alternative culture to male dominated freemasonry. It is important to remember that until 1988, with very few exceptions, male officers did not work in female prisons and female officers did not work in male prisons. The virtually separate female prison service was a safe haven for gay women, one of the few walks of life where one could be openly gay and not face discrimination or social ostracism. The flip side of this could be a dominant and aggressive lesbian culture in which sexuality and more particularly the right choice of sexual partner was a major determinant of professional and personal happiness. The coming of cross sex postings in 1988, controversial at the time, did much to mitigate the unhealthier aspects of gender segregation, although inevitably it brought with it other problems. Even so as a manager, it paid to have a handle on the gay community, which in terms of openness was still strictly female. I learned quickly in my spell at Woodhill (1995–98) that it paid to know not simply who was in a relationship with whom, but who had previously been in a relationship with whom, because there could be found the bad blood and lingering petty resentments that could compromise both safety and operational efficiency.

It took some considerable time for female landing staff to be accepted in male establishments. The service dipped its toe in first with governor grades. However, there were precedents. Borstals had one resident female member of staff employed by the prison department with regular inmate contact. This was matron who ranked equivalently to a Principal Officer. Werrington House Detention Centre still boasted a seamstress, a uniformed post which was graded as a prison auxiliary. The post died on her retirement in the early 90s. Most female staff with prisoner contact were teachers, but they were the employees of the local authority.

A challenge to the status quo came in 1983 when a female catering officer was posted to Werrington House on the closure of Moor Court women's prison. The local branch of the Prison Officers Association resisted the posting but lost the battle in court. It is likely that this decision paved the way for cross sex postings for prison officers which came into force in 1988. The court defeat was not the end of the story and for some time there was guerrilla resistance as the local branch decided that its members would refuse to issue her with keys. The protest fizzled out under the threat of disciplinary action but it was still a major talking point when I arrived in August 1984. My new colleagues were perfectly happy to give me chapter and verse of events. The POA's stated objections were based on privacy and decency given that the catering officers were liable to be called upon to supervise dormitories where fairly obviously there was no privacy and a good deal of communal nudity after PE sessions as trainees dried themselves. As an argument, it had some weight but I would very much doubt that Borstal matrons in their nursing capacity were excused male nudity. Post 1988 as one would expect female officers do not supervise male showers and vice versa, but there are no guarantees when checking on a prisoner's welfare in a cellular environment that he or she will not be in the act of undressing. Indeed for exhibitionists and perverts amongst the prison population being caught in the act of undressing or in sexual activity by an officer of the opposite sex (although this is not essential) is a way of brightening up the day. My own view is that simple sexism was at the heart of the issue for at least some of its protagonists. Stoke-On-Trent in the 1980s rivalled the North East for its Andy Capp stereotypes. Some of my colleagues bought their wives microwave ovens for significant anniversaries. Another colleague objected vociferously to the presence of female staff on the basis that his wife would be unhappy as it might lure him into temptation. Needless to say it was this officer's wife rather than him who indulged in an extra-marital affair. As I recall, the female catering officer moved on within a couple of years and no further female officers were employed at Werrington until the dormitory accommodation was replaced by cellular accommodation in the late 1990s. However some members of the local branch remained vociferous in their objections to the appointment of a female auxiliary to work in the gate lodge in 1990. In due course, she became part of the furniture and her sexuality became of declining interest. Fortunately, she had an excellent sense of humour and dealt easily with the senior officer whose keys just happened to be number 69.

The rank system was the formal culture of the service in 1984 as it still is today, although in a more muted form. Service hierarchy much prefers the term grade, as its connotations are essentially civil service rather than military. Back in 1984, the service was segregated not just by gender but by distinctions of rank which mirrored those of the armed forces with its traditional distinctions of Officers, NCOs and other ranks. In the Prison Service, the officer class were the Governor grades about whom more detail in the next chapter. Suffice it to say at this stage that like the military governor grades had a separate mode of entry to the service and only those under 24 years of age when recruited served a significant period of their training as a prison officer. Governor grades of this era were mainly university educated but the most obvious distinction in the workplace was that governor grades wore suits rather than uniforms. There was an annual competition known as 'The Country House Test' for those prison officers who fancied ascending to the governor grades and were prepared to give up highly lucrative overtime for what as a consequence was the significantly lower monthly stipend of an Assistant Governor. Qualification for the three-day assessment was via an examination which tested arithmetical, verbal and nonverbal skills which I passed whilst still at Officer Training School (OTS). After two years of service, you could then apply for a board. In practice, two or three individuals annually were elevated to the less than serried rank of Assistant Governor and I was not one of them. The NCOs like those in the armed forces had joined as prison officers and occupied in ascending order the Senior Officer, Principal Officer and Chief Officer 2 and 1 ranks which mirrored the military distinctions between senior and junior NCOs in the armed forces. Prison officers at ground floor level were therefore the equivalent of private soldiers, except that they were addressed as mister as the use of surnames was reserved for prisoners.

Formality was the order of the day. You did not address a colleague by their first name in front of prisoners, a good habit I maintained rigorously throughout my service as it sends an on-going message to prisoners about the virtues of respect. Indeed it was deemed unnecessary for prisoners to know the names of staff and a number of my colleagues would hand over a party of prisoners saying 'six to you, sir' rather than 'six to you, Mr Laxton'. Governor grades were always addressed as Sir or Governor and you would be formally addressed in return. My first Governor, Mike Pascoe, still addressed me as Mr Laxton long after I had joined the governor grades myself. Principal Officers were addressed as Sir or PO, and Chief Officers likewise as Sir or Chief. Again you would be formally addressed in return. Only senior officers who were your immediate supervisors were addressed by first name, and only out of the hearing of prisoners. The Chief Officer, who was seen as the equivalent of the RSM in the Army, was a remote and autocratic figure, who may have been loathed as an individual, but whose rank placed him alongside God in the Prison Service hierarchy. God of course was the Governor. Indeed saluting the Governor only went out of fashion a few years before I joined. Prison officers identified with the Chief rather than the Governor. The Chief Officer was seen as the protector of staff against the system. Chief Officers referred to the uniformed ranks below them as 'my officers'. The rank was abolished in 1987 since when old school officers have mourned the demise of the man you could go to if you were in a hole, (provided you were wearing your cap). There is an element of the Chief being remembered in the same nostalgic way as public schoolboys remember the master most prolific with the cane. The Prison Officers Association was founded and given its credibility by Chief Officers which may also account for some of the reverence. However by the mid-80s the POA was no longer the natural habitat of the Chief Officer as they were under significant pressure to act as members of management during the frequent industrial disputes rather than as leaders of the uniformed grades. This tension was one of the strands that brought about the formation of the Prison Governors Association, of which more in the next chapter.

Social change has brought about a more informal society. Outside of jobs such as the Police, Prison and Fire Services it is now unusual for senior managers to be addressed formally, excepting perhaps only the very top bosses. In schools, typically only the Head teacher is addressed formally by subordinates, and that is no longer universal. Tony Blair preferred to be addressed as Tony by his ministers although it was noticeable that Conservative opposition leaders preferred the traditional address of Prime Minister. Like so much of our lives how we speak to people has followed America. We live in the time of the universal Christian name (sorry forename) but the common form of address conceals more than it reveals. It is not a genuine indicator of greater equality, greater democracy or greater diffusion of power. The Duke of Cambridge's servants may address him as William, but it does not make him any less royal than his father whose girlfriends were expected to call him sir. The service itself has consciously sought to break away from the military model and wean prison officers away from being members of a working class organisation with its traditional culture and transform them instead into modern cloned professionals with politically correct attitudes. Old school formality still survives partly because an older generation with traditional values ensures its continuation. For some officers, it has the added bonus of maintaining distance between themselves and management. Clerical grades and other staff working in establishments have long been more informal. During my time as Deputy Governor at HMP Lewes I was always addressed formally by a veteran dog handler but his 22-year-old daughter, a clerk, used my first name from day one as indeed she did with the Governor. I doubt her father would have approved.

Also imported from the military was the system of postings which applied service wide. Recruitment and promotion were both handled centrally and thus until you were halfway through your residential training course, you did not know the name of the establishment at which you would be working, indeed unless you had joined in London it was unlikely to be the jail where you had your initial four weeks familiarisation. Ex-servicemen were familiar with the system having been 'fucked about by professionals' as they described it, but recruits from 'civvy street', particularly those married with families were less impressed at being forced to uproot and move to the other end of the country at the whim of a team of superannuated clerks based in London, although there was an appeal process. The shock was cushioned by the payment of expenses and the availability of quarters. However removal expenses were not paid after 1984 and quarters started being sold off after 1987. It was clear that the system was no longer fit for purpose and impacting on recruitment and retention. When cross sex postings came in the following year, it was another nail in the coffin of the military system. Local recruitment, which was much more cost effective, introduced in the early 90s, was the obvious answer although prisons continued to take people on sideways transfer, but with the abandonment of central postings could now refuse to take staff whose sick record needed a Pickford's truck to transfer it. However as with all reforms it was not an unmixed blessing. The biggest casualty has been the probity and integrity of the promotion and selection process for managers of which more in Chapter 9. The basic rule of thumb is the more senior the appointment the more corrupt the process.

Prison officers were high earners when I joined. The actual basic wage was quite low but a combination of allowances for unsocial hours, premium rates for weekends and almost unlimited overtime in some establishments made for a good standard of living combined with a job security that many workers could only dream about under Mrs Thatcher. Working mid-week rest days was the norm in most establishments and morning only shifts were usually extended. At Werrington House overtime on the opposite weekend (we worked alternate weekends and most prison officers still do) was rarely available, for which I was grateful but in establishments where it was available, overtime ruled peoples' lives. It was not unusual for staff to work seven days a week for weeks on end taking a break only for scheduled leave. Staff on court duties worked a regular 12-hour day and expected to be called into the establishment to work overtime at weekends. This made an 80-hour week the norm and was worth around 105 hours in the pay packet. The obvious downside to this was in relation to the health of staff. Prison officers had gained the right to retire at the age of 55 in the mid-60s as it was demonstrably the case that they lived five years less in retirement. Service in excess of 20 years counted double for pension purposes. In that era, overtime was compulsory and not until 1980 could officers opt completely out of overtime although very few did. Thus although overtime was voluntary there was considerable pressure from management and indeed sometimes from colleagues to work it, just to demonstrate its necessity. Although the long working weeks combined with heavy smoking and a drinking culture were injurious to health the POA fought tooth and nail to hang on to a lengthy essential task list that made overtime automatic and high earnings predictable. The inability of HQ to produce recruits at a rate necessary to fill vacancies caused by retirement and sadly by deaths in service (rarely by resignation in the male service) helped protect staff from the periodic attempts by management to enforce budgetary control of overtime. As budgets were managed centrally, local Governors had no incentive to change the culture. In any event in establishments where overtime was restricted unofficial sick rotas were in place to ensure that overtime was available. In those days, the POA always had the last word. By the time of Mrs Thatcher's enforced retirement in 1990, the POA could truly claim to be the last bastion of unreconstructed trade unionism in the land. The solidarity of prison officers remains impressive to this day.

Nationally industrial relations were rarely anything other than poor. At establishment level they varied across the spectrum from good to awful and a change of Governor or local branch secretary could see a rapid change for better or worse. When I became a governor grade, I found that much depended on the quality of officials. I'm sure local trade union officials hold the same view about the quality of the Governor and Deputy Governor. Those who availed themselves of TUC training were almost invariably better to deal with because at least there was a shared knowledge of the rulebook, if not always a shared interpretation. Certain newspapers would have you believe that the POA is a militant trade union headed by the heirs of Arthur Scargill hell bent on defending the restrictive practices that belonged to the era of shoulder length hair, flared trousers and glam rock. Well there were a small number of officials as there are in any trade union that saw working class organisations as vehicles for Marxist revolution and there were some disaffected and frustrating individuals for which battles with management were their reason for living in an environment which otherwise gave them no job satisfaction apart from the pay packet and the years clocked up for pension purposes. Timeservers are the bane of any workforce, especially when they become union officials. Nevertheless towards the end of my service when I was a national trade official myself I came to understand why industrial relations nationally were so bad, and why the POA refused to trust senior civil servants as a body (there were always individual exceptions) and politicians. It is always difficult to have good working relationships with those whose idea of modernity is to attack hard won pay rates and conditions of service. It is even more difficult when some of those same politicians and officials are unprincipled, contemptuous or duplicitous. In the end, management gets the trade union officials it deserves.

In May of 1986, a national overtime ban brought the service to its knees within 48 hours. Part of the collateral damage was the burning down of Northeye prison, a Category C jail in East Sussex. Subsequent to the 1986 dispute, the Home Office embarked on a more subtle strategy. It bought out weekly pay and overtime making prison officers salaried professionals. Over five years, overtime would be reduced gradually from a 10-hour contractual obligation to zero. It abolished the Chief Officer 1 and Chief Officer 2 grades and likewise did away with the two grades of Assistant Governors. Henceforth they would be Governors 4 and 5 and all would wear suits. Prison service quarters were offered at discount prices to their occupants, mirroring the flagship 'right to buy' policy initiated by Margaret Thatcher's government when it took power in 1979. New recruits would have different conditions of service and not have the right to retire until they were 60. In 2007, new recruits joined on the basis that they would retire at 65 and eventually this will extend to 68. Those with the right to retire at 60 still in service in 2023 will lose that right. Returning to 1987 the most significant change was the creation of the unified service. From henceforward for the first time it would be possible to have joined as a prison officer and serve at every rank up to in-charge Governor and beyond in the Senior Civil Service. Paul Carroll who achieved that feat in 2007 was awarded the CBE in 2012. However for most prison officers this was irrelevant. The package known as 'Fresh Start' was rammed through by virtue of pension provisions that ensured the support of long serving staff.

Although in many respects these were civilised reforms that benefitted the health and promotion prospects of staff, Fresh Start was the first step in restricting the power and influence of the POA. At my own establishment there were very few quarters and none of them met the criteria for a mortgage without significant improvements. As such it passed us by but in reality it was a hugely significant reform. Prison officers became property owners in numbers as quarters were bought and new recruits bought their home in the private sector. Staff communities and the solidarity that went with that were gradually broken up. Atomisation had begun. The simple truth was that prison officers who are servicing mortgages rather than paying peppercorn rents for quarters had so much more to lose during industrial action if they are not being paid. Fresh Start also allowed the department to reduce starting pay for new recruits according to what it perceived as market conditions. The continued presence of a dozen incremental points on the pay spine was no consolation to recruits unable to make up their pay with lucrative overtime. The inevitable impact was to reduce the age of recruits but it also impacted on the traditional recruiting ground of NCOs leaving the armed forces and also former police officers who once formed a significant group. Whether this was the law of unintended consequences or a carefully thought out semi-secret long-term plan, I cannot say. However that which followed, privatisation of new prisons beginning in 1991 and the burgeoning obsession with diversity that manifested itself in a politically correct recruitment agenda after 1997 were deliberate and well thought out.

It is important to remember that distaste for the POA comes from left as well as right. The Prison Officers Association is perceived as part of an ongoing racism that it is desperate to eradicate from society. No other trade union is labelled in this way. Some of it goes back to the 1970s when a small number of prison officers at a London gaol were seen to wear National Front badges. More recently Feltham prison officers were the subject of allegations at the public inquiry into the murder of Zaid Mubarak by a racist cell-mate in 2001, that they deliberately put known racist white young offenders with black young offenders and then stood back to watch the fun. It is important to remember that these allegations were neither substantiated nor were they made by individuals with any credibility. Nevertheless, mud sticks. We also know that Paul Boateng, a former lawyer of Ghanaian extraction, Prisons Minister at the turn of the millennium, was determined to privatise Brixton prison, although in the end there were no bidders. Paul Boateng's antipathy to the POA was well known and it is the best observable evidence that New Labour did not regard the POA as a bona fide working class organisation and therefore one it could treat differently to other trade unions. For the elite movers and shakers of My Generation who cannot forget their Marxist past, Prison Officers like the Police and Non-Commissioned Officers in the Armed Forces are class collaborators who help capital subjugate labour. Of the above-mentioned groups significantly only Prison Officers were permitted to join a free trade union. Prisons therefore are institutions that oppress working people, ethnic minorities who are numerically over-represented in custody, and increasingly, women. It is another example of how My Generation has had difficulty growing up from Junior Common room rhetoric. For the record, the POA is unequivocal in its opposition to racism. Its members elected and then re-elected a black national chairman, Colin Moses, who stood down in 2010. It is also not the only trade union that in the past, in the age of flairs, loon pants and shoulder length hair, has had members it would not wish to highlight in an official history. Back in 1968 it should be remembered that London Dockers marched in support of Enoch Powell after his notorious 'rivers of blood' speech in April 1968.

It would be pointless to pretend that there is not a small minority of prison officers (and for that matter, prison governors) who besmirch the good name of their profession. Like the poor the corrupt, the violent and the venal are always with us. It is exactly the same in any other profession. Prisons continue to house bent coppers and corrupt solicitors. The most corrupt profession of all is investment banking and sadly none of them seem to be in prison. In more recent times, HMP Lewes received a clergyman who had been performing bogus weddings for immigrants so that they could become British citizens. A small number of MPs have been convicted of expenses fraud, and the truth is that many more should have faced justice. We have teachers who connive at examination cheating. I know of no recruitment and selection process that is fool proof. A margin of human error is built into all human endeavour by our very nature as imperfect creatures. It does not help that some of the literature that has been produced by former prison officers in recent years gives the impression that the writers enjoyed using force and regarded their charges with contempt. My own take on these memoirs is that lurid stories of violence and the constant use of inflammatory language to describe sex offenders was expected by publishers as a condition of going into print. They had already decided to aim downmarket, information and education being sacrificed in favour of exaggeration and titillation. Although former POA national official, the late Ron Adams once publicly referred to prisoners as 'the scum of the earth', this was the last roar of the dinosaur. Like other walks of life the prison service has moved on. It is the Liberal intelligentsia that has not. For the record, I witnessed or became aware of very little in the way of gratuitous violence by staff over more than 26 years of service and the bulk of what would now be classed as racist incidents that I was aware of took place almost exclusively in my early years of service and steadily diminished in much the same way as they have in society as a whole. Racist incidents are only perceived to have increased because victims now have the confidence to complain.

It is worth remembering where we have come from. Until 1965 we had the death penalty and until 1967 birching in prisons was permitted. Corporal punishment persisted in schools until 1986, longer even than in priest-dominated Ireland. Police had no hesitation in beating up terrorist suspects (look at the 1974 archive footage of the Birmingham Six) and sadly this was replicated in Birmingham Prison reception. As for racism, Johnny Speight's well-intentioned effort to turn the public against ignorant racism via his creation of the Alf Garnett character in *Till Death Us Do Part*, which first hit our screens in 1965, only succeeded in putting additional racially abuse terms into the public domain. The Black and White Minstrel show remained on our screens until 1978. During John Major's first administration (1990–92) Alan Clark MP was reprimanded for referring to Africa as 'bongo bongo land'. So let's get the world into perspective. The last time I heard a prison officer say that ethnic minorities could not work in the prison kitchen was back in 1989. Three years later when I was at Bedford the Catering Manager actually preferred his work party to be members of the travelling community. When I was a probationer, I heard a colleague call a black prisoner a coffee coloured convict. Of course he got away with it whereas these days he would be sacked but his poor behaviour did not influence others who were well aware of his qualities, or more accurately lack of them, as a prison officer. The word 'jigaboo' was once common currency. I can say with confidence that I have not heard this word on a prison landing since 1993. Returning to the theme of violence it is worth noting that when I joined in 1984 what are now known as Control and Restraint techniques were in their infancy. Up until then the service had no method for dealing with recalcitrant prisoners other than staff pile in and grab what they could. In such free for all situations, it was inevitable there would be injuries, including to staff. The catalyst for change was the death of Barry Prosser in August 1980, who died after being restrained by staff in Birmingham Prison hospital, three of whom ultimately faced a jury on murder charges and were subsequently acquitted.

As life would have it, I actually witnessed an act of violence by a prison officer on the second morning of my induction at Werrington House in August 1984 when I was shadowing the cleaning officer. The party was being marched off the parade square by the officer-in-charge when he smacked a prisoner round the head for failing to march in step. This happened in front of not only other staff and 100 trainees, but also in front of a Principal Officer. I do not recall there being disciplinary proceedings but I do recall being swiftly hauled off into an office to write a report, which I did truthfully. However, sometime later the officer was transferred on special probation, which he was failing badly when he resigned before being sacked. Again I have to say this individual was not typical. He was an alcoholic and a wife beater regularly found asleep in his car outside his quarter by colleagues already on their way to work. In the forces he had reached the rank of Corporal and I have no doubt he was a bully. I had the misfortune to accompany him on my first escort to court, to Warrington magistrates to produce a young offender on further charges. In those days, the police would look after and produce your prisoner and we could go to the pub. Suffice it to say I only managed to get him out of the pub by convincing him that last orders had already been called (this was before all day opening).

On the way back, he uncuffed me from the prisoner an occurrence which I did not dare report on our return. The 'no grassing' culture was much stricter than that amongst prisoners

The drinking culture is something else that has moderated. These days it is inconceivable that staff would drink in the lunch break during a day's Control and Restraint training. Back in the 80s we would knock back a quick half gallon and training would be a shambles in the afternoon. In line with the rest of our society, alcohol consumption has fallen amongst prison staff. Werrington House where I was first posted was one of a minority of establishments that did not have a staff club. Where clubs existed they were the hubs of the social lives of prison officers and even more so if the staff quarters were close by. It was the norm for clubs to open at lunchtime so for the hardened drinkers there was a golden opportunity to knock back 3–4 pints (and sometimes more) with its obvious impact on performance and professionalism. Again I should stress that the prison service was not the only walk of life where lunchtime drinking was considered unexceptional. Memoirs of journalists and retired detectives tell a very similar story. The Home Office produced an alcohol policy which gave Governors the opportunity to forbid the sale of alcohol at lunchtimes. Governors were in a position to override committees as they had on occasion had to bail out clubs with taxpayers' money when they got into financial difficulty. In 2001, this backstop came to an end. During the week I transferred to HMP Ford as Deputy Governor the staff club closed as the Committee were not prepared to take the financial risk on their shoulders. As a consequence, very few staff clubs now remain. A well-intentioned policy has further damaged the cohesiveness of prison officers as a community. Police clubs have gone the same way. Something is lost when working in the emergency services or the prison service becomes just another job.

Prison officers have always known how to have fun. Some of the entertainment once put on at Prison Service clubs would find its way on to the front page of *The Guardian* today, were it still happening. Female strippers complete with audience participation were regular features as were blue (and often racist) comedians. However this kind of white, men only entertainment fell out of favour as the gender-segregated service disappeared and ethnic minorities began to enter the workplace. It is easy to sneer patronisingly at this kind of entertainment, but it should also be remembered that clubs put on Christmas parties for children, and ran fund raising events for staff with serious medical conditions, and also for local charities. High profile charities such as 'Help for Heroes' would have been obvious beneficiaries were the clubs still thriving. Clubs helped to maintain morale.

HMP Bedford where I worked from 1991 to 1993 did not have a club but it did have a cohesive staff spirit. Again there will be much tut-tutting from the lentil eating classes, but the Ugly Bug competition, revived in my time there was the talk of the prison for weeks in the run up to Christmas. The principle was simple. You paid 20p per vote for the ugliest member of staff. Multiple voting was permitted and all the money raised went to a local pensioners' charity. The top three were announced in reverse order in the prison chapel by one of the Governor grades, who incidentally became a funeral director after retiring from the service, the ultimate in black humour. A great cheer greeted the winner. In 1992, the winning officer had actually made the trophy in the carpenter's shop, not realising that he was favourite to win. A sense of humour by-pass resulted in him sawing up the trophy, which was then commemorated on Christmas cards that raised yet more money. The result was posted in the local paper and readers were reminded of his status as Bedford's ugliest officer when he married the following spring. The moral of the story was very much "if you can't take the joke, you shouldn't have joined". I can think of several colleagues who were gutted they did not win. Sadly the competition was banned by the Governor the following year when it was won by a very unpopular female clerk, who complained that it was bullying, unlike the women who worked under her uncomplainingly and had much greater cause to lodge a grievance. The same Governor had to put a stop to another tradition which involved officers celebrating their transfer back to the North of England by sprinting naked through the Barley Mow, then a gay pub. The Bedford Arms, opposite the jail was the substitute club and was handily equipped with blackout curtains. A magazine called *The Lancit*, with its combination of doctored photographs, cartoons and scurrilous gossip met the same fate. As I recall, there was a brilliant cartoonist at the establishment, Officer Frank Settle, one of whose cartoons was gratefully received by the much feared by criminals and much loved by prison officers, Judge Frederick Beezley, on his retirement from the bench in 1993. A former Bedford senior officer, Malcolm Barrett, in his time unofficial social secretary, more than 20 years into retirement still continues to organise reunions. The burdens of a tough job little understood or valued by outsiders always seemed lighter at Bedford than other places I have worked. Even the Inspectorate commented favourably. On this occasion, they were observing the morning staff briefing carried out by a Principal Officer. Those present were duly advised that it was a colleague's birthday and there was a lusty rendition of Happy Birthday, much to his embarrassment. HMIP saw it as morale boosting, as indeed it was.

Prison officers who work the landings still habitually describe themselves as discipline officers. The term is clearly rooted in the quasi-military history of the service and with good reason. With few exceptions prisoners are undisciplined creatures with chaotic life styles that do not include regular work. Prison is the only place where meaningful discipline is imposed. The term is also used to differentiate between discipline officers and specialist grades although the latter are now an endangered species. When I joined, we had uniformed officers on the Works who in a previous life had served an apprenticeship as a plumber, electrician or carpenter and continued these skills in uniform supervising prisoners on the works party. We also had hospital officers, later renamed healthcare officers, who were colloquially known as 'scab lifters'. Unlike their time served colleagues on the works few hospital officers had nursing qualifications. Prison healthcare centres have been run by the NHS since 2006 and prison officers have now virtually disappeared from prison healthcare. There had been a short-lived drive to up-skill drive hospital officers by allowing them to qualify as nurses but again this was perceived as expensive not least because those attending university would need to have their duties covered. Catering officers oversaw the prison kitchens which as one would expect was a significant employer of prisoner labour. There were also specialist Physical Education officers and dog handlers. Each specialism had a rank structure that mirrored that on discipline and in the largest establishments the Works, the Kitchen and the Hospital would have a Chief Officer in charge. In the smallest establishments, a Senior Officer was deemed sufficient. Of those specialists only PE and dog handlers survive intact as prison officer grades and long term this cannot be guaranteed in a ferocious cost cutting environment. The Kitchen at HMP Woodhill was contracted out as long ago as 1992. Where prison officers still work in prison catering departments, they work alongside industrial craftsmen on lower rates of pay. Prison Works departments were contracted out to Carillion, a private company, in 2014, which proved to be an unmitigated disaster. Niche jobs such as library officer have also gone. Although the economies are obvious, they come with risks attached. The use of staff in contact roles who do not receive the nine-week initial course and the mentoring and support which follows, is open to exploitation by manipulative prisoners. One solution had been to take prisoners out of kitchens and also works departments, but the first of these options had the effect of denying them employment and training opportunities with qualifications at the end of them and thankfully was abandoned before the model took hold.

For staff which chose to remain on discipline duties, there have been opportunities to diversify and develop skills as pre-release course tutors, substance abuse course leaders, and as Sex Offender Treatment Programme (SOTP) tutors often working in multi-disciplinary teams with probation officers, psychologists and outreach workers. Establishments now have Offending Behaviour Units (OBUs) which include prison officers, the task of which is to try and successfully resettle prisoners back in the community thus reducing re-offending by anticipating the kind of issues that prisoners will have on release, such as homelessness, such as domestic violence, such as support for those who have made a conscious decision to fight their addictions and have commenced doing so in custody. In training prisons, OBUs will also map out and arrange for the delivery of suitable courses to challenge offending behaviour. Mercifully probation officers and psychologists are more expensive than prison officers so SOTP is unlikely to lose prison officer input, but drugs workers are cheaper as are probation service officers (PSOs), the Probation Service equivalent of 'Blunkett's bobbies' and clerks. I mean no disrespect to any other grade involved in resettlement work, but the involvement of prison officers adds credibility to what an establishment is doing. If prison officers, the largest single work group in a jail and the ones who face prisoners on a daily basis, are not involved in resettlement then they go back to being warders. Sometimes it seems as though senior civil servants want prison officers to return to being simply turnkeys, with all that implies for their professional status and subsequent remuneration.

The modern prison service has a much more diverse workforce than when I joined in 1984, when it was almost exclusively white and amongst prisoner facing staff 95% male. Overall the change in the composition of the workforce has been healthy. The vast majority of prison officers have only a handed down folk memory of what the service used to be like. For them, working on the same wing as female colleagues is the norm. It is not unusual for an entire staff team on shift in a residential area to be all-female. Thirty years ago, the very idea would have caused apoplexy, as would the notion that HIV positive prisoners could live anywhere other than the prison healthcare centre. Ethnic minority colleagues do not have novelty value because any prison officer under the age of 50 brought up in an urban area will have been to school with black and Asian children, played sport with them, and visited each other's houses. The Armed Forces, once the traditional recruiting ground, are themselves no longer exclusively white and heterosexual. The insular communities grouped around a particular industry have gone with the decline of manufacturing. However a workforce with more liberal views also has a more relaxed attitude to the personal use of cannabis and ecstasy although it is not something that individuals admit publicly. New recruits are younger and are recruited mainly from the locality surrounding the prison. In keeping with a less formal society, younger recruits from non-military backgrounds are less clear about boundaries and distance not least because they were often blurred at both home and school. The best ones learn quickly and those who do not become a liability. Although local recruitment is cost effective and has proved an ideal tool for recruiting mature streetwise women with families, there are some downsides, not least that staff may live cheek by jowl with members of the criminal classes and will have often been to school with them with all that implies for personal and professional security. In the south, in particular where house prices and rents are high, moving to a more salubrious area may not be an option on a prison officer's pay. It should also be noted that training prisons in rural areas which take prisoners transferred from inner city local prisons are far more likely to have an almost all white work force facing a very diverse ethnic population. In summary, prison officers remain mainly working class but reflect a working class that is now both smaller and more disparate in its makeup.

There have been calls for the operational prison service to become a graduate profession. There have been similar siren calls as regards the police, and the College of Policing is now seriously taking this forward. One only has to look at the health service to see the disastrous outcome of this policy. Put crudely nursing graduates appear to find bedpans and patients covered in faeces beneath their dignity. Instead this work is devolved to Health Care Assistants, in many respects the prototype for 'Blunkett's bobbies'. Nursing is a gateway to well-paid management jobs which have expanded with NHS bureaucracy. You don't need a degree to walk the beat any more than you need a degree to deal with a distressed or angry prisoner. Degrees are nice to have and open career doors, but they are not necessary for staff whose job satisfaction comes from the daily interaction at ground level and whose ambitions, if they have them at all, go no further than a first line supervisory role. I have three major objections to the Prison Reform Trust's call for graduate prison officers, a recommendation they made to the House of Commons Justice committee in 2009. Firstly it would close down another avenue of reasonably remunerated and secure employment available to ordinary working class people who for whatever reason were let down by mediocre schools and low expectations, and although of at least average intelligence left school with few meaningful qualifications. My second objection is that prison officers would actually be paying for the right to have a decent job given that living costs and tuition fees with the addition of interest would amount to something approaching £70K before the debt is finally discharged. High tuition fees are already having an impact on working class aspiration. My third objection is that degree courses would inevitably be stuffed with politically correct claptrap designed to ensure that working class values are trumped by those of the Metropolitan elite. However at the moment the service seems content to concentrate on the indoctrination of managers of which more anon. A graduate prison officer class would be expensive and there would be significant retention problems. Instead our lords and masters prefer to engage in de-skilling and forcing pay down to private sector levels, or alternatively forcing staff into the private sector itself.

The modern prison officer joining today faces much reduced pay and prospects as a consequence of privatisation, competition and contracting out which became the fashionable nostrums of Thatcherism. The first private prison opened in 1992, the Wolds in Lincolnshire, and in 2010 HMP Birmingham became the first existing public sector prison to be won by the private sector in a competitive bid. It will not be the last. In between all new and re-opened prisons except Manchester were handed to the private sector. The policy continued after Labour took office in 1997. Private sector prison officers were given the powers of a constable and were titled Prisoner Custody Officers (PCOs) which their public sector counterparts soon renamed Privatised Clown Operatives after a series of security blunders took place in the privatised court escort service. The private sector operated very differently. Its PCOs were paid on average £6k on annum less than their public sector colleagues and this for a 44-hour week as opposed to a 39-hour week, and had less annual leave, 28 days compared to 36. If that were not enough, staffing levels were far lower. It goes without saying that pension provision was also far lower. The private sector claimed to pay the market rate but in truth operated mainly in areas that had seen huge job losses from the decline of traditional industry or where local wages were already lower than the national average. Thus the so-called market rate was skewed downwards. As one would expect, the private sector has had retention problems with all that the lack of continuity implies for prisoner care. When I worked at Woodhill prison in Milton Keynes, there was a steady drift from the private sector escort contractor based in the city to the public sector prison service. It is noteworthy that only one private sector prison has opened in London, HMP Bronzefield in the Hounslow area, predictably one of the capital's poorer boroughs. It is nothing short of amazing that despite these advantages, the private sector was unable to win Manchester when it was reopened in 1994, and subsequently lost back two establishments that it had originally won in competitions that excluded public sector bids.

The response of the employer has been to try and force down costs, which given that over 80% of costs are taken up by pay has seen the public sector workforce systematically targeted with below inflation pay rises either side of a pay freeze, and the use of management consultants both internal and external whose briefs respectively have been to abolish and re-grade downwards existing posts, and to come up with management structures that imitate private sector practice. Attacking existing pay structures and employment conditions has proved difficult and TUPE regulations (Transfer of Undertakings and Protection of Employment) have hindered privatisation of existing jails, as the private sector has had no means of cutting the cost of those staff without breaking the law or taking on the cost of redundancy which would have rendered their bids uncompetitive. The logjam was only broken when a private company was able to combine a bid for Birmingham with a bid for a new prison at Featherstone in South Staffordshire, not many miles from Birmingham, which allowed them to transfer 'surplus' staff from Birmingham to the new jail. From April 2013 newly recruited prison officers found the conditions of service to which their senior in service colleagues were recruited, closed. They were recruited on new terms and conditions which capped their salaries at £24k using 2013 figures, around £5k less than the current maximum for pre-2013 recruits. The starting salary will remain around £18k. The reader is entitled to think that £29k is good pay. After all, it places prison officers at or near the top of their pay scale just inside the top 30% of earners, but I can assure you every penny is earned. Prison officers face very similar dangers to the police from the same sort of clientele. If you still think it is too much, then imagine yourself on duty during the Ford riot. On promotion to senior officer, they will again be denied access to a closed grade with a similar pay differential to those doing the job before April 2013. However, it doesn't end there because existing staff are also affected. While their terms and conditions are protected in their current grade they will not be protected if they take promotion or if they transfer sideways. Staff will be trapped and there will be nothing to stop the pay review body from recommending an extended freeze to the pay of closed grades. Indeed HMPPS has asked them to do this as they claim this will give them a measure of insurance against equal pay claims. As can be seen, it is a fiction that the only poor employers are in the private sector. In addition, promotion opportunities out of the uniformed grades will become significantly more difficult, something I will expand in the chapter on promotion and selection. The upshot of this is that Prison Service has become just another job and that will be reflected over time in the quality of the workforce.

Chapter 5
Prison Governors

As I have said earlier, the operational Prison Service I joined in 1984 in many ways reflected the structure of the armed forces with its division into those who were commissioned as officers and those who enlisted as private soldiers and their naval and air force equivalents. The vast majority of recruits to the gubernatorial class came from outside the service. The only crossover was the handful at the most of prison officer grades which ascended to the dizzy heights of Assistant Governor via the annual closed competition. There was, of course, no movement the other way. Just as an army officer could not be demoted to the ranks, neither could an incompetent or ill-disciplined governor be demoted to a prison officer grade. The service was effectively divided into two castes, not by visible marks on the forehead, but by visible distinctions of dress. Governor grades did not wear uniform and despite periodic recommendations that they should do so, not least from Sir John Learmont after the Parkhurst escape in January 1995, they remain in suits. Their private sector equivalents do, however, wear the company logo. However, when I joined the service, the real distinctions were of class and education.

Most prisons have a board somewhere on which are engraved the names of past Governors, and in the case of Dover, Deputy Governors. One thing that is very striking is the preponderance of former military officers as incumbents, a trend which continued right through to the end of the 1960s. The same phenomenon can be observed with the police whereby former military officers entered borough and county forces at what we now call ACPO ranks. Given the military ethos of both services it seemed entirely natural to recruit sometimes straight from the forces members of the officer class who were seen to have immediate transferable skills. It was also perfectly normal for former army officers of Major and above to continue to use their military rank in civilian life, a practice which died out as its use and cachet was overwhelmed by the forces of social change and the triumph of the professional over the gentleman amateur. In those far off days management ranks were much thinner and a Governor, Deputy Governor and Chief Officer were considered perfectly adequate. Assistant Governors had their origins in the Borstal system and were not seen in adult establishments until the 1967 Parole Act was implemented and caseworkers with direct knowledge of prisoners were required. In the Borstal system, the Assistant Governor was a Housemaster, very much modelled on the public school Housemaster. Borstal Rules stated: "A Housemaster shall, with the assistance of a matron and such other staff as shall be appointed, be responsible to the Governor for the administration of each House, and for the personal training of the inmates in it." Note the absence of the word management, and note also the personal responsibility for the training of the inmates under his command.

In adult training establishments, the Assistant Governor would have a specific focus on casework, assessment and the writing of parole reports. In local prisons, this type of work was largely absent so the role was largely administrative with a limited managerial role. Assistant Governors in adult prisons did not run the wings on which their offices were housed. The 'AG', as he or she was known, carried little authority. The wings were run by Principal Officers reporting to the Chief Officer, all of whom were jealous of their professional status, and often viewed junior AGs as wet behind the ears convict loving do-gooders. The Assistant Governor knew he was in trouble if the Chief Officer addressed him as 'Sir'. It indicated that there was a problem, and that for whatever reason, perhaps because it was weekend or a bank holiday, no one more senior was available. The role therefore was very varied carrying very considerable weight and kudos in Borstals, carrying out what is part of the modern role of the Probation Service in training establishments, through to being the lowest form of managerial life in the large, squalid local prisons where prisoners were simply warehoused until they were dealt with by the courts. Assistant Governors did not exist in the 'short, sharp shock' detention centres where there was simply no role for them.

Back in 1967, adverts for Assistant Governor were aimed at those with an interest in social work. Training, of which the theoretical part was carried out at the former staff college in Love Lane, Wakefield, made it clear that the primary responsibility of the Assistant Governor was to the prisoners, (although the word 'inmate' was in more general use at the time). They were expected to act as role models and have some responsibility for the training and supervision of staff, although as I have said, these powers were jealously guarded by the senior uniformed ranks. In adult jails, the military comparison broke down. By no stretch of imagination could Assistant Governors be compared with an Army Second Lieutenant. Trainee Assistant Governors studied the Sociology of Institutions, Social Psychology and Criminology. Management training came later. On one day a week, trainee AGs were attached to their local Probation Service to learn offender casework. The probationary period for trainee AGs was two years and they were supernumerary in establishments during that period. Only after successfully completing the probationary period could they call themselves a substantive Assistant Governor and have the bracketed 'T' for trainee, removed as an appendage to their rank. Assistant Governors were not remotely recruited for a fast track promotion scheme. It was not unusual for a recruit to spend 10 years as an Assistant Governor before entering the hallowed ranks of a Governor IV, which only in a smaller establishment granted Deputy Governor status. In the early 70s, recruitment language changed a little and talked of management with a social purpose. The reality was rather different. The social purpose in Borstals remained although along with rest of the system it was gradually undermined by defeatism and institutional neglect. Britain was not a happy place in the 1970s and for different reasons not happy in the 1980s when I joined, and this was reflected in the morale of staff, the poor industrial relations, and 'happiness is door shaped' philosophy that saw relationships between staff and prisoners gradually break down and take us on the road to the cataclysmic destruction of Manchester prison (Strangeways) in 1990. Indeed looking back it is a wonder that the idealism, the belief that bad people can change given support, encouragement and opportunity, and the personal sense of mission felt by many AG recruits of the 60s and 70s through until the final course passed through the staff college in 1987, survived at all amidst the resigned acceptance of mediocrity and worse that held the system in thrall.

Until the demise of the AG scheme in 1987, there were two types of external recruit. Those under 24 who usually joined direct from university and had to serve 12 months as a prison officer in uniform, and those older than 24 joining from other occupations and professions but still normally university educated, who spent only a nominal three months of their training on prison officer duties. Quite why this sub-distinction was made eludes me. No doubt it can be found in some obscure Home Office tract. Thus there was an obvious distinction between the Secondary Modern educated prison officer and the University educated Governor. The other divide was class. This is not to say that there were not Governors from working class origins. In fact their numbers grew exponentially as the products of the Grammar Schools took advantage of increased and free university places and made their way in the professions. The point is that they became middle class by virtue of their education, even if they were not quite gentlemen in the eyes of some of their colleagues. Thus they were a class apart and it is fair to say that some behaved like it.

The corporate clone did not exist in 1984. The gubernatorial class contained the charismatic, the sociopathic and the plain eccentric. It housed the deeply religious and the sexually promiscuous. It housed the straight and the gay (though rarely openly). There were innovative and inspirational Governors with real missionary zeal and those who simply administered the status quo. There were the comic and the terrifying, sometimes contained within the same person. There were those who could handle trade unions and those who found them a complete mystery. Despite being authority figures themselves, there was often a healthy contempt for authority. Although all political views were accommodated, liberal humanitarian views predominated, as one would expect from people with social science degrees and/or social work backgrounds. From more senior leaders came a sense of entitlement to respect that came with having earned their position and status. The service could also attract some towering intellectuals, people with the capacity to think, to conceptualise and to subject the prevailing orthodoxy to challenge. Back in 1984, the Governor was also a very visible, if remote individual, and carried out a daily round of the prison accompanied by the Chief Officer.

My second Governor, Peter Salter, was probably the most charismatic I have worked for. He also liked a pint in the days when lunchtime drinking was a normal activity, not that it ever affected his demeanour or efficiency, although the same could not be said of some of those who accompanied him in a bid to get the Governor's ear and establish themselves as members of an 'in crowd'. Peter Salter was a risk taker who not only rescinded the smoking ban that was part of juvenile YOI rules that were implemented in 1988, he also began granting temporary release, known colloquially as home leave, for trainees to visit their parents or resolve domestic crises, which was to say the least a creative interpretation of temporary release provisions. Trainees were also sent out to court appearances escorted only by one officer and unrestrained by handcuffs. As I recall, this was not explicitly forbidden, but it was certainly a little used form of discretion. Within a few short years the expression of discretion over matters like smoking, temporary release, and the use of handcuffs would become almost inconceivable. Peter Salter also did something else that would be inconceivable today. When Werrington was threatened with closure in the early 1990s, he campaigned openly and indeed successfully to keep the establishment open. 20 years on such behaviour would result in immediate removal to a desk in headquarters pending disciplinary action and possible dismissal. Not that prison governors are ever likely to get the opportunity to behave in this way in the modern service. When the closure of HMP Wellingborough was decided upon in 2012, the Governor, Ali Dodds, was told only hours before she was required to make the announcement to staff and was not even permitted to inform her deputy.

It should be noted that in civil service terms, prison governors are actually quite low in the food chain. They are not classed as senior civil servants. The in-charge Governor's immediate line manager is a senior civil servant, but is at entry level in terms of civil service hierarchy. Bringing prison governors back into line and ending their perceived privileged status came quickly with the establishment of Area Managers in 1992, whose power was swiftly reinforced by a series of reports in the mid-90s which exposed security and management failings that were laid firmly at the door of the hapless prison governor. Thus when the then Governor of Brixton, Bob Chapman, went public in October 1999 about the establishment's squalid hospital and the chronic underfunding, his reward was to be removed from his post and transferred to HMP Downview, a job normally held by a lower grade of in-charge Governor. The peremptory strike against Bob Chapman, whose retirement was not long delayed, sent a shudder through the ranks of prison governors.

Another man of high principles I worked for was Brodie Clark. He was my Governor when I transferred to Bedford in the spring of 1991. Mr Clark is perhaps the best-known former prison governor in the land having found himself on the front page of the *Daily Mail* and other newspapers in 2011 when undertaking his final civil service role as Head of the Border Agency. All that I can say is that the vast majority of prison staff who worked for Brodie Clark would have grave difficulty in accepting that Brodie exceeded his authority and relaxed border controls in respect of non-EU citizens without ministerial approval, and then lied about it. In the end, the Home Office chose to settle Mr Clark's constructive dismissal claim for a figure reputedly more than twice that originally offered to him to leave quietly, which probably tells us all we need to know despite no admissions of liability from either side. Brodie Clark had also been in the news in 1994 when he had the misfortune to be the Governor of Whitemoor during the IRA escape from the special secure unit at that establishment. As he had been in post only a short time, he escaped the blame from the Home Secretary if not from sections of the press. Mr Clark has never been given the credit he deserves from the restoration of discipline, morale and the reputation of the prison. In due course, he was promoted to the senior civil service. I did not work under him at Woodhill as he had moved on a few months before I arrived, but his vision and ethos were alive and well under his successor. Woodhill which opened in 1992 was a great forcing house for young talent. John Hewitson, Tony Corcoran, Andy Rogers and Andrea Albutt, the current President of the Prison Governors Association have all gone on to enjoy stellar careers. Paul Whitfield went on to be Head of the Home Department in the Guernsey Civil Service and Paul McDowell after governing three establishments graduated to be CEO of NACRO and then HM Chief Inspector of Probation. All owe a debt to a man who deserves to be remembered as one the most influential leadership figures in the prison service over the last 25 years. Each of those individuals served in the uniformed ranks under his leadership. Further up the Woodhill food chain at the time as members of the Senior Management Team were Martin Lomas, who later served as Deputy Chief Inspector of Prisons and David Wilson, Professor of Criminology at the City of Birmingham University and also vice-chair of the Howard League for Penal Reform.

David Wilson had also left by the time of my arrival although I did meet him occasionally. He also had a significant reputation as a mentor for young ambitious staff. Martin Lomas was my immediate line manager when I came to Woodhill as the junior governor grade in May of 1995. He did not court popularity and had little patience with the kind of prison service tradition that involved serving meals or locking prisoners up earlier than the times published. Similarly if unlock for association was scheduled for 1800 hours, he expected that to happen and not be delayed for spurious reasons. Supervisory grades were expected to ensure that the regime was delivered on time and could expect to answer for it if they didn't. Martin Lomas may not have been the most clubbable of men but he was perfectly straightforward to work for. He was clear what he wanted from you, when he wanted it by, and to what standard. You were held accountable and as such you made sure that those below you were also held to account. There were no cliques and no favourites. It was spelt out to me on my first day that I was there to lead, and that involved setting a personal example as well as delivering on management tasks. As a junior governor grade, I could not have had a better introduction.

Indeed it was brought home to me on my very first weekend home back in Wakefield (I did not complete a move of home until several weeks after transfer) when I bumped into a group of former uniformed colleagues on a Friday afternoon pub crawl and joined them for a couple of drinks. Some of them were already very well oiled and upsetting bar staff in one of the city centre pubs. Out of the corner of my eye I spotted the landlady pick up the phone and at that point swiftly downed my drink and departed. I like to believe that I would have done the same thing without the pep talk from Martin, but where drink is concerned there are no guarantees unless there is something to prick your conscience. Wakefield had a drinking culture that at one time had extended to governor grades although they tended to use Henry Boons, the nearest pub, rather than the staff club. One Wakefield governor grade was reputedly banned from Henry Boons on account of drunken behaviour. In keeping with the times, there was no disciplinary action.

It was another member of the Woodhill Senior Management Team who set me off on another significant road in my career, the Prison Governors Association (PGA). As the junior governor grades, Denis Keeler and myself were not members of the Senior Management Team. Apart from the brief morning meeting held by the Governor, the only time we got together with our senior colleagues was at the PGA branch meetings. Late in 1995 at a branch meeting Martin announced his imminent departure on promotion. John Cann, the formidable and authoritative Deputy Governor promptly suggested that as I was the junior governor grade, I should be branch representative. That was approved without a vote and so began my career as a union rep which led me to the NEC and to the editorship of *The Key,* our association magazine. The PGA was founded in 1987. Previously governor grades were typically members of the Governors branch of the Society of Civil and Public Servants (SCPS) since renamed the Public and Commercial Services union, better known by its initials, PCS. Governors were increasingly feeling unrepresented by a body they perceived as both too militant and too happy to take the subscriptions but without offering much return as a representative body. Almost parallel to this was the increasing discomfort of Chief Officers in the Prison Officers Association. The implementation of Fresh Start in 1987 abolished the Chief Officer rank and re-designated those individuals who remained in service as governor grades. This was the opportunity for governors and former chiefs to come together and despite efforts by the PCS and POA to render the infant trade union stillborn, the PGA obtained certification and then recognition by the Home Office of its right to represent Governor grades 1–5 as they then were, although recognition for grades 4 and 5 was shared with the POA. In practice, very few of these remained in the POA any more than governors remained in the PCS in any significant number. Like the BMA the PGA has a hybrid role, acting both as a professional body to be taken seriously for its expertise in the criminal justice system, and as a fully-fledged trade union representing its members individually in grievances and disciplinary matters, and collectively for purposes of consultation and negotiation. My own contribution was mainly on the trade union side although I was the NEC speaker on the controversial resolution to the 2009 conference which called for the cessation of wasteful and pointless short terms of imprisonment which we believe contributes to further reoffending rather than reduces it. I joined the NEC in 2007 after many years as a branch rep and served out a full three-year term before retiring. During that period, I was also editor of *The Key* and brought my own distinctive style to the role. I also had the privilege of chairing our national conference in 2006 and

2007, and to my stunned surprise was awarded Distinguished Life Membership on my retirement in 2010.

In reality, my own role was a mere footnote when compared to that of Paddy Scriven OBE who served on the NEC continuously from 1987, firstly as Finance Officer and from 2007 as General Secretary being re-elected for a further three year term in 2010. She retired in 2014 and sadly passed away in 2018. Paddy left a huge hole to fill as she had an unrivalled historical knowledge of every precedent set over a quarter of a century, was a one-woman authority on the civil service code, and very pertinently knew where all the bodies were buried. She was also the repository of so much of the credibility of the association. Her successors have had big shoes to fill, and their task has been made harder by government proposals to reduce facility time which have disproportionately penalised small trade unions such as the PGA and could potentially lead to the unintended consequences of merger, amalgamation or federation, all of which come with the risk that governors will once again be represented by organisations that provide an umbrella rather than a voice. Did ministers seriously want to see junior governor grades falling into the arms of the POA? Thankfully, the PGA has continued to thrive.

As with the Chief Officer, the Assistant Governor grade was abolished in 1987 as a consequence of what was called 'Fresh Start' and with it went the separate Assistant Governor recruiting scheme. 'Fresh Start' was a response to the events of the previous year in which there had been national industrial action by the POA and Northeye prison had been partially destroyed by rioting inmates. Perhaps not before time the Prisons Board had come to the conclusion that the old caste based service was no longer fit for purpose. For most prison officers, the most significant change was the change from variable pay packets paid weekly in cash to predictable salaries paid monthly into the bank. Prison Officers were now to be professionals and no longer members of the working class who could conceal their true earnings from their wives. The end of overtime and its replacement by 'time off in lieu' put paid to that. The other significant change particularly for the ambitious like me was the creation of the unified service. The distinction between gentlemen and players was abolished and all staff would have a common line of promotion from prison officer. The Chief Officer rank disappeared. Chief Officer 1's migrated across to the Governor IV rank. Chief Officer 2's and Assistant Governors merged to form a newly created Governor V rank. The changes were controversial, not least among existing chief officers and principal officers looking for promotion, for which the career summit was the chief's insignia and pace stick. Although now uncomfortable in the POA, they did not necessarily wish to wear suits nor did they wish to be anonymous governor grades. For them, it represented demotion and loss of status, even if the pension at the end of the day told a different tale. It is no exaggeration to say that it was the equivalent of the abolition of the sergeant's mess and the merging of senior NCOs with the officer class in the army, something one could never imagine happening in that institution. As most were over 50, many Chiefs took the opportunity to retire early. A select few, including John Cann, Gerry Ross, Ted Butt and the redoubtable Veronica Bird took up the challenge and made it to in-charge governor, something that was previously inconceivable.

As far as prison officers were concerned, the Prisons Board's hope that the unified service would put a swift end to the cultural apartheid was misplaced. In truth, the opportunity to breach the historic divide was lost by not creating an all uniformed unified service. The law of unintended consequences took over. Now that no hour in the week was better paid than any other, prison officers went sick at weekends, creating a brand new management problem for prison governors. Staff could now go sick without the loss of weekend premiums, shift disturbance allowance, and the probability of an extended shift at penal rates, which had previously pertained. Loyalty that was no longer bought and paid for was only grudgingly granted. The former Assistant Governors were the main beneficiaries of Fresh Start. Their pay was raised in line with that of the former Chief Officers. The other advantage was that the increase in the number of governor grades reduced the amount of weekend commitment and evenings spent on call. In anybody's language, more pay and less unsocial hours is a result but the joy was short lived as the long hours culture developed in the service as it did in other walks of life.

The breaking down of barriers allowed the flourishing of previously stifled talent. Of the six names I quoted earlier that worked under Brodie Clark at Woodhill only Paul McDowell benefitted from the Accelerated Promotion Scheme (APS) introduced in 1988 as the successor to the Assistant Governor scheme. Andrea Albutt, a Health Care Officer in 1995, found herself in-charge Governor of Low Newton 10 years later. It seems amazing that a report in 1972 had come to the conclusion that there was no untapped talent pool amongst prison officers yet promotion from the ranks enjoyed a heyday that lasted at least a decade until APS graduates grew sufficiently in numbers, experience and credibility. However, I should point out there were concerns not necessarily about the managerial skills of former prison officers making it through to Governors IV and V, but about literacy skills. At that level report writing skills are crucial as one of my former line managers, Barbara Treen, herself an AG recruit, pointed out to me one afternoon in discussion. I have to say that she was quite right and my own experience would prove it, managing otherwise able individuals who for all their other talents and drive could not be trusted to conduct a serious disciplinary investigation because their report writing skills were so deficient as to put the credibility of the report and subsequent proceedings based on it at risk. This was the downside not just of a Secondary Modern education, but also of a bog standard comprehensive education. The most ambitious staff set out to up their skills. Tony Corcoran, who back in 1995 was a senior officer under me, enrolled with the Open University. He was not alone. Former Assistant Governors now making their way in general competition came with almost guaranteed standards of literacy and continued to prosper in career terms especially if combining those skills with the harder edge increasingly required in the service as it came under greater duress from the press, ministers and pressure groups in the final decade of the 20th Century.

The first APS course commenced its management training at the staff college in Wakefield in October 1990. There were a mere two external graduate recruits on that first course, Of the remaining 14, all but one had joined as a prison officer, the exception being a female clerical officer, a grade now known as administrative officer. There were only two women on the course, the other being Ingrid MacAlpine a native of Northern Ireland who was invalided out of the service after a car crash a few years later. However it was the remaining female, Colette Kershaw, who was the first to make it to substantive in-charge Governor, ten years after commencing the year as a prison officer that all external and non-prison officer recruits were required to undertake. Sadly both Ingrid and Colette died of cancer before their fiftieth birthdays.

Amongst the former prison officers were four graduates including myself. Thus less than half of the course members were graduates, not quite what the Home Office had intended, but that would change fairly rapidly. The gender balance would also change markedly as I discovered when I was put in charge of the APS welcome week at the Prison Service College in September 1999. External candidates now not only dominated, but were largely female. Indeed in this cohort all bar one of the external candidates, I think there were 15 of them, were female. I have written about recruitment, promotion and selection in detail in chapter 9.

It would be remiss of me to leave out my own experience of the Accelerated Promotion Scheme, even though I would prefer to forget it. Prior to its introduction during our officer training we were offered the opportunity to sit the Assistant Governors Examination which I passed easily. After two years of service, I could apply for a board and be called automatically. Thus in January 1987 I attended the last Assistant Governor Selection Board for internal candidates, held over three days at Wakefield and duly had a nightmare. Two years later came an opportunity to apply for the new accelerated promotion scheme. The tests in Maths (mainly statistics to interpret) Verbal Reasoning and Non-Verbal Reasoning were more difficult than the old AG's exam. I passed, but unlike the AG's exam we were not told our scores. The Assessment Centre was held at the new Prison Service College near Rugby and I can remember starting the first task at 08.30 on a sunny September Sunday Morning. Much to my surprise I was selected. I am under no illusion that I would have had any chance a few years later as competition became much stiffer. After a six month training course, I transferred to Bedford as a Principal Officer. We all swiftly discovered that plans for us to be supernumerary had been abandoned. Not only were we no longer in a training grade but also we had taken away a promotion opportunity in the establishments to which we were posted. The welcome was less than ecstatic not just from staff but also from some of our bosses who either preferred the Assistant Governor scheme or were not believers in accelerated promotion at all. It was straight in at the deep end where the piranhas were circling. There was not the all-round buy-in of establishment senior management teams that would have ensured effective mentoring for all course members. This was only corrected when HQ became concerned about the attrition rate of their pet scheme.

My own immediate boss was the Deputy Governor, David Addison, whose chief concern was that I should concentrate firmly on being an effective Principal Officer as he could not afford any weak links. My big mistake was to accept that advice and to concentrate almost exclusively on making it at least in my own mind as a Principal Officer. It left me completely unprepared for the Governor V Board twelve months later and I duly failed. Twelve months later I passed but below the now elevated standard required and was duly invited to leave the scheme. The only consolation was that in the final 12 months of my 30-month stay I achieved a degree of professional acceptance that would have otherwise passed me by. The loss of my place on APS 1 hurt but it did not prevent me from getting two promotions in the next four years, not dramatically slower than the successful members of my peer group. The real loss was that of patronage, a subject covered in detail in Chapter 9.

It is always difficult when you are the bottom of the heap to know exactly what the big boss does. Back when I was a young man growing up in Blackburn typically management and administrators started work later than the factory floor and often finished work earlier. We believed that the biggest bosses took long liquid lunches and spent afternoons on the golf course. How true that was I do not know, but it certainly had more than a grain of truth. Journalists enjoyed a reputation for alcohol consumption during the working day. The pace of life in city stock broking firms was also known to be leisurely. I can remember being amazed by how crowded the pubs near Liverpool Street Station were by early Friday afternoon. Gentlemen did not do toil and expected to enjoy leisure in accordance with their station. Work was for the working classes. I exaggerate to some extent for effect but historians and commentators have drawn attention to the indolence of British management and its role in our decline is as important, and related to the industrial militancy that plagued Britain as the decline became apparent in the sixties and seventies. All that would change under Mrs Thatcher. One of the great historical ironies of the 20th century is that it was the radical Tory Prime

Minister who did the most to break down the old class structure as we knew it. Those parts of the public sector which escaped relatively unscathed until after her fall were the slowest to change. Keith Hellawell, former Chief Constable of West Yorkshire observes in his memoirs how one particular Superintendent was never at his desk before 10.00AM. The Governor and Deputy Governor in my first establishment, Werrington House, were both very keen golfers. However I have no memory of them sneaking off to play golf on a sunny afternoon and would be quite certain that they never did.

Indeed in small establishments with small management teams establishment cover was often quite stretched. At Werrington back in 1984 there was only one governor grade, Mike Pascoe who obviously was governor in charge, and his deputy was the Chief Officer. In 1987, when Chief Officer 2's were merged with Assistant Governors, Jim Smith formally became Deputy Governor. Only later when the bureaucracy surrounding the custody of juveniles expanded were extra governor grades added. Thus the Governor and Deputy Governor worked alternate weekends. During summer leave one would work three consecutive weekends and all the days in between covering the time off. Thus the duty governor commitment was 100% as indeed was the liability to be on call. The duty governor popped in most evenings and there was a weekly night visit. This sort of situation was replicated at countless smaller jails up and down the land. It was an ideal job for a teetotaller. Even though the demands of HQ were much lighter (much, much lighter), there was an unavoidable culture of 'presenteeism'. It helped that in those days Governors lived much closer to the prison, often in quarters although a Governor's quarter would be a rather grander affair than that of a bachelor prison officer. Pre Second World War the in-charge Governor was permitted to have domestic servants.

Where possible the hierarchy preferred the in-charge Governor not to work weekends. Indeed at Werrington dispensation was eventually granted to allow a Principal Officer to double as duty governor at weekends. When I transferred to Bedford in 1991, a small local, there were four governor grades including the Governor in-charge, the 'number one'. Here the Deputy Governor only did weekends when it was necessary to cover the holiday commitments of his two junior colleagues, who otherwise worked alternate weekends. Their working pattern was ten days on followed by four days off. At Wakefield where I also served as a Principal Officer, my memory is that the duty governor role was delegated entirely to Governor V's during the week, but there would always be a more senior colleagues on duty in this high security, high profile establishment. A Governor IV, who in a large establishment was a grade below the deputy, was always present at weekends and would act as duty governor on one of the days. This commitment occurred one weekend in four. As a governor grade myself, I worked one weekend in four at Woodhill, and similarly at Dover where I was Deputy Governor. At both Dover and Ford, the number one chose to go on the weekend roster. At Dover, we had only four governor grades which stretched cover perilously thin, so I can only imagine what it was it was like for earlier generations. My second Governor at Ford did not go on the weekend roster, so it was back to one weekend in four.

In my time, working a weekend could be a pleasant bonus with none of the stresses present during the week, unless you had a major incident. HQ and Area Office work Monday to Friday so you were not pestered with demands for information, for papers you had sent weeks ago and the external telephone was therefore also very quiet. In more recent times, it did mean some respite from E-mails. At Woodhill where two governor grades were rostered for weekend work, the one not duty governor and therefore excused a full round of the prison could catch up with all the paperwork and the routine administration that gets neglected in the week. It was a time when reports could be written and staff appraisal documentation completed. If you were not the senior person on duty, then so much the better as you would not be carrying out adjudications which are the disciplinary hearings into prisoner misconduct, heard every day except Sundays and some Bank Holidays. If, as in most establishments, you were flying solo at weekends, then there was the routine of Governor's rounds. Again this was more relaxed at the weekend as prisoners were not permitted to make routine applications. There was more time to speak to staff. At Ford I could spend time drinking coffee with the farm manager and on a pleasant summer Sunday watch cricket. It was the custom at Ford and no doubt at other open establishments that friendly matches, all at home by then, were played against local sides. Cooked breakfasts were another tradition at many prisons. At both Ford and Woodhill the duty governor was welcome to partake, one of the few exceptions to the more usual apartheid that prevailed; governors did not use staff tearooms. Under the terms of the 1952 Prisons Act every establishment is required to have a Governor (for a time in Detention Centres the term was 'warden') and also a chaplain. Logically every prison must have a Deputy Governor as someone is required to be in operational charge when the Governor is on leave even if in practice most Governors will interrupt their leave, assuming they are in the country, to deal with a high profile major incident or a sudden arrival of the Inspectorate. There is no such requirement for anyone else's job to carry the appellation of Governor. Indeed a number of current and former Governors share the unease of HQ that the term 'Governor' is applied to what in a large establishment are more than a dozen senior and intermediate managers. It is confusing for the press as well as for the public. Nevertheless, Headquarters only has itself to blame. It created the Governor IV and in 1987 subsequent to Fresh Start created and added the Governor V. Around half of all governor grades are Governor V's. From that date there would be five grades of Governor, numbered one to five. Briefly and somewhat absurdly HQ then decided that it would abolish the familiar ranks altogether and thus a Governor 2 simply became a grade 2 and a prison officer became grade 8. A former colleague working in Werrington gate lodge decided to try that out one morning when the Deputy Governor, now minus his Chief Officer's uniform, entered the prison. He greeted him with a cheery 'Good morning Grade 5' to be told very bluntly that the correct forms of address were 'Sir', 'Dep' or plain 'Mr Smith'. Dep as the form of address is considered both respectful and accurate and the Governor will often use that form of address to his or her immediate subordinate in front of staff or prisoners. Describing every member of operational staff in this way was soon abandoned probably because it would have been confused with senior civil service grading, also numerical, where to be a Grade 1 is to be one of the most powerful civil servants in the land, the people who really run the country. In any event, it would never have caught on. The service also tried describing Deputy Governors as Heads of Custody. No one really used the term in an establishment and it existed only in job adverts. It was just another way of saying that the Deputy Governor was in charge of the day-to-day running of the prison.

During one of the numerous reorganisations so favoured in the public sector, the service introduced the term 'Operational Manager'. There would be Senior Operational Managers, almost but not entirely in-charge Governors, and Deputy Governors in large establishments, and Operational Managers in two pay bands, E and F which corresponded with Governors IV and V. It didn't really solve the problem. Governors V continued to refer to themselves as Governors. The press, when they could be bothered to report accurately described them as junior governors, as indeed often did their own in-charge Governor. The Prison Governors Association put forward a simple solution: there should be Governors, Deputy Governors and all other operational managers would be known as Assistant Governors. Some former members of the Assistant Governor scheme were a dissenting minority. Presumably the hoi polloi who had graduated from the ranks should not be allowed the use of an otherwise redundant but venerable title. In fairness that job had changed radically but that did not make it unique in an organisation where reorganisation is the default substitute for meaningful change, displacement activity cunningly camouflaged as action. Staff can always see when the Emperor has no clothes. It would have been easy to understand for everyone but the Prisons Board preferred to resist. There is little doubt that if some senior civil servants without a Prison Service background at the Home Office and now at the Ministry of Justice would prefer to get rid of the title 'Governor' altogether and put Prison Governors back where they seem them as belonging, somewhere below the salt. Thankfully the 1952 Prisons Act is there to thwart them. Now you know how the Civil Service spends chunks of what should be productive time. Staff and prisoners quite naturally show no interest in this kind of arcane discussion. As far as prisoners are concerned, they want to see a Governor, preferably the Number One Governor. I have yet to meet a prisoner who asked to see an operational or senior operational manager. Similarly the operational manager pay band F conducting adjudications (prison disciplinary hearings) will be addressed as Governor by segregation unit staff and prisoners, as he is carrying out Governor's Adjudications, which have been delegated by the Governor in-charge. He or she will follow adjudications by conducting the Governor's round of the segregation unit. Again this is a delegated role, although the in-charge Governor is expected to adjudicate and conduct the segregation unit round once a week.

Similarly the role of Duty Governor retains its name despite attempts to give governor grades new and unthreatening titles. There have been attempts by HQ and some in-charge Governors to go over to a Duty Manager as opposed to a Duty Governor but the latest round of reorganisation seems to have killed that one off. The role of Duty Governor is well understood by staff and prisoners. He or she is the first port of call when someone senior is needed to approve segregation, check a sentence calculation, speak to a member of the public, or take a Governor's application from a prisoner. The Duty Governor is at everyone's beck and call, which allows various statutory duties such as sampling the prison food and others laid down in Prison Service Orders and Instructions to be carried out by one individual whose day is forfeit to the role, thus allowing colleagues to get on with their own jobs, until their own turn comes round. The Duty Governor is also on call in the evening and overnight. In larger establishments, it is unusual for the in-charge Governor to go on the roster and take the radio, and often the Deputy Governor will not be on the roster either. In smaller establishments, it is often very different as teams are small. At both Dover and Ford my boss carried out the Duty Governor role. The most important part of the role is the complete round of the prison.

Again going back to when I joined the in-charge Governor always did a full round and in his or her absence the Deputy Governor undertook the job although in practice the Deputy Governor would have been equally visible which was the whole point. To be effective, leadership has to be visible. The bureaucratic demands of Head Quarters and in particular those of Area Offices have made an in-charge Governor's daily round almost impossible. My last Governor, Robin Eldridge at Lewes, solved this problem only with iron monastic discipline and a minimum 12-hour working day. A Governor's working week is supposed to be 42 hours inclusive of meal breaks, not 60 or more. The same problem applies to senior police officers. Former Chief Constable of North Wales, Richard Brunstrom, gave up a weekend day off most weeks to do a full shift with traffic officers. No doubt his Deputy and Assistant Chief Constables (the designation is good enough for the Police) were expected to do the same.

A Governor's day (I am referring to all governor grades) has familiar contours but not predictability. Many HQ roles will be highly predictable because they will not have prisoners or local trade union officials to worry about, although there will be exceptions that do not just affect the most senior staff. Some in-charge Governors arrive early in order to tackle the mountain of E-mails that accumulate daily as it is the best time to work undisturbed, although a cunning plan of this nature can be thwarted if a prisoner is found hanging at morning unlock. Other Governors I have worked for arrive early so that they can observe the unlock routine and also visit reception, which in local prisons is the busiest time of the day with prisoners being processed for court and short termers being discharged back into the community. Early starters often live some distance from the prison. It makes sense to get up early to beat traffic. All Governors have a personal secretary usually shared with the Deputy Governor. One of her first jobs on arrival will be to ensure that the Governor and Deputy Governor are provided with a steaming mug of tea or coffee. The Personal Secretary acts as gatekeeper to the Governor keeping his/her diary up to date and also arranges for mail, almost all of which by convention is addressed to the Governor, to be distributed to the relevant department. During her working day she will have access to the Governor's E-mails and redistribute them accordingly but typically the Governor will read them all anyway, unlike written correspondence. E-mail has gained a stranglehold on public sector management. It is not unusual for members of the Governor's senior management team to return from a week's holiday to 200 plus E-mails, all of which have to be read just in case. E-mail is the all-consuming monster. Only the Governor will have the luxury of someone to forward and/or delete E-mails during his absence, but many will not risk having them deleted. Because of the sheer volume of traffic generated by HQ, mistakes do get made. Towards the end of my time at Lewes HQ got very animated about the absence of our returns for the staff survey. Somewhere along the way an instruction demanding that we produce a 90% response rate had got lost in the ether. I had never seen it and the Governor was distinctly unhappy that no other member of the senior management team (SMT) had seen it either, not least because he would have to explain it to the Area Manager.

Governors are besieged by bureaucratic demands. All establishments have a morning management meeting, but there is no set format and what information is exchanged or passed on varies from establishment to establishment. At some the pace is very leisurely. My own preference is for short meetings where key information from the previous day is shared, such as the prison roll, significant incidents, staff sickness, planned or unplanned regime reductions (usually caused by sickness), colleagues' diaries for the day including visitors and external engagements and any information which may affect public confidence in the prison service and therefore needs to be shared and also transmitted up the food chain. Generally speaking the Duty Governor will either complete a standard form or use the traditional Governor's journal. Often this form is required by Area Office and where such a form is not available the secretary will do a digest from the journal. It is staggering how badly such business meetings can be conducted. A former colleague at Ford boasted that in the reign of one particular Governor, morning meetings could last over an hour with much tea and coffee consumed and much hot air expended over which prisoners were suitable for temporary release to wait on at Masonic dinners. I should swiftly add that such abuses have been ancient history for the best part of 20 years.

Nevertheless I can still recall wasteful discussions about problems that never got resolved such as the distribution of newspapers to prisoners. I was always taught that one should argue to a decision, not merely to a conclusion, so found this kind of thing very frustrating. However despite the fact the lines of communication were shorter and decision making by committee was less fashionable when I joined there was still ample evidence to those of us at lower levels of a management that seemed paralysed in the face of simple problems. As a junior officer at Werrington, I can recall that our mess orderly (a prisoner who made our brews at break times and kept the tea room clean) was forever being moved to another job just as we had him trained and trusted. Another seemingly intractable problem was prisoner cutlery which the catering officers refused to wash and make ready for distribution at meal times. Thus prisoners lost and stole cutlery, didn't bother to wash it, or kept in the same drawer overnight as their week old underpants. The lost and stolen cutlery was the biggest problem as staff had two choices; deplete staffing levels and go the store in a different part of the prison or tell the prisoner to eat with his fingers. I should add that we are talking about cheap plastic cutlery. I struggle to remember how many years it took before this problem was solved.

In my time at Bedford, even the great Brodie Clark seemed reluctant to deal with bureaucratic obscurantism. The problem was that prisoners discharged to court had any unspent earnings moved into their private cash account, the two being separate in those days, and it was taken with them to be handed over if they were bailed, acquitted, discharged on appeal, or satisfactorily purged contempt, whatever the proceedings may be. Back in 1991 convicted prisoners could only purchase tobacco from earnings and unlike un-convicted prisoners could not have it sent in by post. In the week, this was not a problem as if the man returned to Bedford the morning was simply restored to the earnings account and he could purchase tobacco at the prison shop on the next canteen day. However administrative staff did not work weekends and therefore could not deal with prisoner accounts, so under the strict letter of Standing Orders convicted prisoners returned from court on a Friday could not purchase tobacco until Monday. Every fifth Saturday when I was Orderly Officer prisoners complained and I overruled the canteen staff and gave permission for the affected prisoners to purchase tobacco, which was the common sense humanitarian thing to do. Every Monday morning without fail the disgruntled canteen staff denied the pleasure of winding up prisoners without putting themselves at risk whinged to the Head of Finance who duly raised that matter at the Governor's morning meeting. Brodie Clark never once instructed me to cease and desist, but neither did he tell the Head of Finance to stop raising the matter. The problem only ceased when I became line manager of the canteen staff who were uniformed prison auxiliaries, issued the appropriate instructions and made it clear that going behind my back was wholly unacceptable. They had a cushy job, much better than yard patrol in winter, something I could soon arrange.

Under a different Governor different frustrations could arise. One in particular allowed morning meetings to make policy. I have always believed that SMT meetings are the correct forum for policy making with advance agendas and supporting papers as opposed to policy being made on the hoof. The upside of Eoin McLennan-Murray's leadership at Lewes is that he genuinely wished to hear vigorous argument about the way forward on major policy matters. You felt not just consulted but included, although he remorselessly shredded weak arguments if you were ill prepared. Indeed there was nothing he enjoyed more than the total intellectual destruction of someone from HQ up at the establishment to sell the latest wheeze to practitioners on the ground. The result of course was very long meetings although Eoin did encourage the bringing of cakes to meetings to celebrate birthdays or other significant anniversaries, a civilised custom practiced by many Governors which cements team spirit. Nevertheless, team building although it has official support and is a core competence for every level of management, is not necessarily the preferred style. Colleagues may be grateful for short meetings, but will be unhappy that SMT meetings do little other than scrutinise performance reports and data with little or no discussion permitted about the strategic direction of the prison. A Governor of this inclination often manages his immediate subordinates negatively. Interaction is limited to short formal meetings with individuals where coffee is most definitely not served. Under this sort of boss you can expect public as well as private criticism as this makes people watch their backs and thus it stifles debate. This type of Governor will focus on transactional management rather than transformational leadership, of which he or she is largely incapable. A climate of suspicion and mistrust builds up as colleagues seek to insinuate themselves into favour and protect their careers at the expense of colleagues. I have known Governors who insist on all senior managers working with their office doors open and another who asked her secretary to give her information about who had spent significant time with me in my office during her frequent absences from the prison.

Earlier in the chapter I said that back in 1984 there was no such thing as the corporate clone. There were of course dictators and tyrants but they were operating as individuals in an era when individualism was encouraged and management from the centre was remote and weak. The modern dictator by contrast is a corporate creature. I discuss recruitment in more detail in Chapter 9 but a recent advert for the NOMS (National Offender Management Service) graduate programme seeks people 'who love being set and beating targets' and 'organising and maximising performance'. The layman would expect to find this kind of requirement in the job spec for a sales manager in a company selling washing machines. The target culture is at the heart of what is sometimes referred to as 'New Public Managerialism'. Sadly, the public failures of the service exposed in the years after the Manchester riot, rendered it vulnerable to this apparent panacea. Its philosophy, if I can be excused for dignifying it with the term, is that management is a science rather than an art, an activity that is rational rather than intuitive. Where there is leadership it is controlling and transactional, rather than empowering and transformational. It is about compliance not initiative. There is no room for people for people who can intellectualise outside the tramlines or otherwise ski off piste. Reward is linked to achievement narrowly defined using pseudo-scientific measures to monitor, analyse, audit and evaluate performance. It borrows from the private sector with its emphasis on cost reducing market orientated competitive discipline and a bonus culture for the highest earners. It's obvious weakness in the public sector is that markets and therefore many of the targets that people are incentivised to reach and beat are artificial and therefore measurement of performance is simply a mathematical construct with no objective external meaning. I have heard its leading protagonists in the service say that only that which is measured will be valued. All that I can say is that most well-adjusted men do not measure their penis, but they sure as hell value it. I have read recently in the paper about the management style of the former Head of the Royal Bank of Scotland, Mr Fred Goodwin as he now is, and the dread that his subordinates reportedly felt at morning meetings if they had failed to achieve impossible targets or failed to drive down costs far enough to satisfy their demanding boss. There is now a breed of governor, both in charge and at lower levels for whom success is about the extent to which artificial targets are achieved, the extent to which blame for failures can be unloaded on to others, and the extent to which costs can be cut regardless of the damage done to infrastructure, the additional burden on workloads, and the inheritance for future managers. In order to deliver on targets that purport to measure humanity and decency, the service employs individuals whose own humanity and decency to put it charitably, is at risk of being compromised by a set of values they are either forced to embrace, or much worse, embrace willingly.

My first harsh lesson in the way in which the service was changing came when I moved to Dover in 2000, my first Deputy Governor post. Until this stage I had given no thought to Area Managers, who were the immediate line managers of the Governor, and even less about more senior civil servants with whom I had only the most occasional contact. The Governor was the late Colette Kershaw for whom this was her second in-charge appointment, a higher-grade post that was her reward for her efforts at Cookham Wood, a female prison. The Area Manager was the abrasive Irishman, Tom Murtagh, who would achieve national fame or notoriety according to taste as a consequence of the Blantyre House raid that resulted in the removal of the Governor, Eoin McLennan-Murray, of which more in Chapter 10. The problem was the inheritance. The previous Governor had cut costs, for which he was reputedly paid a handsome bonus, but had done so in a way that had avoided conflict with the Prison Officers Association. Thus the gate lodge which in most establishments was now staffed by support grades was staffed by prison officer grades who were excused prisoners. Similarly there were no support grades working in reception, the administrative work of which does not require a prison officer. On the other side of the coin, security was very poorly staffed. Despite the fact that the establishment had failed its previous security audit, there was often no staffing available from Friday to Monday, a problem exacerbated by poor work profiling. As one would expect, security information reports remained unprocessed for days in breach of security requirements, a fact soon picked up by the Area Office Performance Team who were constantly on our backs about this and other failings. Staff sickness was a major issue and another crunch point with Area Office was our constant borrowing of supposedly ring fenced drug strategy resources simply to staff house units. This was an establishment that still had dormitories, which from time to time were smashed up by the young offenders. Cancellation of Association periods, particularly on weekends came with huge risks.

Working days at Dover could be hugely demanding, particularly Mondays and Fridays. As Colette Kershaw was studying for her Master's degree in Criminology which involved an authorised six weeks per year away at Cambridge in addition to annual leave, it was often the case that I or a colleague was the only Governor grade on duty on a Monday or Friday. In a four-person team, it was always someone's rest day on one of these days, so if another colleague was on annual leave and Colette was at Cambridge then you were on your own. Assuming there were no issues from the night before you could spend an hour on routine paperwork at the beginning of the day. After morning meeting, it was adjudications. The level of adjudications in Young Offender Institutions is always higher than in adult establishments. They are still very much adolescents heedless of consequences unable to back down in front of their peers. They represent a harder test for staff which as a consequence reinforces any tendency to pass the problem up to the Governor. Prisoner disciplinary proceedings regularly took all morning and often staff had to be diverted so that we could continue securely into the lunch break. After tasting the meal, I could finally get back to the office, often to an exasperated secretary wanting to know why I hadn't answered the radio and broken off what I was doing to prioritise a call from one of Tom Murtagh's minions at Area Office. The radio was of course off during adjudications and quite properly there was no phone in the adjudications room. Kent Area Office was a black hole that regularly lost paperwork that you had sent them. The most common phone call was a demand for something you sent weeks ago. In the afternoon, I would then do rounds. Back then workshops opened Friday PM. The Duty Governor, because of course you were Duty Governor as well as Acting Governor, was required to visit them all, and quite rightly so as instructors often felt quite beleaguered and isolated with a shop full of unmotivated young men more interested in mischief and mayhem. There were numerous workshops and by the time you had visited the residential areas as well it would not be far off 5PM. All this assumes you could make progress around the jail without incident and without any union representative wanting a piece of your time. If you were really unlucky, someone from Area Office would drop in to offer unconstructive criticism about establishment failings or demand an action plan to make up training hours not completed. I can remember one Friday afternoon returning to the office only to find a gentleman from Area office whose anonymity I will preserve, carping about some paper failing or other, and sharply telling him, "Can't you see I've got a fucking prison to run." Going home was certainly not an option. Letters had to be signed, correspondence read and calls returned. As Duty Governor, you needed to be around for the first part of the evening regime and make it clear that Association needed to start on time. There was no time for thinking, reflecting and planning.

The pressure was constant. Tom Murtagh was a former Governor of the jail and therefore always felt he knew better. Within the service he had a fearsome reputation. I found the best way to get his respect was to stand up to him but many of my colleagues could not conceive of going toe to toe verbally with an Area Manager as it was considered disrespectful. In the end, he did me no harm and even supported my application to attend the Assessment Centre to select those considered 'Suitable To Be In Charge' (STBIC as it was then known). When Tom visited, you all assembled in the Governor's office and remained there at his pleasure while he reviewed performance and the written reports you were required to send every month. You got no protection from the Governor and were very much on your own. None of this was good for relationships. The late Colette Kershaw would not accept that Dover was not just structurally incapable of delivering good performance as measured by targets, but also of delivering a decent environment in which prisoners felt safe and reoffending could be reduced. Resources were either not available, in the wrong place or protected by vested interests. She was reduced to shouting and paranoid suspicion of non-existent plots. The Accountant was absolutely terrified of her and actually admitted that to her face. Tom Murtagh's view was that "The senior managers are not a team…The Governor needs to address this". Although at the time I was unsympathetic, in retrospect it must be one of the harshest criticisms a Governor can see of her own performance in print and can only serve to make the pressure almost intolerable, especially when Area Office is part of the problem rather than part of the solution. However she did not help herself by working on her course assignments in the privacy of her office whilst the rest of us were struggling to keep up with the ferocious pace of a typical day. It was the classic 'do as I say not as I do' and it gave her the appearance of being a semi-detached dilettante. The end for me came in March of 2001 when Tom Murtagh announced he was sending in a Standards Support Team to assist us with the forthcoming audit. This was the ultimate humiliation. By this time Colette Kershaw and I were barely on speaking terms, and after a blistering row I was transferred. As they say at the BBC, deputy heads must roll. This is another feature of the culture of entitlement and of modern governance; the perceived right to appoint one's own deputy.

There was no lingering animosity between Colette Kershaw and myself. Breakdowns are what happen when a system of patronage replaces a system whereby people are allowed to develop expertise via a series of structured career moves before being pitched into difficult roles. In Colette Kershaw's case, a critical developmental gap had left her exposed; she had never been a Deputy Governor before being parachuted into a number one job. Although it is still relatively rare to promote people to head establishments without having been a Deputy Governor there are forces at work that are propelling people into jobs they are not sufficiently rounded either personally or professionally to discharge successfully, without being carried by their subordinates. The cult of youth is one force. The other is the recruitment of people into senior management roles direct from external organisations in the belief that somehow running a supermarket has any bearing on running a prison. The lucky ones are never found out which only reinforces any sociopathic tendencies already present, which in turn only reinforces the Head Quarters view that they have successfully cloned the DNA of the senior prison service manager. I use the term deliberately because these people are Governors in name only. As for Colette Kershaw, divine providence intervened professionally. There was a major riot at Dover and the audit, which if failed would have seen her exiled to a desk in HQ, was cancelled. Dover ran for months with a much-reduced number of prisoners and she was transferred to HMYOI Rochester as Governor in-charge. As regards her personal welfare, there was no divine intervention. Sadly she died of cancer in the summer of 2006 which puts all professional differences into perspective.

Sometime after I transferred from Dover to Ford, I was in conversation with my own Governor, Ken Kan and Mike Conway, Governor of Swaleside. Mike departed the public sector a couple of years later and became Director (the private sector equivalent of Governor) at Peterborough, a huge local which also housed female prisoners. He had had enough of the public sector with its sclerotic bureaucracy and stifling of initiative. Mike did not leave for the money, unlike some others. The conversation was about who was 'a company man' and who was not. Being labelled a company man was not a compliment. In this discussion, owners of that label were school sneaks, lickspittles or careerists, or a combination of all three. I am open to being told that I am completely wrong but it is difficult to conceive of a conversation of that nature taking place 15 or even 10 years earlier. Although Governors of an earlier era were probably more rebellious they had an immense pride in their work. They saw it as a vocation. Ambition and the desire for promotion were not ends in themselves. Promotion offered opportunities to lead and inspire staff and to make a difference to the lives of those unhappy souls we keep in custody. It offered the opportunity to take risks and empower people with talent. It was not about targets, audit box ticking and performance league tables. All that I can say is that some of our Young Turks who have embraced this culture should look at the fate of Sharon Shoesmith, one time Director of Social Services in Haringey. As she discovered, performance targets are false gods. After the death of Baby P, it was revealed that Sharon Shoesmith had praised her department's performance against a whole series of Child Protection Performance Indicators. That revelation swelled the media firestorm and fuelled the determination of local and national politicians to procure her dismissal. The lesson is that embracing the all-pervading 'managerialist' culture offers no protection when scapegoats are sought. Governors beware.

Chapter 6
Prison Workers Miscellany

In March 2010, some six months before I left the prison service, there were 1,434 operational managers (governor grades to you and me), 32,528 prison officer and officer support grades (uniformed staff), 2,669 non-operational managers, and 12,594 staff who are below the grade of non-operational manager, mainly administrators, instructors and tradesmen, but also including psychologists and chaplains. The nursing grades included in the figures are employed by the NHS. At first sight these figures may have no real meaning and sometimes conceal rather more than they reveal. Perhaps the most obvious statistic is that only around 70% of staff fall into governor or prison officer grades, although not all of the remainder are in non-prisoner contact roles. Firstly as I have said in Chapter 5 the service prefers the term operational manager to governor and the reader can see that those classified as non-operational managers are about double in number those classed as operational. So what is the distinction, does it matter, and who are they? The distinction is actually important. The 1952 Prisons Act requires that each establishment has a Governor and chaplain. The operational authority of the Governor can only be delegated to someone accredited as a Governor grade (operational manager in service speak). Normally this is the Deputy Governor but at weekends and overnight the person in-charge on the ground will be the Duty Governor, who will most frequently be a Governor 5, the lowest grade of prison governor. In practice, either the Governor or Deputy Governor will always be available by telephone. Thus if there is a major incident the Duty Governor will assume control until relieved by someone more senior. This could also occur on a weekday if the Governor is on leave and the Deputy Governor is standing in on an external commitment. Operational accreditation comes via a Job Simulation Assessment Centre (JSAC). Candidates for assessment will undergo a written qualifying test and at the centre will undergo a series of exercises designed to test suitability for the role. Incident management and issues that will routinely be thrown up by prisoners and staff will be realistically tested. Further up the food chain is the Senior Operational Manager JSAC, designed to identify those suitable to be in-charge, although this level of accreditation is also required for deputy posts in large jails. Thus a manager without operational accreditation can never be in temporary command, no matter how senior they may be. Nor can they carry out the adjudication of reported infractions by prisoners of rule 51, the prisoner disciplinary code.

It is perhaps unfortunate that the Prison Service chooses to use negative labelling. I doubt that the estimable people who are lumbered with this label are terribly impressed. Historically non-operational managers were middle ranking treasury grade civil servants with their own separate career structure and avenues of promotion. I can remember a careers talk from school when I was about 16 years old. Back in 1969 the mainstream Civil Service was divided into Clerical, Executive and Administrative classes, as indeed it still was when I joined in 1984. The Administrative Class was largely recruited from university and had its own complicated grade structure up to the apex as Permanent

Secretary. We now know it as the Senior Civil Service. The Executive Class had three divisions: Executive Officer (EO), Higher Executive Officer (HEO) and Senior Executive Officer (SEO). In a prison, the grades and numbers of staff in the Executive Class would vary with the size and complexity of the prison. Promotion to this class was normally via the clerical grades. When I joined in 1984, the most senior of these at an establishment was referred to simply as the 'AO', which stood for Administrative Officer, although of course he or she was not a member of the Administrative Class. Neither were they entitled to be addressed formally. They were in charge of the back office functions. The Clerical Class also had three divisions: Clerical Assistants, Clerical Officers and Higher Clerical Officers, although I don't ever recall meeting one of these. By the end of the decade, clerical staff had been re-designated as Administrative Assistants and Administrative Officers. It is confusing. The AO would become Head of Management Support Services, swiftly renamed Heads of Management Services (MSS) as the former title suggested a rather inferior role when in fact they were members of the Prison's Senior Management Team (SMT). By the time I reached Woodhill in 1995, another reorganisation had divided administration into Personnel and Finance, each with its own head at Higher Executive Officer level. The inevitable downside of specialisation was that internal moves of staff became complicated by territorialism.

As ever in the Civil Service, this was not the end of change. In 2000, the Prison Service brought in what is referred to as 'Pay and Grading'. The title is anodyne, the reality rather more complex with a definite agenda. The service in common with other government departments has a great love of expensive management consultants. This particular bunch recommended a merging of governor grades with treasury grades via a common pay and grading structure. The only significant difference would be whether the manager concerned had operational or non-operational status. Thus a Head of Personnel or Head of Finance in an establishment became the equivalent of a Governor IV. Henceforth both would be regarded as Prison Service Manager E, operational or non-operational. To demarcate the distinction financially, the operational manager would receive an additional allowance, although in fact he did not receive it, part of his/her salary was simply re-designated, and could be lost if taking on a HQ role for more than three years. The real winners were the Heads of Personnel and Finance, and other non-operational managers, with access to a far higher top of the pay scale than previously applicable. With unification in theory there could be crossover. A Governor grade could be Head of Finance if he/she had the qualifications, Head of Personnel if a member of the Institute of Personnel via the requisite qualifications, and Head of Learning and Skills if a graduate and a qualified teacher, which incidentally I am. However, it would be necessary for anyone crossing over to remain on the Duty Governor roster and carry out unsocial hours in order to keep what is called RHA (Required Hours Allowance which is pensionable) thus retaining operational pay and status. To the best of my knowledge only the last of these has seen any crossover from the operational ranks. A movement the other way would require the manager to accredit and join the operational duty roster to get the pay and status. Without wishing to denigrate non-operational managers the attractions of unsocial hours and excrement-smeared prisoners on dirty protest have proved a less than irresistible lure for the sake of another £5k per year. It was not quite the same for an earlier generation who moved across the grade structure 20 years ago when there were considerably less opportunities for advancement outside London in administration and the extra money in percentage terms for accrediting and moving across was rather more lucrative. Probably the outstanding recruit of this generation was Mike Shann who went on to govern Birmingham and shared the healthy scepticism of his generation for those who sold out their values on reaching senior civil servant status.

A not terribly well hidden agenda amongst the upper echelons of the service was to weaken still further the perceived power and status of governor grades. In the private sector which now has 14 of the 121 prisons, the equivalent of the duty governor is the duty manager, with the important difference being that the designated individual either does not necessarily occupy a conventional operational role. In other words, the equivalent of the Head of Finance could not merely be taking phone calls from prisoners' solicitors about facilitating a legal visit out of normal hours which is an operational matter, but also be in operational command of the establishment at the start of a serious incident involving prisoners, despite having no background at the sharp end of the operation. The former is the thin end of the wedge; the latter is taking major risks with safety and security. Sadly dangerous precedents of this nature only seem to encourage our political masters to be even more daring, evidence of which is the crazy proposal to bring people into our police forces directly at Superintendent level. Chapter 9 covers in more detail so called workforce modernisation. Prior to the workforce modernisation programme was the outsourcing of personnel functions to a Shared Service Centre based in Bridgend. Personnel clerks were for the most part redeployed and Heads of Personnel were invited to apply for a new role that of Human Resources Business Partner. For the uninitiated Human Resources has replaced Personnel as the fashionable term for those who deal with issues like recruitment, sickness monitoring and staff training. Clerks deal with the transactional work and the departmental head the strategic side. On the face of it, it is very simple. However, sample job descriptions revealed that it was intended that the new style Heads of HR would have responsibility for industrial relations, traditionally the day-to-day responsibility of the Deputy Governor. They would also have taken over the Deputy Governor's role as commissioner of investigations. And of course, there would be some external recruiting from industry. No governor in their right mind would let loose anyone without an operational background anywhere near industrial relations with the Prison Officers Association unsupervised. As it turned out, the HR Business Partner in every jail went the way of much flesh with the ferocious round of cost cutting that followed the 2010 election, yet another example of civil service short termism that NOMS, as it was now called, could have been much better managed without. The few HR Business Partners that remain are now an area resource and therefore field based.

Alongside the changes in titles and management structures there have been significant changes in the work carried out. When I joined in 1984, there were no Heads of Finance. There was a very simple reason for this; budgets were not devolved to prisons. The Governor therefore had no incentive to curb overtime or indeed any other form of costs. I can remember back in 1988 when premium phone lines first became fashionable. Colleagues were happily listening to telephone commentaries of horse races and to sex chat lines based in America. Part of the fun was connecting Sexy Sadie the Spanking Queen or similar personage to a colleague elsewhere in the prison. It was all the more fun on speakerphone. This kind of abuse ran unchecked for years in some establishments to the extent that it became an unofficial perk. It took devolved budgets, the introduction of technology to monitor calls, and most importantly, the will to get a grip on this kind of thing, to stamp it out. The system at Woodhill was much tighter. Terry Phillips, Head of Management Services at the prison, sent a monthly memorandum to all middle managers with calls costing over 50p highlighted, and more importantly, the internal extension number. It was our job to account for them which was usually not terribly difficult if someone was known to have a girlfriend in Grimsby or wherever. Modern managers have never known anything other than devolved budgeting which says everything about the old Civil Service culture of inept central control. However, some might ask whether anything has changed. At one of my former establishments the

Governor had elected not to pay for the telephone monitoring service. Thus when a female prison officer found her home besieged by reporters after being discovered visiting a serving prisoner at HMP Ashwell we had no means of discovering whether her home address had been leaked by someone using an official Home Office telephone. To this day I am convinced I know who was responsible and that they were stupid enough to use an office phone even though it was not common knowledge that the call monitoring facility was not active. However, despite that loophole long being covered, leaking to the press remained endemic at Ford, and judging by events since my retirement, it still is.

Jails may not have had a budget but they still handled plenty of money. Up until 1987, prison officer grades were still paid weekly, and the majority who requested it were paid in cash. Indeed I was one of the few who had his wages paid into the bank. The pay clerks were therefore very important people as was the cashier who physically handed over the money. In the smallest establishments, they were often one and the same person. Cashiers were noted for assuming airs and graces by restricting the times at which staff could collect pay and expenses. Woe betide any officer who knocked on the cashier's window when it was closed, even though she was probably having an unofficial fag break, these being the days when smoking in offices was still permitted. Payday was Thursday, but night patrols and those officers out of the jail on court duties could apply to go on the early pay list and get their money on Wednesday. It used to baffle me that our elderly night patrols would carry their pay packets around the dormitories every Wednesday night without fail. Fortunately, the young offenders remained blissfully ignorant. However, a plumber did have his pay stolen from the works department by a trainee. It was recovered intact from a hiding place 24 hours later, but people were still not deterred from carrying large amounts of cash.

At this time prisoners were also paid in cash. They had only two means of preventing theft or coercion. These were either spend the lot, which most did, or make application to have savings deducted and retained for release. It may seem rather shocking now with the benefit of hindsight but prisoners as young as 15 were able to purchase pornographic magazines out of earnings or private cash under youth custody rules. The separation of juveniles when the sentence of Detention in a Young Offender Institution replaced Youth Custody in 1988 put an end to that particular abuse. It was the job of the Library Officer to go into Hanley to WH Smiths, having drawn the correct amount of cash from the cashier to go and purchase top shelf magazines such as *Penthouse*, *Playboy* and the gruesome *Readers Wives*. I covered this duty only once, on my motorcycle. You needed to have no shame to walk up to the counter, uniform and key chain concealed by an overcoat, to deal with the stares from fellow customers and the shocked face of the cashier as you paid in cash for upwards of a dozen of these magazines that in those days were not covered by cellophane. I rode back to Werrington with them in my top box. The regular library officer made sure he read them all first. Quite why a prison officer was sent out to do the porn shopping I will never know. I can only suggest that it was not considered a suitable job for a teenage admin assistant.

The system for paying expenses was also bureaucratic. In a large establishment, up to a hundred officers per day were engaged on court duties. Almost all were entitled to subsistence depending whether or not they were out of the jail for more than 5, 10 or 12 hours on official duties. All these claims had to be paid in cash and all had to be countersigned. As prison officers, we made the system work for us. If there was any danger of getting back from court in just under 10 hours, the taxi driver would be instructed to slow down or take a scenic route, much to the amusement of the handcuffed prisoner. I know of former colleagues who took more drastic measures and stopped off at the pub, complete with prisoner by now un-handcuffed, (prisoners wore civilian clothing for court) and bought the prisoner a drink as an incentive to keep quiet. It was vital to be one minute over the 5, 10 or 12 hours as otherwise the cashier would not pay out under the strict letter of the rules. Relationships between clerical staff and prison officers could sometimes be very poor and beating the system became an article of faith. However, there was usually an easier way than clockwatching as the Senior Officer or Principal Officer in charge of the court would often tell you to put in your own departure time, which of course the officer in charge of the escort would not write in until approaching the prison gates. In 1995, the service began handing over court escorts to the private sector which put prison officers back on the landings and put an end to lucrative subsistence payments which mounted up significantly for officers on a 20-week stint at crown court. It put an end to another source of income that could be hidden from spouses. One former colleague frequently regaled us with a story of what occurred when his wife asked about subsistence. His response was "Don't worry about subsistence, I'll pay it". Whether he actually got away with that only he knows. Most of us just kept quiet and pocketed the cash.

Detached duty at other establishments was also quite lucrative. The modern system is that accommodation is booked via a contractor for a set maximum cost and the staff member has no need to pay up front themselves, or ask for an advance as many did. An additional allowance of £26 per night is paid to cover the expense of living away from home. Back in the 1980s staff booked their own accommodation and were able to claim both the maximum cost for a room and the overnight incidental expenses allowance. Needless to stay staff booked into virtual doss houses or if in a group asked for a room with four bunks. The service eventually got wise to this but staff simply upgraded to single rooms in the best hotel they could get. The modern system belatedly introduced I think in 2005 cuts out the needless bureaucracy. The system generates payments into your bank based on the information entered and broadly assumes honesty although receipts need to be retained for a period for spot compliance checks.

For a period, the employment of accountants was fashionable in the Prison Service as opposed to career Civil Servants on promotion to Head of Finance. They came and went not least because there was no further promotion for them in the public sector. A return to the more lucrative private sector swiftly beckoned for those for whom higher salaries now was of more interest than a secure but distant public sector pension. These days one cannot become an in-charge Governor without being financially literate, even though at least 80% of costs are beyond the control of the Governor with national pay bargaining and national contracts for essential supplies. All members of senior management teams see the full prison accounts monthly and often have delegated responsibility for their own department.

The average citizen would no doubt like to think that the outsourcing of personnel and the large-scale replacement of paper systems by electronic ones has had a serious impact on salary costs by reducing the number of clerks in NOMS. Well the average citizen could not be more wrong. Complexity swept away in one area has been replaced by complexity in another. Every prison has a Custody Office, in recent years subsumed into Offending Behaviour Units (OBUs), but formerly known as the Discipline Office. Custody Office is one of those rare new names (and more accurate ones) that actually caught on. One of the principal jobs of the Custody Office was and is sentence calculation. Without accurate sentence calculations, there may be people in the community who should still be in prison and vice-versa. Failure to release a prisoner on time attracted compensation of around £90 a day when I left the service in October 2010. Area Managers, now re-titled Deputy Directors of Custody tend to get upset about releases in error, not least because the press get very animated, particularly if the individual commits a serious offence. For this reason, those staff who work routinely on sentence calculation are under particular pressure as there is no hiding place from mistakes. There is a system for checking and crosschecking, but it relies on knowledge of complex instructions being up to date and training courses being available for the clerks and their supervisors who carry out the role. In some prisons, the Duty Governor signs for the final check which is a pointless ritual as most are not trained in sentence calculation, nor indeed should they be as that is a clerk's job. Historically sentence calculation wasn't difficult. After all if a year in prison has to be served, it isn't hard to work out. The advent of remission was the first complication. When I joined it was one-third rather than one-half as it is now. The sentence of say three months was calculated in days, one third taken off, (I can't remember if it was rounded up or down) and the prisoner was then given an Earliest Release Date, known universally as the EDR, a day which is actually part of the sentence. Unless he received loss of remission from the Governor, release on this date was, and remains, an entitlement. In the days when loss of remission was a Governor's award, this generated plenty of recalculation work for clerks. That power now lies with District Judges who normally visit monthly, so that work now comes all at once. If the release date falls on a Saturday, Sunday or Monday Bank Holiday, it is brought forward to the previous Friday. When Christmas Eve falls on a weekend, it sees the single largest discharge of prisoners into the community. That is not an entitlement that attracts a financial penalty, but it is a convention built around the fact that clerical staff do not work weekends.

So far it appears straightforward. This is the part where clerks need to concentrate. Prisoners can and do receive overlapping sentences. On the face of it, not too difficult, you just take the longest. It is rather more difficult if there is a mixture of concurrent and consecutive sentences received when they are already serving a custodial sentence for a different offence. Then there are appeals. A sentence may be reduced and on occasion increased. It may even be necessary for the prison to be contacted to do an urgent recalculation as a reduced sentence may mean release at court. Furthermore, over the years there have been of wheezes conceived to reduce the pressure on an overcrowded system. One of the most staff intensive of these wheezes was the inclusion of police custody time, every single day of which prior to attending court being taken off the time in prison in respect of a single offence. Thus if a man was arrested and arrived in custody just before midnight on a charge of affray and released, say at 4AM, then he would have been entitled to have two days off any custodial sentence given back to him. However, if he had been convicted of an offence for which a) he received a longer sentence and b) was charged at a different police station, he would have received only the time spent in custody at a police station for the first offence, even if this was less. Custody Office clerks spent hours trying to get confirmation from individual police stations that prisoners firstly spent time in their cells, and then how long. Some prisoners simply could not remember which police station they were taken to in respect of a particular offence or offences, but if a man had made an application to have police custody time credited, then the clerk had no choice to pursue what could have been a very time consuming matter, which if the sentence was very short would have needed to be prioritised. Not surprisingly the Police did not regard such matters as urgent. They want villains in prison, not exploiting legal loopholes to get out early. Thankfully in more recent years, time spent in police custody after arrest can only be credited with the permission of a judge. Nevertheless, this scandalous loophole had been available for over two decades before it was closed.

I suspect many prison officers never mind the public have the first idea what goes on in the back office and certainly not the pressure under which some of the admin staff work. Custody Office clerks in local prisons are also busy dealing with the courts in respect of productions. Every day the list is prepared. Again mistakes are frowned upon. Even though private sector contractors are paid for conveying prisoners to court, the Governor is responsible for ensuring that prisoners appear. Thus if an error is made that results in a non-appearance when one is scheduled, the Governor will have to find staff to produce the prisoner out of his own budget. Court lists are juggled throughout the week as cases overrun or collapse. Production orders can come very late in the day. Thus at least one clerk in a local prison will always need to work late though at least they have the benefits of flexi time.

Another wheeze to reduce the prison population was Home Detention Curfew (HDC) introduced under the last Labour government. It has been tinkered with on and off but the maximum time on curfew (usually 7PM to 7AM) is now 135 days. Thus a prisoner sentenced to 18 months obtaining full remission and being granted HDC will serve just four and half months in custody. The work is not in providing a fresh calculation, the work lies in the risk assessment that has to be prepared before the go ahead for release, signed off normally by the Deputy Governor, is given. For clerks, it is yet more paper to pull together. For the Probation Service, along with other reforms designed to balance protection of the public with getting prisoners back into the community it has led to the increased secondment of probation officers into prisons. Needless to say Offending Behaviour Units are harried relentlessly on the telephone and on E Mail, always with a read receipt, by solicitors demanding to know why their client is late out on HDC, despite it not being an entitlement.

In 2004, the Prison service was subsumed into the National Offender Management Service (NOMS), renamed Her Majesty's Prison and Probation Service (HMPPS) in 2017, which sought to merge the work of managing offenders in prison with managing offenders in the community. The intention was that services to offenders would be 'joined up' and integrated and thus provide greater protection for the community. The left hand would know what the right hand was doing. The very different cultural traditions of the prison and probation services would go into the melting pot and out of it would emerge a single correctional services culture. In particular, the government sought to change the perception that those in custody were the only ones being punished whereas those offenders carrying out community penalties or released early on licence were being let off and handed over to an ineffective, inherently liberal probation service that had a vested intellectual interest in soft justice. I exaggerate for effect, but for the average *Daily Mail* reader, not by much. However, the government did not make probation officers civil servants, and they remained organised locally rather than nationally, with probation trusts replacing the former county based services, until 2014 when the thirty-five probation trusts were replaced by the National Probation Service, which manages high risk offenders, and the privatised Community Rehabilitation Companies, which manage low risk offenders

The Probation Service has its origins in the London Police Courts Mission, a Christian and temperance organisation typical of the Victorian era. The formal history begins in 1907 when probation officers were given status as officers of the courts in London. The 1925 Criminal Justice Act required the establishment of probation committees throughout the country and they were required to appoint probation officers. Thus philanthropic voluntarism was nationalised. The 1948 Criminal Justice Act introduced prison aftercare and provided for the funding of probation homes and hostels. The central purpose of probation officers remained to 'advise, assist and befriend'. A period of probation is simply a period of trial that allows an offender to demonstrate that they can be a fully-fledged and trusted member of the community. With the advent of the Criminal Justice Act 1967 which provided for parole introduced the following year, only part of the sentence was served in prison and the remainder in the community under supervision if parole was granted by the Parole Board. Despite numerous legislative and administrative changes, the principle that part of the sentence may be served under supervision in the community has not only held but been expanded and has most recently been extended to those serving a prison sentence of twelve months or less, in a bid to deal with the recidivism of serial petty offenders. Thus all prisoners released partway through a custodial term for all but civil matters such as contempt of court, are on licence for the remainder of the term imposed by the courts. The Parole Board now only deals with the most serious offenders almost invariably serving indeterminate sentences. The granting of parole by the parole board requires an evidentially supported belief that the prisoner can be returned to the community as a probationary member. The law provides for parolees to be returned to prison even if they have not committed an offence if the probation service is concerned about their behaviour. Risk Assessment has evolved as the key tool for determining whether discretionary release on licence on parole or Home Detention Curfew can be permitted. What has happened over 50 years is that the system has become ever more bureaucratic and costly as successive governments have groped for an answer to reducing re-offending by the criminal classes as more and more prisoners have fallen into its orbit. Now there are very few prisoners not subject to some form of release on licence. In the case of life sentence prisoners, they will be on licence for the rest of their lives. The cynic might argue that this is the trade-off for the refusal of successive governments to have a genuinely deterrent criminal justice system which would mean meeting the costs of imprisoning more people and for longer. However, it is worth noting that if we imprisoned at the same rate as our co-linguists across the pond, we would be locking up over 600,000 people at any one time, which is a sobering thought.

One of the ironies of the changing role of the probation service is they are no longer perceived as the prisoners' friend. When I joined, probation officers seconded to work in prisons were still referred to as 'The Welfare'. An earlier designation was the Probation and Welfare Service. Prison officers saw them as convict loving do-gooders who addressed prisoners by their first names, permitted them sneaky use of official phones and found flats for those whom no one would want as neighbours. Welfare work differentiated probation officers from prison officers, and they were perceived unfairly as those who rescued prisoners from the consequences of their actions. Probation officers in prisons were not primarily concerned with re-offending and the term risk assessment had still not made its way into the lexicon. The change in recent years has been dramatic. The culture clash of graduate probation officers with secondary modern educated militaristic prison officers is ancient history. Probation officers and prison officers have never worked together more closely and it is probation officers who take the lead in seeking to block early release as a risk averse culture has taken hold. As Deputy Governor, I found myself overruling over cautious risk assessments. The overruling of the recommendation of a board chaired by a Senior Probation Officer and substituting a decision in favour of a prisoner would once have been inconceivable, not least because probation officers are excellent and cogent report writers. Whereas once prisoners would have seen prison officers as the villains of the piece if they did not secure early release, that mantle now belongs to the probation service. In the community, they are expected to very tough with those who do not co-operate with community penalties or ignore licence conditions. This is known as 'breaching' and has almost made the probation service as unpopular with prisoners as the police.

The biggest source of bureaucracy is Headquarters of which more in Chapter 9. At this stage if the reader remains mystified as to how non-operational managers and clerks are so numerous compared to those who face prisoners or maintain the running of prisoners that is where the answer will be found. Within establishments there is one other team of clerks and their supervisors that needs to be mentioned: the Performance Team. Every prison has one, usually under the Deputy Governor in current management models. Every Area office has one also. Every month they turn out graphs and pie charts showing how the prison is performing in relation to what was when I left 16 Key Performance Indicators (KPIs) and 46 Key Performance Targets (KPTs). Sharon Shoesmith no doubt had something similar at Haringey Social Services as did Mid-Staffordshire Health Trust. They will also monitor progress on the Inspectors recommendations and provide administrative support for internal audit with yet more eye catching colourful diagrams. At HQ Standards Audit is the equivalent of garden Leylandii, hugely resistant to all attempts to trim it back.

As was noted earlier under the terms of the 1952 Prisons Act, every prison must have a Chaplain. At one time Chaplains were on a par with the Deputy Governor and the Senior Medical Officer. Indeed they fought a long losing battle to retain the right to have their annual appraisal carried out by the Governor. For some years now their reports have been written by a governor grade in the third tier of management. I have never had the dubious pleasure of appraising a Chaplain but what I can say that like any other prison worker all types of humanity are represented. I have known the saintly and the serene, the devout and the devoted, and thankfully only in a small minority of cases the ill-tempered and the uncharitable. I can still remember the Reverend John Humphries at Werrington House stood outside the chapel in his cassock, bible in hand, smiling inscrutably as a prison officer marched the church parade down to the chapel, letting off volleys of ferocious four lettered and unfettered abuse at those trainees who dared to march out of step. As no colleague of that era ever suggested that they had received a rocket as a consequence, I can only presume he never complained. Back in 1984 the Chaplain was always a Church of England minister. Other Christian members of the chaplaincy team were prefixed by their denomination, hence the Roman Catholic chaplain and the Methodist chaplain. Members of the chaplaincy team (not that they would have operated necessarily as a team in that era) would have had no difficulty identifying members of their flock behind their cell doors. Church of England prisoners had white cell cards, Roman Catholics had red cell cards, and it was blue for Jew, not that I saw many of them. Atheists, Rastafarians, Muslims and others who did not fit the mould were given white cell cards. It reflected the military traditions of the service and mirrored the experience of former national servicemen in the armed forces. That system has long been overtaken by social change. Although as you would expect cell cards are still issued showing the prisoner's name and faith (if any) there is no attempt to colour code religious adherence. Indeed we would probably now run out of colours.

The Chaplaincy itself has also changed. It is no longer mandatory for the co-ordinating chaplain to belong to the Anglican faith. There is now nothing unusual about the Head of the Chaplaincy team being a Roman Catholic priest or the local Muslim Imam. Although there are still some individuals precious about sectarian identity, the norm is multi-faith ecumenical teams working together united in the knowledge that they worship the same god rather than being divided by doctrine and different roads to paradise. The RC chaplain at Werrington simply took the covers off the statues before celebrating Mass so shared facilities are nothing new. Most jails now have multi faith rooms and washing facilities provided for Muslim prisoners. In terms of practicing their faith as opposed to being nominal adherents, Muslims are now the largest single faith group in prisons and with the growing influence of Islamist extremism amongst young Muslim men, they are a prime target for radical elements. Countering the growth of militant Islam is one of the biggest challenges facing the modern prison service, which again demonstrates my oft-repeated mantra about prisons reflecting the society they serve. However, there are ways in which the chaplaincy has not changed at all. It is still the job of the chaplaincy to deliver messages about deaths in the family outside and offer comfort and consolation, not just to the faithful. However communicating messages about deaths in prison is a job for governors rather than priests. Not unreasonably where death is self-inflicted or there is a suspicion of foul play, families want to hear from someone with earthly authority. When at Woodhill, I once had to ring a nun in an Irish convent with bad news about her brother who had been smashed around the head with a PP9 battery and subsequently died. The assailant got an extra 15 years. The chaplaincy plays a key role in suicide prevention, at which the service has got much more proficient since the tragic self-inflicted death of 15-year-old Philip Knight in Swansea prison in July 1990.

The Senior Medical Officer is now an extinct role in the English prison service. In large prisons, the Senior Medical Officer would be supported by two or more medical officers and the prison would constitute a medical practice on its own. All prisoners have to be examined by a Doctor within 24 hours of arrival. The full time medical officers would be fully qualified doctors and unlike their counterparts in the NHS would be civil servants and therefore subject to the authority of the Governor. Back when the NHS was founded in 1947 the BMA had successfully resisted proposals to make all Doctors civil servants which they saw as impinging on their professional independence. As I have mentioned in Chapter 4, in 1997 the Governor of Woodhill was in a position to resist a demand from the SMO to issue condoms to prisoners. In smaller prisons, the Senior Medical Officer was a local GP and the establishment was a part of his practice. The part time medical officers were not civil servants and relationships with prison management and the quality of care given to prisoners could vary significantly. I have encountered visiting Doctors who were rude or under the influence of alcohol, and on occasion both at the same time. At little Werrington House, the part time medical officer was supported by two hospital officers (later renamed health care officers), one of whom held supervisory rank. As I recall, the ward facilities would go unused for months on end, partly because young men were probably healthier in 1984 as the drug culture had not yet fully exerted its grip, and partly because they were actively deterred by a management culture that regarded reporting sick as on a par with malingering in all but the most serious cases. The best time for a trainee to get a hospital bed was when the Inspectorate was visiting. At the very largest establishments, the most senior uniformed member of hospital staff would hold the rank of Chief Officer. The military ethic was not diluted by membership of a caring profession.

When Woodhill opened in 1992, other than a Principal Officer to manage the staff it did not recruit traditional hospital officers. Instead it recruited nurses who were almost entirely female much to the joy of male prison officers. However although it got much greater professional expertise there were other significant problems, primarily recruitment and retention. The grading of nurses was too low and for whatever reason the Governor was deaf to pleas to ignore the Head of Personnel, and instead go to the market and pay the market rate for the expertise needed. Recruiting Doctors and Nurses directly as employees came to an end a few years ago as local Primary Care Trusts were contracted (commissioned in NOMS speak) to provide Health Care Services. At Lewes successive Heads of Healthcare were NHS managers who had progressed through the nursing grades. At one time the Head of Healthcare was my predecessor as Deputy Governor, who was dual qualified by reason of his former nursing career. More recently still modern Matrons have been appointed, as in the NHS, though not with remotely the power, influence and prestige enjoyed by the former Borstal matrons. The aura of matron as portrayed by the late Hattie Jacques has survived so long in popular consciousness that it is hard to believe that they disappeared from the NHS at the end of the 1960s.

Unlike Healthcare staff prison teachers have never been civil servants. They have always been the employees of a contractor. At the beginning of my service the provider was usually a local Further Education College. As they were paid out of central funds rather than locally, they called the tune as regards the curriculum. It would be difficult to call it a contract in any meaningful sense. Gradually this would change as the service got its act together as regards the central role of education in the reducing re-offending agenda but also with the development of contracting out as large organisations emerged to bid for lucrative contracts. Manchester College is probably the single biggest provider in the English prison system and is represented far from its own original regional boundaries. Teaching staff, or more accurately lecturing staff, have seen their employer change on a number of occasions and found their terms and conditions gradually worsening, always assuming that they haven't been made redundant. Unlike prison officers who can rely on being transferred if their prison closes, teaching staff face compulsory redundancy on terms much inferior to those of civil servants who as yet have only been faced with voluntary redundancy.

As with every other employee working within a prison, most teachers are very professional and only a few let them down. School age offenders have compulsory education so the challenge is similar to that of an inner city sink school classroom filled mostly with the children of the nation's underclass. The main difference in prison is that they cannot truant. Just like a conventional classroom they will attempt to probe for weakness. Shortly after Werrington became a juvenile establishment in 1988 one thirty something female teacher made a classic error inviting her class to ask absolutely any question they wished she got the almost inevitable 'Miss, when did you last have sex?' After that, getting respect was an uphill battle. At Dover the issues were rather different. The staff, which were employed by the local college, were exclusively white and middle class and almost entirely female, whereas the offender population contained a well above average population of black youngsters. There was little meeting of minds, a constant stream of disciplinary charges laid, and more than a little tension. On my recommendation, the Governor excluded one particular teacher and made it clear to her line manager that disciplinary action for racist remarks was appropriate. Unfortunately, the College declined to take action. However her departure from the establishment did improve matters. With adults the situation can be different again. Teaching staff are less likely to be perceived as the enemy and there is a more adult relationship. Sometimes prisoners would like it to be even more adult. It has to be remembered that Education is popular for more basic reasons, not least because the staff are largely female, and unlike female prison officers they wear civilian clothes, not an unflattering uniform.

Another significant group of professionals in need of mention are psychologists. Where there are lifers or prisoners serving indeterminate sentences for public protection there will be psychologists assessing them. They are very powerful people in the lives of those prisoners who have no definite release date. No life sentence prisoner can contemplate release or transfer to a lower security prison unless the psychology team are in agreement. In a main lifer centre, the Principal Psychologist will be a member of the Senior Management Team. It is fair to say that with that power comes enormous responsibility as they control the destiny of serving sex offenders. All except around 75 lifers who have a whole life tariff are likely to be released back into the community at some point, and old age may not weary them. One of the more practical and scientific tools available to psychologists is the penile plethysmograph, which measures the blood flow as it affects the size of body organs, in this case the penis. It is used to discover whether or not the offender remains stimulated by the type of pornography most closely related to his offences by measuring the level of arousal. It is reckoned to be at its most accurate with child molesters. How it is fitted and calibrated I do not know and have never asked.

The downside to the power held by psychologists is the daily diet of perversion and horrendous abuse that is contained in reports and the self-justifications provided by offenders. It was part of a residential Principal Officer's role to be one of the interviewers of sex offenders when their progress reports were due so I have some idea what sort of filth prison psychologists have to endure from my stint at Wakefield which housed the largest concentration of sex offenders in Europe, so much so it was known locally as 'monster mansion'. One snippet will suffice. More than one sex offender justified incest with his daughter on the basis that it was his job as a father to introduce her to sexual intercourse. Fortunately, I am one of those people who can switch it all off at the end of a day's work. We lost one prison officer early in 1995 who was a Sex Offender Treatment Programme tutor working in a multi-disciplinary team with psychologists. There was no note and no other clues but most of us believe that the balance of his mind was disturbed by daily exposure to the most shocking perversions. Since that time the support and counselling services available to staff carrying out that work has improved. One of the most immediate improvements was that prison officers were no longer expected to go straight back to landing duties at the end of a class. Readers are probably not aware that sex offenders have to take their turn in the 'hot seat' where they are required to detail their offences and their motivation, and take criticism from others in the room. I have never attended one of these sessions but have observed it simulated on an awareness course that I attended. It is emotionally harrowing.

All establishments had a Works department which did what it said on the tin. I say "had" as in 2014 maintenance was contracted out to Carillion, a private company as a cost saving measure. Carillion went bust in 2018, primarily as a result of underbidding for this and other contracts, leaving HMPPS to sort out the mess. When I joined a typical Works department contained plumbers, joiners and electricians under the control of a Head of Works, who prior to 1987 was always a uniformed member of staff. No unskilled labourers were employed as that was what prisoners were for. Sometime before I joined the service the apex of the rank structure was changed in line with the rest of the uniformed service. The Senior Foreman of the Works, known colloquially as 'The Engineer' gave way to a Principal Officer or Chief Officer depending on the size of the workforce. After the scrapping of the rank of Chief Officer, the Head of Works in a larger prison was a Governor V and in the most complex of establishments a Governor IV, and they would be members of the Senior Management Team. Until the Reorganisation of Works Departments (ROWD) the workforce was a mixture of prison officers who doubled as tradesmen, and employees who were known quaintly as 'civilian workmen'. The initials 'CW' would appear on their payslips in front of their surname. I am told the designation has its origins in what were known as free workmen, to distinguish them from convict labour. In 1984, the title reflected the in-house distinction between 'screws and civvies'. It always struck me as bizarre given that prison officers were simply another grade of civil servant and as much a civilian as any other non-armed forces walk of life, notwithstanding the powers of a constable in certain circumstances. After all was not the unarmed Police force conceived by Peel a civilian rather than a military body. Civilian workmen were paid what was called a lead allowance for supervising prisoners in the same way as their uniformed colleagues.

Inevitably the cost of employing prison officers as tradesmen came under scrutiny given that a prison officer's pay at the top of the scale exceeds that of an Industrial Craftsmen, to give them their modern name, by several thousand pounds per annum. Senior civil servants felt that trades officers (T.O.s), as prison officers in the Works department were titled, should be back handling large numbers of prisoners rather than a small number of the more trustworthy offenders who were on the Works party. And so under the ROWD (Reorganisation of Works Departments) programme the roll out of which began in 2001, prison officer grades were gradually eased out of Works departments, and they became almost entirely civilianised. At Ford the surviving trades officer became Health and Safety Advisor where as one would expect Works Departments had a great deal of expertise. Works Departments were now overseen by Area Office rather than individual Governors which on occasion caused tensions. Heads of Works who equated to Prison Service Manager E now theoretically had a further promotion avenue, Prison Service Senior Manager D at Area or Regional Office, the equivalent of the Deputy Governor in a high security gaol. As a consequence, Heads of Works were no longer necessarily employees who had progressed from Trades Officer. The Industrial Grades began to break through that which was once not just a glass ceiling but a permanently closed roof, and become Heads of Works in establishments. What privatisation did for their prospects I cannot say.

The same effect can be observed in prison kitchens where civilianisation began earlier. The privatisation option has also been chosen. Back in 1992 Woodhill opened with its kitchens contracted out to a firm called Aramark. The downside and it took four years to change, was that prisoners were no longer employed in the kitchen, which is one of the most obvious avenues of training and skilling prisoners for the outside world. There was also no requirement for prisoners to be employed on the Works although they continued to be in my time at Ford. On one ludicrous occasion, during a hostage exercise being run by me, an industrial grade came to cordon off the area around the incident, accompanied by a prisoner carrying the cordoning tape. You couldn't make it up. There were times when I despaired of Ford open prison joining the rest of the Prison Service and this was one of them. The best that can be said is that it was an exercise and to my knowledge didn't happen again. Mistakes of this kind were one of consequences of this form of de-skilling. In certain parts of the country and West Sussex was one of them, the salary for Industrial Craftsmen was well below what they could earn locally in the private sector. As with the under graded Healthcare centre at Woodhill, the only answer was the expensive and counterproductive use of agency staff to fill the gaps. It could only happen in the public sector.

Prison Service instructors, not to be confused with teachers, also fall into the old division between screws and civvies. Believe it or not there are Officer Instructors who are prison officers, and Instructional Officers who are referred to as civilians in the same way as industrial grades and clerks. Few if any Officer Instructors now remain as they are both expensive and much less likely to have formal skills qualifications. At Werrington, the concrete shop was run by an Officer Instructor. Although there was plenty of heavy work my old colleague Derek Fielding would not have been happy to call it unskilled. Someone has to prepare concrete moulds. The motor cycle repair shop, known as the Mechanics shop, was run by an Instructional Officer. Vocational courses such as Bricklaying, Plastering or Painting and Decorating would normally have been staffed by Instructional Officers, unless they were contacted out to the education provider. Mailbags are no longer sown but there is plenty of low-grade monotonous assembly work. Somewhere in between falls work like furniture repair, important in a penal setting where the inhabitants do not particularly respect government property. Ford employed horticultural craftspeople for its extensive floristry operation and also maintained a sewage farm, both of which provided institutional employment for prisoners. I imagine the latter would be one of the few things to please penal hard liners about Ford.

I have mentioned contractor's employees on a number of occasions. Contractors supply drug workers in addition to those already mentioned, charities supply volunteers with NACRO (National Association for the Care and Resettlement of Offenders) the best known. As a breed, they tend to regard suits and ties as just another uniform. Every day is dress down Friday.

I can't end this chapter without mentioning night patrols. I write as one who hated night duty. They were formerly a separate uniformed grade below prison officer and the modern designation is Operational Support Grade. They are a breed of men, and occasionally women, who actually choose to work permanent nights for a living. In my working life, they were usually older than prison officers, not least because under their terms and conditions they could work until they were 65, which they virtually all seemed to do. Until the Employment Equality (Age) Regulations were introduced in 2006 prison officers and prison governors were normally required to retire from those grades at the age of 60, so re-grading was a means of continuing in harness for those staff who could not yet face life out of uniform. The default age of retirement for all workers, 65, was abolished in 2011. In my time at Werrington House, we had just three night patrols to support two prison officers, of which two were always on duty. Thus they worked two weekends in three (prison officers worked alternate weekends) and inevitably two Christmases in three. A colleague's leave provided an overtime facility which until OSGs superseded Auxiliaries and Night Patrols in 1997, paid double time for Sundays and time and a half on the remaining nights. After 1997, existing night patrols could retain their old terms and conditions or join new employees in either working overtime for time and one fifth, or taking time off in lieu, known universally as TOIL. I would doubt that many original night patrols now remain in service given the age profile of this group of staff in 1997.

As one would expect, the service likes to be sure that the night staff do not go to sleep. When I worked at Werrington they had large clocks which they carried on their shoulders with a key attached which had to be turned in what were called pegging points so that a night patrol's visit to a dormitory or landing was recorded. It should be remembered that this was evidence only that the person was awake, not that they had checked on prisoners. The print outs were checked the following day by a Principal Officer, indeed they still are. With such a small night patrol contingent at Werrington prison officers were often called upon to cover sick leave or annual leave that could not be realistically be covered in a group of three if they were to have any time off at all. Most of my colleagues resented carrying the clock. Pegging every 15 minutes left no time for any clandestine rest and some resorted to throwing the clock in a bath of water which tended to stop it, so of course there was now no point pegging. Another trick was to ask the gatekeeper who changed the tapes on which the times were recorded, to not fit them back properly so the times would not record at all. Yet another trick was to unscrew the pegging points from the wall, take them into the office, and peg from there. Unlike the other two tricks, it didn't give the opportunity to sleep, and unlike the other two scams needed to the co-operation of the night orderly officer to work. The modern system is electronic, but still beatable by those determined to avoid legwork. At Lewes we suffered a spate of damage to these expensive pieces of kit. Our belief was that the electronic pegging gun was being cooked in the microwave, but proving it and catching the culprits was another matter. In all prisons a team of prison officers and dedicated night staff under the command of an officer, senior officer, or principal officer in the high security estate staff the prison.

At Ford just like Werrington in my day there were just two prison officers on duty, supported by a minimum of four and a maximum of six regular night patrols. This was for 550 men. If sufficient patrols were available, one was designated to cover the other side of the road to the accommodation, patrolling around the offices (which had been known to suffer burglaries!), workshops and grounds on that side of the prison. It was a one-man job and over an 11-hour shift he would see no one apart from the Night Orderly Officer on an occasional short visit to check on his welfare and switch the alarms on, and then off in the morning. There was a rudimentary shelter, really just a sentry box which offered some protection from rain but none at all from cold. You really have to be a different breed to do that job permanently.

Chapter 7
Prisons and Politicians

From joining the Prison Service on 8 May 1984 until retiring on 14 October 2010, I served the Crown under ten Home Secretaries and two Secretaries of State for Justice when that office was created and combined with the role of Lord Chancellor and took over from the Home Office responsibility for the nation's prisons. Both of the Justice Secretaries, Ken Clarke and Jack Straw were previous Home Secretaries so in total I served the Crown under ten different Cabinet ministers and innumerable and largely unmemorable junior ministers, with the assiduous Ann Widdecombe being the only exception to this roll of anonymity. Indeed perhaps the next best known was one not appointed to junior office with responsibility for prisons, Edwina Currie, who famously turned down the job offer from then Prime Minister John Major, with the full story only emerging some years later. During our 4 week induction at Stafford our Training Principal Officer, the late Roy Sanders made it clear to anyone forced to listen (us), that Roy Jenkins, Home Secretary 1965–67 and again 1974–76, was the biggest disaster ever to hit the penal system having abolished the disciplinary awards of bread and water and the birch, and the death penalty. It is true that he abolished the use of the birch in our prisons but for the record he was not yet Home Secretary when the death penalty was suspended in November 1965 and in any event the suspension was carried on a free vote. According to his obituary Robert Carr, who died in 2012 at the great age of 95, was the Home Secretary who abolished what was known as the 'Number 1 diet' in 1973, before Mr Jenkins returned for his second stint at the Home Office the following year. Nevertheless Roy Jenkins remained his pet pantomime villain. Roy Sanders also took great delight in informing us that the Governor, Colin Heald, was on first name terms with former Labour Home Secretary, Merlyn Rees.

Leon Brittan was Home Secretary when I joined. The following year he moved to Trade and Industry before being forced out in January 1986 as a result of a cabinet leak against Michael Heseltine who had just resigned over the Westland affair. Mr Brittan never held office again in the UK and went off to make his career in the EU, becoming a European Commissioner in 1989. He is remembered for his tenure only for being forced to sanction early releases to solve a population crisis, caused not unexpectedly by the Government talking tough, the courts getting tough, and then finding out that there wasn't enough space for those on the receiving end of the newly toughened sentencing. It did not save him from being savaged by the Tory press who had begun to get their teeth into Conservative Home Secretaries starting with his predecessor, William Whitelaw (1979–83) who was also Deputy Leader of the party. Despite his legislation for the short sharp shock for young thugs, he was branded 'Willie Wetlaw' by his critics in the right wing press. Leon Brittan's successor was the urbane Douglas Hurd.

Mr Hurd was faced with a crisis in 1986 when the Prison Officers Association called an overtime ban which in a service entirely dependent on overtime crippled it within 24 hours. The action was called off very swiftly but not before HMP Northeye, a Category

C prison in East Sussex was partially burned down by rioting inmates. What remained of the prison was closed in 1992. Douglas Hurd was shrewd operator who got both sides back round the table by fudging over the distinction between negotiations and consultations by simply arranging for discussions. For the uninitiated trade unions normally hold negotiating rights for pay and conditions but everything else is consultative. Problems start when the employer does not listen when consulting, or when the trade union seeks to make that which is consultative, negotiable, or the employer vice-versa. My own experience is related in more detail in Chapter 9. Nevertheless as related earlier 'Fresh Start' which made prison officers monthly paid professionals and abolished overtime was successfully negotiated and introduced on a rolling programme around 12 months later. However, the interpretation of the national agreement known to all as 'Bulletin 8' has bedevilled the service for 30 years. The end of overtime successfully decommissioned the lethal, legal and almost unbeatable weapon of the overtime ban. Douglas Hurd also conducted a more direct assault on the POA, when he abolished 'check off' the system by which trade union membership subscriptions were deducted from pay by the employer on behalf of the POA and other trade unions recognised for the purposes of collective bargaining. This system was once a common feature of agreements between employers and trade unions, and still survives in some workplaces strange though that may seem in 2019. However, it did not have the impact on trade union finances that it might have had with a workforce paid weekly in cash. Now that all prison officers had their salary paid directly into a bank, direct debiting was a simple solution.

Mr Hurd's unusually lengthy tenure was also noteworthy for two other changes. Firstly, the 'short, sharp, shock' so beloved of Mr Whitelaw was abolished. As was discussed in detail in Chapter 2, the Detention Centre and Youth Custody sentences made way for one sentence, Detention in a Young Offender Institution which in reality bore none of the punitive features of the former. Thus all young offender establishments now needed new signage which was made in a workshop at HMP Coldingley. A rather less liberal but long overdue reform was the abolition of the un-convicted prisoners' alcohol privilege. I would guess that there are many serving prison officers as well as most members of the public who did not know that until 1987 un-convicted prisoners could receive one pint of beer per day via visits, except on a Sunday. In practice, only cans were accepted as bottles were potential weapons. Instead of the expected disorder, there was no reaction from prisoners and it went the way of the naval rum ration, except that it was relatively un-mourned.

Douglas Hurd (Lord Hurd since 1997) was replaced by David Waddington in a cabinet reshuffle for a brief tenure that lasted only 13 months before being elevated to the House of Lords when John Major replaced Margaret Thatcher as Prime Minister. David Waddington was unusual in that he was the first incumbent of the office to openly favour the return of capital punishment in the quarter of a century that had passed since Henry Brooke had allowed the last judicial hangings to go ahead in August 1964. To students of miscarriages of justice, he is better known for his career as a barrister, more particularly as the QC representing the wrongly convicted Stefan Kiszko in 1976. Kiszko was convicted of the murder of Lesley Molseed, which took place in October 1975 and served more than 16 years in prison before being released in May 1992. Sadly, he enjoyed only 18 months of freedom before collapsing and dying of a massive heart attack two days before Christmas in 1993. Mr Waddington has been criticised both for running a defence of diminished responsibility and for not demanding an adjournment when the prosecution disclosed a huge pile of documents to the defence only on the day the trial was due to start. Mr Waddington was also hampered by the fact that his highly suggestible client had confessed to the killing, although he subsequently withdrew the admission. Juries of that era had no understanding of the pressures faced by innocent but naive people in police custody. If I am perceived by readers to be over generous to David Waddington, it should be remembered that what characterised this case, as with a number of miscarriages of justice that occurred in the 1970s, was police wrongdoing. As we now know and David Waddington could not have known, West Yorkshire police deliberately withheld evidence that Kiszko was sterile, and therefore could not have been the murderer.

David Waddington's other misfortune was to be Home Secretary at the time of the Strangeways riot, which started with a protest in the chapel on Sunday 1 April 1990, when the authorities seemed powerless to end 25 days of mayhem by rioting prisoners, which resulted in the near total destruction of the establishment. It would be four years before Strangeways (HMP Manchester) would reopen for business. Lord Justice Woolf was commissioned to conduct a public inquiry into the riot which spawned copycat disturbances elsewhere in the system most notably at HMYOI Pucklechurch on 12 April, which resulted in the loss of another prison. The deep-rooted causes as opposed to the immediate triggers have frequently been rehearsed. Conditions were utterly squalid with prisoners being forced to spend up to 22 hours per day confined to their shared cells with no choice but to defecate into a plastic pot if they could hold on no longer. Visits facilities were appalling and for remand prisoners, i.e. those still innocent in the eyes of the law, they were even more restrictive at just 15 minutes per day. A prison designed for 970 people held 1,647 prisoners on the day of the riot. Education was for the lucky few. It is important to remember that it wasn't just Manchester. Most local prisons were equally squalid and in some cases even more overcrowded. April 1990 was the nadir of 'nothing works'.

There were also allegations of mistreatment. It is no secret that Largactil, known as the liquid cosh, was used throughout the system to control the behaviour of those with disruptive mental health problems. There is no corroborated evidence of a widespread culture of staff brutality, but it is important to remember that a dysfunctional system brutalises and corrupts the integrity of staff and prisoners alike. Staff and prisoners as a whole had ceased to engage meaningfully. For prison officers, happiness became door shaped and having prisoners out of sight and contact became perceived as the preferred method of completing a shift safely. Writing as one who was working in a jail where the young offenders lived in large open dormitories, we did not have this luxury and therefore had to deploy our interpersonal skills on a daily basis in order to manage the environment. 29 years on dormitory conditions in Young Offender Institutions would now be unmanageable as a consequence of social change and murders in custody would become common, but the importance of interaction and making relationships with one's fellow human beings can never be overstated, not just because it is the most effective way to manage, but also because it humanises institutions in which one body of people is tasked with locking up another larger body of people. The Home Office took the decision, against the advice of the Governor, Brendan O'Friel, not to attempt to retake the prison. It is difficult to know whether an attempt to retake the prison by force in that first week could have succeeded without fatalities, but the Home Secretary had to live with the political consequences of playing the long game, played out as it was on the nation's TV screens for 25 seemingly endless days. Amongst the hidden consequences were the psychological effects on staff, some of whom were never the same again. Staff were dispersed far and wide to new jails, and those who returned in 1994 when the prison finally re-opened after being completely rebuilt, came back to a very different establishment.

By coincidence, the Roman Catholic Chaplain at Manchester at the time was a former classmate of mine, Father Peter Wilkinson. In prison, Mass is normally celebrated on Saturday so it was his Church of England colleague whose service was disrupted. Mr O'Friel had already initiated regime improvements which were opposed by a minority of staff. One interesting theory of insurrection is that the incendiary outburst of the kind that occurred at Manchester is more likely when hope has been raised a little by reform rather than when conditions are at their worst. Thus impatience takes over from sullen demoralised acceptance. It is speculation and certainly not a reason for continued repression. There has to be a positive moral dimension to imprisonment and Brendan O'Friel, at the time President of the Prison Governors Association, was the leading light amongst the majority of Governors who shared that view. 'The explosion of evil...' as he called it, was an accident waiting to happen and arguments about the timing are irrelevant. Strangeways brought an end to an era of less than benign neglect by politicians of a system that taken in the round was patently unfit for purpose. However, it did not resolve the debate about the purpose of imprisonment nor has it prevented our politicians from treating the events of April 1990 as an aberration whose lessons can be increasingly ignored with passage of time. Strangeways has not improved the behaviour of our politicians any more than it has improved the behaviour of prisoners. Indeed with some honourable exceptions it has made it worse.

Lord Woolf took evidence from June through until the end of October 1990. He and the Chief Inspector of Prisons, Judge Stephen Tumim, sent letters to every prisoner and prison officer in the country. 1,300 prisoners and 430 prison officers responded. A selection of responses was appended to the report. The report was submitted to David Waddington's successor, Kenneth Baker, who remained in office until the General Election in April 1992. Woolf was critical of the handling of intelligence prior to the riot and critical of the breakdown of the chain of command and of tactical errors made on the day that allowed prisoners to seize control of parts of the prison that might otherwise have been held and the riot contained, individual acts of great heroism notwithstanding. He also described conditions as intolerable and blamed successive governments for failing to 'provide the resources which were needed to enable the Service to provide for an increased prison population in a humane manner.' There were twelve key recommendations and it is instructive to see what has happened to them.

Woolf recommended firstly closer co-operation between different parts of the Criminal Justice system. He recommended that the Director General should be a visible public figure, should have a published contract or 'compact' with ministers, and should be responsible for the performance of that contract or compact. The DG should be publicly answerable for day-to-day operations. Admiral Raymond Lygo was given the task of reporting on Prison Service management. Consequent on the Lygo report into the management of the Prison Service, it was floated off as an Executive Agency in 1993. The idea of Executive Agencies was to give them the freedom and responsibility to deliver, whilst ministers retained responsibility for policy and overall accountability to parliament, thus creating a theoretical distinction between policy and operations. Greater integration and co-operation did follow. Martin Narey who headed the service 1998–2005 was created Commissioner of Corrections in 2003 which united custodial and community interventions under a single line manager. The following year the National Offender Management Service (NOMS) was created. There have obviously been consequences and not all for the better. It is fair to say that senior management was professionalised, although it took a circuitous route to get there. Prior to 1992 when Kenneth Clarke replaced Kenneth Baker as Home Secretary, the Head of the Prison Service was always a career civil servant. The top job was not open to prison Governors.

Ken Clarke broke with tradition at a point when the infatuation with all things private sector, (privatisation is covered later in this chapter) was probably at its height and appointed Derek Lewis, former Head of the UK Gold TV channel as Director General. Practitioners saw the appointment as both a gimmick and a slap in the face. It would end in tears when Ken Clarke's successor, Michael Howard, of whom more anon sacked Derek Lewis in November 1995 after the publication of the report by Sir John Learmont into the Parkhurst escape earlier that year. Mr Lewis won his case for wrongful dismissal and breach of contract. The upshot was that no outsider would take the job and risk being used as the fall guy to protect a minister from the press and perhaps the Prime Minister, looking for a scapegoat. Subsequent Director Generals Richard Tilt, Martin Narey, (both of whom since knighted) Phil Wheatley and Michael Spurr have all been career Prison Governors. As civil servants, the Secretary of State has no power to fire them, although Michael Howard is known to have wanted to dismiss Andy Barclay, former Governor of Whitemoor, even though he had moved on before the attempted IRA escape, and is also known to have intervened and procured the suspension of the Governor of Parkhurst after the January 1995 escape, against the advice of his Permanent Secretary. Michael Howard's actions in dismissing Derek Lewis have had the effect of creating an enduring career opportunity for prison service insiders.

Michael Howard set the tone for subsequent Home Secretaries. Like David Waddington he had previously voted to reinstate the death penalty for certain types of murder. He made no pretence of being a penal liberal, was noted for his controlling style and frequent excursions into the day-to-day operation of the service, and was extraordinarily concerned to guard his tough guy reputation in the party against the whims of the popular press. Thus it was never a failing of policy, but the failing of those charged with operational execution of policy. As a distinction, its meaning is always arguable, but it protected Michael Howard's political career, as it would protect Theresa May's a decade and a half later. Unlike many ministers including those in his own party, Michael Howard was also protective of the public purse and had no compunction about cutting budgets. The political backdrop was that public finances had been strained by an overvalued pound, followed by the fallout from 'Black Wednesday' in September 1992 when the UK was forced out of the European Monetary System. The Chancellor of the Exchequer, Norman Lamont, paid with his job the following year, and the subsequent reshuffle saw Kenneth Clarke go to the Exchequer, and Michael Howard to the Home Office. Kenneth Clarke, a noted penal liberal, had been ideologically committed to Wolfe, whereas his successor was almost the dream choice of his party's law and order wing. The recommendation for increased delegation to individual Governors went the way of all flesh under the rising tide of 'managerialism'. Indeed the trend was already underway before Michael Howard had taken charge. A key development had occurred the previous year. The four Regional Directors who were usually fairly hands off career civil servants gave way to ten (later twelve) Area Manager posts which in fairly short order became the default promotion avenue for insiders i.e. Prison Governors. The Lygo report recommended a more proactive role for Area Managers and spawned the monster of which more towards the end of this chapter and also in Chapter 9. In summation, the combination of their creation and the Lygo recommendation ensured that power would flow away from Governors rather than to them. You can now govern a penal establishment without any leadership skills.

Similarly the recommended enhanced role for prison officers was slowly strangled. I have already described the demise of trades, catering and healthcare prison officers in favour of cheaper substitutes. Money dictates the extent to which prison officers have a role in treatment programmes and other interventions designed to tackle offending behaviour. More recently NOMS has taken managerial responsibility away from first line managers reducing them to shift supervisors. Quite how this squares with an enhanced role is a mystery.

Prisoner compacts are one of the few success stories from Woolf. The Incentives and Earned Privileges scheme piloted in 1995 did for the most part deliver better prisoner behaviour and a willingness to participate in programmes. It was particularly effective in getting a grip on what were known as the 'dispersal' prisons, now known as the High Security estate. Until the introduction of this scheme the seven training prisons which housed Category A and Category B prisoners serving more than five years imprisonment were bedevilled by different entitlements to privileges which caused enormous friction when prisoners were transferred, and by the fact that the privileges were virtually automatic. The idea of a liberal regime within a secure perimeter led to appeasement and powerful prisoners calling the shots and obstructing security in certain parts of the dispersal estate. With the exception of Wakefield staff posts were hard to fill and inexperience and lack of continuity played their part. The escapes from Whitemoor and Parkhurst were the catalyst for regaining control of the lawless parts of that estate. The Incentives and Earned Privileges scheme ensured that it was done positively. Mr Howard would not allow in cell television to go on the privilege list, a decision reversed by his Labour successor, Jack Straw in 1997. Since then there have been rumblings but the scheme had survived press criticism and ministerial discontent until Chris Grayling announced reform of the scheme, adding another ingredient to the dangerous cocktail brewed in our prisons by this government which is covered in more detail in Chapter 11.

Michael Howard also refused to make Prison Service Standards mandatory, which with the benefit of hindsight is something of a surprise. In fairly short order that was reversed by his even more controlling successors but their value was seriously traduced by excessively forensic auditing and box ticking. When I left, there were 65 standards covering everything from staff appraisal through to catering, chaplaincy and race relations but good audit results provided no reliable indicator of the quality of custodial care. It is rather like the health service where a short queue for a minor operation tells you nothing about your chances of catching MRSA or some other flesh-eating bug as a consequence of ingrained filth. Each standard would have numerous, in some cases scores of baselines with different weightings. Standards Audit Unit became probably the most powerful HQ bureaucracy of all, resisting regular attempts to rationalise the system with the ferocity of Japanese Knotweed. It was truly a monster. Auditors who were often fairly junior in the organisation could make or break the careers of those much senior to them. Getting things written became far more important than getting them right. In the managerialist climate created by politicians one of the most crucial posts to be filled in a prison was that of audit manager whose job was to ensure that there was a local self-audit system which was itself subject to assessment. This middle ranking individual would have significance out of all proportion to grade such was the power of audit over careers. Get a good one and you could breathe a sigh of relief. It was not only Governors who lived in fear, but also Area Managers. The solution, you've guessed it, create an area standards audit team. A good audit and high compliance with the 16 Key Performance Targets became a very effective way of disguising major cultural faults within a prison and thus deflecting criticism when it came, always helpful if you are a minister under pressure.

However, ministers of whatever hue were forced to take seriously integral sanitation. Public opinion may have little regard for prisoners, but even the most reactionary drew the line at defecating into pots and slopping out. Nevertheless politicians still managed to water down the requirement (no pun intended). Very few refurbishments and only some new builds had discreet toilets. For most the water closet is as much a part of cell furniture as the table, chairs and portable television. Although he no longer has to squat over a plastic chamber pot, the average prisoner still has to defecate in the presence of his cell mate because politicians will not pay for elementary decency. At my last prison, Lewes, the much-maligned F wing was being refurbished as I moved on. At the beginning of the millennium it was used as a dumping ground for sex offenders in denial who refused to attend programmes. The poor law principle of less eligibility was clearly applied from above despite the protests of Governors and the jail's independent monitoring board. Eventually, the sex offenders were moved out to facilitate refurbishment, but then that was postponed and the wing filled again, although not with sex offenders, as politicians pulled the plug on funding. As I have said, eventually the refurbishment took place but not with discreet sanitation as that would have entailed a loss of one third of the cells.

Perhaps the most critical recommendation in terms of humanising the system was the proposal for a prison rule that no prison should hold more prisoners than its certified normal accommodation (CNA). Any material departures from that rule were to be truly exceptional. Even Kenneth Clarke baulked at that recommendation. In fairness to Mr Clarke, he did preside over a fall in population and seems hard to believe that in 1993 our Home Secretary was content that crime was sufficiently under control for the prison population to be barely half of its current figure of 82,706, as recorded on 5 April 2019. The peak figure was actually 88,179, recorded in December 2011. The failure to adopt this rule allowed overcrowding after the brief hiatus under Mr Clarke to regain its position as the norm. As noted in Chapter 2, prisons have both a CNA, and an Operational Capacity, a higher figure which incorporates permitted overcrowding. Just as in 1990 overcrowding in our local prisons is institutionalised with the obvious effect it has on facilities for prisoners and opportunities to tackle their offending behaviour and thus halt the revolving door. In short overcrowding makes the community less safe. It will probably take another Strangeways before politicians get the message, and even then it is not guaranteed.

Returning to Woolf the situation with regard to visits did improve. Convicted prisoners gained the right to have fortnightly visits, when previously they were monthly. The Incentives and Earned Privileges allowed additional visits for those with enhanced regime status. At Bedford a large new visits facility was created although it did take staff a little time to adjust to the luxury of having the space to allow all visits to continue until the end of the session. Convicted prisoners were entitled to a visit of just half an hour in length (since raised to one hour) and although things were usually much better in training and young offender establishments, in local prisons the minimum entitlement was often all that had been granted. Longer than the statutory minimum soon became the norm across the system, and indeed the statutory minimum was often reserved for less well behaved prisoners who had to dropped to basic regime, leaving them to explain to less than impressed relatives why their visits were of truncated length. However, the recommendation for maintain family links via serving sentences in community prisons came to nothing. Only prisoners serving short sentences who are unsuitable for open conditions can expect to complete their sentence at their local prison, i.e. the one that received them from court. The rest will be transferred and it is largely an accident of geography and building history whether or not they are able to serve their sentences close to home. It was never a practical recommendation and the cost to the public purse of providing prison places in the most accessible locations could not be justified. Some training prisons are in such remote locations that prisoners from that area can be counted on fingers and toes. Haverigg Prison near Millom, Cumbria, and Dartmoor in rural

Devon are exceptionally remote. Suffolk has two remote establishments, and Acklington and Castington now combined as HMP Northumberland is also in a remote location. These all have spaces that need to be filled. Convicted prisoners from London would often find themselves in places such as Blundeston near Lowestoft or on the Isle of Wight with the consequent need for the ferry. It should be added that there are no good grounds for closing these perfectly serviceable prisons and it should be remembered that they are an important source of jobs for law-abiding people in areas where employment is often at a premium. HMP Blundeston was, however, closed in 2013.

Woolf also recommended division of prisons into smaller and more manageable units. The population spike has put paid to that. Both new and old prisons have seen building programmes put new accommodation on to existing sites. HMP Lewes, a Victorian prison which opened in 1853, added 174 spaces in a new house block in 2008, during my tenure as Deputy Governor. Amazingly it was single occupancy accommodation and has remained so. HMP Woodhill, where I served from 1995 to 1998 only opened in 1992, but within four years it had a new house block with double occupancy in its cells. HMP Wayland in rural Norfolk which opened a little earlier in 1985 has expanded subsequently on three occasions with five new house blocks added, the most recent in 2008. The prison can now hold just over 1000 inmates. There are now 25 prisons holding in excess of 1000 offenders. In 1984 when I joined there were less than 10, as indeed there still were at the time of the Strangeways riot. Indeed we have come close to even larger establishments, so called 'Titan' prisons as recommended by Lord Carter in 2007. Plans to build three establishments with a capacity of 2500 were dropped in 2009 ostensibly on the grounds of difficulty in obtaining planning permission, but also in the face of near unanimous hostility from criminal justice professionals and academics. Nevertheless, the UK's largest prison, HMP Berwyn, with an operational capacity of 2,106 when complete, took its first prisoners in 2017.

As far as remand prisoners are concerned, they have benefitted only from change only to the extent that it has benefitted the population as a whole. There is no separate statement of purpose, no separate conditions, and they are still held in Category B conditions of security, except for those ranked as potential Category A, if convicted. Unconvicted prisoners remain the poorest relations of the system.

Woolf's final recommendation was for improved standards of justice within prisons. Again going back to when I joined Adjudications, as prison disciplinary hearings are called, were based on the military model of COs (Commanding Officer) Orders, or its naval equivalent, Captain's Table. Having being given earlier a docket setting out the nature of the disciplinary charge, the prisoner would be marched in front of the Governor and ordered to give his name and number. The prisoner would remain standing throughout proceedings faced by two officers, one on each shoulder, peaked caps pulled down firmly staring intently at the inmate. This procedure was known as 'eyeballing' and was a prime target for prison reformers. The Governor effectively acted as a magistrate as he/she had the power to take away remission or as it was later called, award added days, and therefore lengthen the offender's stint as a guest of Her Majesty. As a consequence, the standard of proof was beyond reasonable doubt, the same as in criminal trials. How rigidly that standard was adhered to would no doubt be disputed by former prisoners. There is well travelled and presumably well embellished story of a Governor informing a prisoner that 'if one of my officers was to say you were riding a motorcycle on the landing, then you were riding a motorcycle on the landing.' The maximum Governor's award (another military term) of lost remission was 28 days but the Board of Visitors (BOV), an independent watchdog that each prison is required to have, now renamed Independent Monitoring Boards (IMB), could add up to 180 days loss of remission equivalent to the maximum power of a lay magistrate in the community in respect of a single offence for more serious infractions referred to them, such as gross personal violence to staff and possession of illegal substances. Woolf recommended that the Board of Visitors lose their adjudicatory powers which he believed compromised them in the eyes of prisoners and concentrate on the watchdog role. This was accepted and these powers were duly abolished in 1992. Prisoners also gained a local complaints procedure which was a great improvement on the impersonal system of petitioning the Home Secretary which saw complaints answered almost invariably with a knockback by some middle ranking civil servant who would not have known one end of a prisoner from another.

However the politicians could not keep their hands directly or indirectly off the disciplinary procedures. The charge 'In any way offends against good order and discipline' was removed from what is now Prison Rule 51 in 1999 ostensibly on the grounds that it was unfair and punished infractions that were not specific offences. If we were to be consistent, then the common law offence of Misconduct in Public Office should be removed from the statute book since it has exactly the same weakness. In reality it is an excellent weapon against corrupt public officials. Neither did Governors get all of the Board of Visitors powers although Michael Howard did raise the Governor's maximum award to 42 days. Earlier in the decade the Criminal Justice Act of 1991 which came into force the following year abolished Forfeiture of Remission (FOR) and replaced it with Added Days Awarded (ADA). This move was welcome by the Prison Reform Trust and is referred to in their commentary on the major revision of Prison Rules enacted in 1999. Quite why the change of terminology was made I am unable to divine. It does, however, have the advantage of sounding tougher. As ever when there is agreement from polar opposites on the political spectrum, we should be very afraid. I will remain convinced until my dying day that it was this change in terminology which allowed the successful challenge under the Human Rights Act in the court at Strasbourg in 2002 which saw the Governor's powers to award added days declared a breach of human rights on the basis that an independent tribunal was needed when a prisoner's liberty was at risk. The fact that the 50% discount on time spent in custody was and is a privilege cut no ice. The Home Secretary, David Blunkett, was forced to restore all added days awarded in the two-year interval that had elapsed between the Human Rights Act being enacted and the judgement in Strasbourg. The law of unintended consequences had intervened to create prison places. In 2003 there was a below the radar change under Rule 51 and its Young Offender equivalent. The disciplinary charge of 'is indecent in language, act or gesture' was abolished which de facto legalised homosexual acts in prison. This has been covered in more detail in Chapter 3. Whether this was the intention we shall only know when Home Office papers are released under the 20-year rule.

The year following Michael Howard's elevation to the Home Office, Tony Blair succeeded the late John Smith as Leader of the opposition Labour Party. After four successive defeats at the hands of the Conservatives, Mr Blair took advantage of the Tories ripping themselves to pieces to skilfully reposition Labour on a number of issues prominent amongst which was crime. Whether it was Mr Blair himself or one of his speechwriters that coined the phrase 'tough on crime, tough on the causes of crime' it sparked off what effectively became a depressing populist auction conducted to secure the support of key newspapers and more pertinently that part of Middle England, sometimes referred to as 'Mondeo Man' that had previously trusted only the Conservatives to deliver on crime. Until the return of Kenneth Clarke in 2010, a succession of Home Secretaries (from 2007 Justice Secretary) competed with each other and their opposition shadows as to who could be toughest on crime, and no matter how tough they were it was never enough for some sections of the press. With capital and corporal punishment firmly off the agenda, toughness equated to only one thing, prison. There followed the seemingly inexorable rise in the prison population. At one point the Labour government was planning for a prison population of 100,000 and some projections suggested it would rise further still. Perhaps the most repressive penal measure of the New Labour era was the introduction of Indeterminate Sentences for Public Protection in 2003. This allowed serial offenders whose individual offences were not serious enough to merit a life sentence to be detained indefinitely until deemed safe to release after the expiry of their tariff, i.e. minimum period to be served before being considered for release by the Parole Board. In some cases the tariff was a matter of months. The upshot of this particular piece of legislation was that by 2012 when IPPs as they are known were abolished, (although not retrospectively,) there were some 6,000 prisoners serving them (around 7% of the population), of whom 3,500 were over tariff. Why were so many prisoners detained beyond their tariff? There are two reasons. Firstly, the Government massively underestimated the extent to which the courts would use the sentence, and secondly it did not provide the resources to allow these prisoners to address their offending behaviour in custody. Unsurprisingly ECHR ruled IPPs to be incompatible with Human Rights when it was not possible for a prisoner to access the interventions that would help rehabilitate him. This judgement was delivered in 2012 and compensation was awarded. Further claims inevitably followed. While the offenders concerned are often squalid nuisances who attract little sympathy, in no respect can their being left to rot count as justice. I should add that our own courts had already forced modifications of the 2003 Act before a foreign jurisdiction got involved.

Mandatory life sentence prisoners, known as mandatory lifers, in plain language murderers, as no other sentence is available on the statute book for those convicted of murder and no other offence attracts a mandatory sentence, also scored a significant victory under the Human Rights Act. After the suspension and then abolition of the death penalty, the Home Secretary gained the right to set the tariff, the minimum period required for retribution and deterrence before the parole board could recommend the release of a prisoner on life licence, itself subject to the approval of the Home Secretary. Detention after tariff was for the purpose of public protection. That a life sentence had two parts was a well-understood principle in government and legal circles (but not by the public as a whole) unless it was a 'whole life' tariff which does exactly as it says on the tin. There are only around 75 such prisoners in the system, many of whom are notorious and convicted of the most heinous and shocking offences who will only leave prison in a coffin. The tariffs were normally set some months after sentence after consultation with the trial judge by the Home Secretary. I went to work at Wakefield in October 1993, less than six months after Mr Howard became Home Secretary, which was my first experience of a large concentration of such prisoners. However, Mr Howard did not content himself with merely raising tariff levels when compared with his predecessors, he also revisited those of serving prisoners and raised a number of them, which as one would expect caused considerable disaffection and much consulting of solicitors for those who could obtain one. It was my job as a wing Principal Officer to hand over to prisoners their copy of the tariff when it arrived from the Home Office. As you would expect prisoner reactions varied along the spectrum from stoicism or mute incomprehension, through to tears and absolute outrage. In those days there was no further legal aid after a prisoner had exhausted his appeals against conviction. One prisoner I recall in particular, John Taylor, had his tariff raised from 16 to 30 years. Despite the difficulties Taylor together with his co-litigant Anthony Anderson, who had his tariff raised from 15 to 20 years, found a solicitor to take their case through the English courts, albeit unsuccessfully, though their day would come.

The ultimate victory of Anderson at ECHR in 2002 can be traced back firstly to the government's determination to single out murderers as evidenced in the 1991 Criminal Justice Act which distinguished them from discretionary lifers, i.e. those lifers for whom the judge had at least in theory the option of a fixed term of imprisonment. The life sentence was available for serious offences other than murder, most notably manslaughter, rape and other serious sexual offences. Under the 1991 Act discretionary lifers were treated differently. The power to set the tariff where an indeterminate sentence was handed down was given formally to the trial judge and it was announced in open court on sentencing. Secondly, the convention that the Home Secretary accepted automatically the recommendation of the parole board regarding release was given statutory force. On the other hand, the Government was firmly of the view that murder was a uniquely heinous offence requiring the Home Secretary, at the time Kenneth Baker, to exercise a judicial function on behalf of the public. As I have said, Mr Howard took this duty very seriously. In 1993, he went a stage further and added an additional criterion for the length of time a murderer should spend in prison; public acceptability, defined as that which maintained public confidence in the criminal justice system. Whichever way you cut it, this is a political function not a judicial one. Michael Howard's Labour successor, Jack Straw, confirmed his own intended adherence to the principal in 1997. The incorporation of the European Convention on Human Rights put paid to that, barely two years after the Human Rights Act came into force.

Also in 2002, the Home Secretary lost the power at Strasbourg to overrule decisions of the parole board in the case of mandatory lifers. Dennis Stafford, convicted as long ago as 1967 and twice recalled to prison was denied parole by Mr Howard formally in February 1997. Stafford initially petitioned the British courts and lost, to the satisfaction of Home Secretary Jack Straw whose powers were confirmed by the House of Lords before Strasbourg intervened. Thus in a short space of time populist Home Secretaries were stripped of powers they claimed as of right by the most lethal source of all of the law of unintended consequences, the Human Rights Act.

Few of these cases registered significantly above the radar as far as the general public were concerned, at least until they came before the European Court. However, there was one major exception: the ten-year-old boys who murdered James Bulger in February 1993. The case horrified the nation. The idea that two small boys could torture and murder a toddler was virtually without precedent, with only the Mary Bell case in 1968, in which 11-year-old Bell was convicted of the manslaughter of two younger boys on separate occasions, bearing any similarity within living memory. She served 12 years before being released on licence. Mr Howard raised their tariffs from eight years to fifteen years, in order to ensure that like Mary Bell they would serve at least part of their time in jail. The passing of the Human Rights Act and with it the incorporation of the European Convention on Human Rights into British law saw public outrage and that of James's campaigning mother, Denise, frustrated, as both their trial and Mr Howard's raising of the tariff were deemed breaches of their human rights by the House of Lords in November 2000. As a consequence, the Home Secretary lost his tariff setting powers over juveniles and both murderers, Robert Thompson and Jon Venables, were released from secure children's accommodation in June 2001 on the recommendation of the parole board without serving a single day in a penal institution. As has been said, a further blow came in 2002 when the ECHR ruled against the Home Secretary setting or raising tariffs for adult offenders. The Attorney General can appeal against an unduly lenient tariff but this does not alter the fact that the final decision lies firmly with the judiciary.

Since the 2003 Criminal Justice Act, there have been stringent guidelines for the judiciary as regards tariffs for particular kinds of murder, as Home Secretary David Blunkett (2001–04) who succeeded Jack Straw attempted to close the stable door after the human rights horse had bolted and tie learned judges down with a list of prescriptive tariffs. As piece of legislation, it was straight from the managerialist textbook.

My own personal view is that since the abolition of the death penalty there is no place for politicians interfering in individual sentencing decisions and it would have been better had they given up those powers back in 1969, when the suspension of the death penalty for murder was made permanent. There was no evidence that during the period of suspension, 1965–69, that the judiciary had failed to reflect legitimate public outrage in their recommendations to the Home Secretary. Reprieved murderers had typically served just ten years but this changed dramatically from 1965 onwards. The Judiciary proved itself perfectly capable of reflecting public outrage when the Moors Murderers were convicted in 1966 and when three policemen were murdered in Shepherd's Bush in the same year when 30-year tariffs were recommended. Indeed Harry Roberts, the one surviving member of the gang that murdered the three police officers, remained in prison until November 2014, without any interference from politicians. Similarly after 1969 when policemen were murdered or innocent citizens died at the hands of terrorists, successive Home Secretaries had been content to accept their recommendations and 30-year tariffs became the norm for these top end cases of murder. Frederick Sewell who murdered Superintendent Gerry Richardson in Blackpool in 1971 served this length of time before being released in 2001. The upshot of the failure of politicians to appreciate the principal of the separation of powers held by the executive on the one hand and the judiciary on the other hand, has brought about interference in our internal affairs by a foreign court for which the concept is entirely alien. In 1989 a House of Lords Select Committee recommended that the Home Secretary give up his powers to set tariffs. However, I am not naive enough to believe that adoption of this course of action and the eschewing of populist grandstanding by our politicians would have been sufficient to prevent the erosion of sovereignty of our own criminal justice system by the judicial Praying Mantis in Strasbourg. I do, however, accept the view as expressed by the Homicide Review Advisory Group that the mandatory life sentence for murder should be abolished. The truth is that the mandatory life sentence was a compromise designed to fool the public that the life sentence was actually followed by life in prison when in fact, as has been said, that never had been the case. It was a fiction that gradually unravelled as the press took an interest in lifer tariffs and Home Secretaries felt constrained to advertise their law and order credentials. This gave birth to the 'whole life' tariff, which by some Euro miracle was upheld at Strasbourg in the case of Jeremy Bamber. However, ECHR does not work on precedent and it came as no surprise in July of 2013 when ECHR did a somersault and ruled in the case of four appellants including Bamber that 'whole life' tariffs breached their human rights, as there was no procedure for review. ECHR actually went further and expressed the view that 25 years should be the maximum tariff before a prisoner became eligible for review by the Parole Board. Most recently in 2017 ECHR ruled that whole life tariffs did not breach human rights as there was now a review procedure in place, which appears to settle the matter.

There is no doubt that some murders are particularly heinous, but murder itself cannot stand alone in gravity when the category includes for example the mercy killing of an elderly spouse. An offence of that nature cannot stand comparison with the worst offences of rape or paedophilia which effectively leave victims destroyed and often wishing they were dead. The 2003 Criminal Justice Act is a classic piece of unplanned British legislation passed to shore up the government's position in the face of opposition to its plans, this time from the foreign judges to whom the Blair government had so graciously ceded ultimate sovereignty over our criminal justice system. The differentiation in the Act between types of murders is explicit. In this respect it goes back to the principles of the 1957 Homicide Act which distinguished between capital and non-capital murder, and was passed specifically to buy time against the strengthening forces that favoured the abolition of the death penalty. However, unlike the 2003 Act, the key purpose of the 1957 Homicide Act was to constrain Home Secretary rather than the judiciary, for it was he on behalf of the Queen who exercised of the royal prerogative of mercy. This was to be done by restricting the death penalty to those most heinous categories of murder that would not merit a reprieve. Nevertheless only 35 out of the 65 death sentences passed between July 1957 and suspension in November 1965 were carried out, only a marginally lower reprieve rate than the 50% or so that had been the norm. The law of unintended consequences had triumphed again.

Politicians have not limited themselves to the purpose of imprisonment and the sentences that can be seen to reflect that. They turned increasingly during my service to the organisation of the prison system, as the Thatcher government focused on the power of trade unions, the perceived inadequacy of the senior Civil Service and the size of the public payroll. Privatisation or contracting out whichever term you prefer became the weapon of choice in effecting change and altering the balance of power between the government and those it saw as the enemy of change; principally the public sector trade unions but also local government and a 'can't do' and overcautious Whitehall culture. State industries were returned to private hands after 40 or more years as public enterprises. Whole functions of local government such as refuse collecting were subjected to compulsory tendering to force councils to contract out. Ministers took their cue from economic gurus such as Friedman and Hayek rather than the pragmatism of departmental Permanent Secretaries. It came as a shock when the Prison Service was slated for a taste of the new discipline. Douglas Hurd had specifically ruled out private sector management of prisons but Kenneth Baker under the new Premiership of John Major, took a different view. Like so many bad ideas it was imported from the USA. To Britain's everlasting shame it became the first European country to hand over state prisoners to the tender mercies of a private company.

In the USA, a company called CCA (Corrections Corporation of America) was awarded the first contract to run a private sector establishment in 1984 in the southern state of Tennessee. To the company it was a logical development given the number of contracts it held for the outsourcing of services. For the state government, it was a chance to offload costs, risks and pensions. In the same year, the Adam Smith Institute in the UK, a little known right wing think tank, recommended the contracting out of prisons to the private sector. One of the think tank's key members was John (since 1993 Sir John) Wheeler a hitherto obscure backbencher who was also a former Assistant Governor and a man with a potent hostility to the Prison Officers Association. After leaving parliament in 1997, he later became Chairman of Reliance Custodial Services, a private sector company that sought Government contacts for the court escort services which were privatised in 1995. Within a few short years a policy rejected by Douglas Hurd Home Secretary 1985–89 under Mrs Thatcher, was embraced by John Major's first Home Secretary, Kenneth Baker (1990–92). The contracts for the early private prisons were for the management only of new prisons built at public expense and ran initially for five years. HMP Manchester, completely rebuilt and finally reopened in 1994 was also offered in open competition, but this bid was won by the public sector. Two of the early private prisons, Blakenhurst and Buckley Hall were won back by the public sector after the expiry of the first five-year contracts. The very first private prison, The Wolds, lasted

20 years before being competed for successfully by the public sector. For those ideologically committed to prison privatisation, the ability of the public sector to win competitions rather defeated the object. As early as 1993, even before the success of The Wolds could be evaluated, the Government determined that in future all new prisons would be built and run by private companies.

Stunningly within months of its landslide election victory, New Labour with Jack Straw as Home Secretary did a complete U-turn on its policy of returning all private prisons to the public sector, by renewing one contract and launching two new ones restricted to the private sector. The following year it announced that all new prisons would be Designed, Constructed, Managed and Financed (DCMF) under the Private Finance Initiative. Contracts would be awarded for 25 years, thus tying the hands (and the purse strings) of future governments. Jack Straw's U-turn angered the Prison Officers Association and the Prison Governors Association, both of which trade unions now had to confront the reality of private prisons being permanently part of the penal furniture. One of Jack Straw's successors, John Reid, would become a consultant to G4S which in 2018 hold contracts for five private prisons. Their main competitors, Serco and Sodexo, hold the other nine between them. The private sector thus has 14 of the 121 English and Welsh prisons incarcerating more than 10% of the inmate population, more even as percentage than the USA.

For those not familiar with PFI, its greatest attraction is that it does not appear on the balance sheet of the relevant Government department despite the fact that public funds are at risk, because the debt has to be underwritten by the government and should it be necessary to terminate a contract for non-delivery or continued under performance, the government again is responsible for the debts. Thus the protection of the public interest is dependent on how well or how badly the original contract was written, and the ability of civil servants to ensure that the private company honours its obligations. Ultimate government responsibility for debt particularly in these austere times loads the dice massively in favour of the oligopoly of contractors. Government departments have already been very badly stung by expensive IT contacts and NHS trusts driven deeply into debt by one-sided PFI contracts for new hospitals and maintenance services. Since the banking crisis of 2008, bank lending has gone into virtual deep freeze so the government is now forced to fund PFI contracts itself. Even before the banking crisis, government liability under PFI was a terrifying £215 billion.

The privatisation lobby's first opportunity came when a new prison was to be opened in East Yorkshire, HMP Wolds. The prison was put out for tender to the private sector only and G4S, then known as Group 4, the security firm better known for guarding vans full of bank notes, won the contract in 1991. At the time I was working at HMP Bedford and one of my senior colleagues was David McDonnell who when Duty Governor one weekend broke the news to me that he had been recruited as Deputy Director of the new jail. Stephen Twinn, who subsequently returned to the public sector, was appointed as Director. (Private sector senior managers do not use the term Governor although there is nothing to stop them doing so). The new establishment poached its senior managers from the public sector, but recruited its prison officer equivalents from the local community, on significantly lower pay. The new private sector also refused to recognise trade unions. With wholly inexperienced staff there were major teething problems, to put it charitably.

Competition in order to raise standards and improve efficiency was the new mantra. The new private sector had the considerable advantage of only opening new prisons with modern facilities that made it much easier for them to claim brand leadership in terms of decency. Prisoners were being booked into a low budget hotel (still with locks) rather than being processed through the dank and depressing human warehouses that were many of our local prisons. Private sector prisoners were addressed as 'Mr,' had more time out of cell and better visits facilities, including in the evening. Naturally there was integral sanitation and in the early days, single cell accommodation. There were good sports facilities including well-equipped gyms. Classrooms were bright and cheery. Nothing was too good for the private sector. The downside was suppressed from the public by the doctrine of 'commercial in confidence'. The only information came either from prisoners who had served in The Wolds or from off the record chats with members of the Home Office Controller's team who monitored compliance with the contract and could levy fines, and who also carried out adjudications as private sector managers were not at this stage permitted formal disciplinary powers. The reality of the brave new world was rather different. Prisoners not unexpectedly took full advantage of inexperienced poorly paid staff. Whilst at Wakefield we heard hair-raising tales about the insecure pharmacy and the naiveté of health care staff at HMP Doncaster, the second private prison which opened in 1994. It is no coincidence that with the single exception of HMP Bronzefield, a female prison opened in Ashford, Surrey, new private prisons have opened in areas where wages were lower and unemployment higher than average, as a consequence of the erosion of the UK's traditional industrial base. Despite high local unemployment, staff turnover was terrifyingly high and continues to be high to this day. Staffing levels were and are very tight, with staff being bullied by managers under the duress of low basic pay into working overtime at short notice. This was the world the public sector had proudly abandoned as recently as 1987.

HMYOI Pucklechurch, near Bristol, the scene of a major disturbance in 1990 after which it closed, reopened as a refurbished private sector juvenile young offender establishment in 1999. Quite who believed it was remotely possible that staff recruited from the street on salaries of £15k per annum could exercise meaningful control over this extremely volatile age group, god only knows. Its early years were a disaster area marred by rioting and bullying. According to the Inspectorate staff even resorted to using the stronger young offenders as quasi staff, or more accurately Capos. For the uninitiated, a Capo is a head prisoner. They were used extensively by the Nazis in concentration camps to enforce discipline, usually brutally. In Ashfield, it must have made *Lord of the Flies* seem like a walk in the park. It became so unsafe that in 2003 the Youth Justice Board, responsible for commissioning juvenile places, began a phased withdrawal of 172 juveniles. Martin Narey, Head of the Prison Service at the time called it the worst prison in England and Wales. As an act of political stupidity, opening a private sector Young Offender Institution from scratch was only one step short of the ultimate folly of opening a private sector high security prison, which mercifully has never happened, and as far as I know, was never seriously mooted. Although it remained in the private sector, a leading public sector Governor was put in to sort it out and restore confidence. In fairness it has improved massively since, but the learning curve was steep and the collateral damage on the way unacceptable. All that glittered in the private sector was not gold but very base metal. For many years, the much-trumpeted greater decency of the private sector ran only skin deep. The National Audit Office in 2003 stated that private prisons as a whole were less safe and less secure than those in the public sector. It seems that nothing much has changed in the intervening years. In July of 2013, it was revealed that two of three worst prisons in the country were in the private sector, performing at unacceptable levels against the criteria of public protection, reducing re-offending, decency, resource management and operational effectiveness.

The last brand new built public sector prisons for 25 years, Woodhill, High Down and Lancaster Farms were opened in 1992–93. There were attempts to use Woodhill as a public sector comparator with The Wolds. I was certainly surprised at the staffing levels on the main residential units at Woodhill when I arrived in 1995, which were more typical of a Category C prison rather than a Category B local which also held a small number of prisoners graded as Category A. I was told that staffing levels had been deliberately slashed by HQ taking advantage of the fact that until the newly transferred and newly employed officers arrive at a new prison, which normally occurs in stages, there is no local POA branch to oppose them. Thus the POA were on the back foot from the beginning. However in 1996 it was announced that Woodhill would join the High Security Estate the following year. This was a year of cuts in the service but after the disastrous escapes from Whitemoor and Parkhurst in 1994 and 1995 and the subsequent inquiries conducted by Sir John Woodcock and Sir John Learmont, money was no object. Charged with leading the re-profile of establishment staffing it is my proud boast that I was able to divert some of those extra resources to the house blocks which did not house Category A prisoners. It was an opportunity too good to waste given that the kind of intrusive surveillance by Area Offices that would become the norm by the millennium was not yet established. Whether that legacy lasted I cannot say. What I do know is that not until 2010 when the first existing public sector prison, HMP Birmingham, was privatised, did NOMS succeed in significantly forcing down staffing levels in a large local prison with a powerful trade union branch.

The Private Sector also fails the value for money and efficiency tests, despite its competitive advantages on pay and staff to prisoner ratios. Until the benchmarking programme which forced public sector prisons down to the same unsafe staffing levels that pertained in the private sector, the ratio of staff in the public sector (all staff not just landing staff) was 1 to 3.03 prisoners, whereas in the private sector it was 1 to 3.78. The pay for private sector landing staff is on average three quarters of that of public sector staff. They have 8 days less holiday and typically work a 44-hour week compared to the conditioned 39-hour week in the public sector. Final salary pensions are not available. At the other end of the scale senior managers are paid rather more than their public sector counterparts. The money obviously did tempt some leading public sector governors to defect, but others such as Mike Conway left to escape the strangling bureaucracy and the hot breath of Area Office. The freedom to manage and innovate was a significant attraction. Guy Balfe, one of my predecessors as Deputy Governor of Lewes, became Director of Lowdham Grange, a Category B training prison in Nottinghamshire and was able to put telephone facilities into individual cells, something which would have been impossible in the public sector. The downside for prisoners was the ending of weeknight association. The savings on Mr Balfe's budget available were available for him to spend on regime improvements elsewhere in the prison. In the public sector, Area Office would have simply confiscated part of the savings and probably spent it on expanding the team of Diversity advisors or on other non-jobs such as Head of Social Inclusion. For those unfamiliar with non-jobs and their jargon in the public sector, take a look at *The Guardian* weekly jobs pull out.

Yet despite its ability to innovate the private sector at best has had a neutral effect on the taxpayer. The theory is that privatisation drives up quality and drives down price. However, unlike the private sector the public sector does not have shareholders with an insatiable desire for dividend payments. The more a company is reliant on public contracts, the greater the taxpayer subsidy to shareholders. Those who are not worried about this will argue that it is better off in their pockets than those of public sector trade unionists. The truth is that a workforce will spend its income mainly at home or save it in British banks whereas the institutional shareholder may put his money in any company or bank in the world. It is argued that private sector prisons are consistently cheaper in terms of cost per place, but this is achieved mostly at the expense of the workforce.

Additionally if you are running a shiny new prison rather than a crumbling Victorian relic, then it is obvious to any halfwit that the private sector has an advantage. When the Labour government decided to market test (i.e. invite both the public and private sectors to tender) HMP Brixton in 2001, there were no private sector bidders. In terms of performance as measured by ministry league tables, although far from all measures apply to the private sector, typically private sector prisons have languished in the bottom quarter. The private sector is also very inflexible in terms of responding to new policy priorities. Public sector prisons are simply told to do things often with no extra resources. Such a luxury is not available with the private sector which will do nothing extra without payment. Between 2006 and 2012 an extra £54 million has had to be given to the private sector to get it do extra work that the public sector has been told to do for nothing. There is no evidence that the private sector is better at reducing re-offending any more than it has shown itself to be better at running railways. The effect on the national debt has been discussed elsewhere. The prison system sits largely under the radar as I have argued earlier. However the public is well aware of the downsides of the privatisations of utilities and the aforementioned railways which have proved decidedly mixed blessings. Mercifully we have avoided US style corruption whereby judges have been bribed to incarcerate in order that private prisons will be full enough to maintain the cash flow from government contracts.

The onward march of privatisation was slowed only by the switch of emphasis to existing public sector prisons. New prisons however financed cost money and having presided over record numbers and competed with each other to raise the temperature and at the same lower the tone of the debate on crime and punishment, both major parties have effectively accepted a cap in prison numbers, whatever the rhetoric says. We now actually have old establishments being closed. As I have said earlier, the market testing of Brixton collapsed ignominiously. Partly it was because of the crumbling infrastructure, but also it was down to the cost of taking public sector staff on to the payroll. TUPE (Transfer of Undertakings) requires employers taking over a business to respect existing terms and conditions. In the public sector and particularly in the Prison Service, these are aggressively policed by the trade unions. Existing terms and conditions not only included pay and holidays, but also pensions. The Civil Service scheme remains one of the very best. Shorn of its advantages the private sector struggled to compete. The Gordian knot was only cut when the 2009 round of market testing gave the opportunity for a private company to bid for both Birmingham and the new prison in South Staffordshire, now known as Oakwood, simultaneously. Thus they could slash staffing at Birmingham and move surplus staff to the landings of the new prison. This is in fact what happened and as a consequence of a successful bid for both prisons, Birmingham joined the private sector, the first public sector jail to do so. The only other public sector prison to find itself transferred to the private sector was HMP Northumberland before market testing was replaced by benchmarking.

That does look likely to be the last round of prison privatisation, at least until the austerity in the prison service ends, which could easily stretch beyond 2020. This is because private companies face heavier costs over the earlier years until inevitably staff leave or retire and can be replaced by new staff on lower pay and worse conditions. This is unattractive to government that typically wants savings now, if only so that tax cuts can be offered at election time. Instead the MOJ was attracted by the major slashing in the cost of prisoner places at Birmingham achieved by G4S as a consequence of winning two contracts geographically close to each other. That new lower cost became a benchmark for other prisons and eye watering staffing reductions most of which were achieved by voluntary redundancy. There were major concerns about staff safety at

Birmingham almost from the outset and the chickens came home to roost in 2016. I refer the reader to Chapter 11 for more detail. Added to that the public sector is also employing new staff on salaries (if not hours and pensions) which are broadly in line with those of their private sector counterparts. The maximum for a new prison officer is around 5k less than his colleagues employed before April 2013. Thus, if and when competition via market testing resumes, the public sector will be well placed in the continuing race to the bottom.

The government was perhaps fortunate that the privatisation of Birmingham did not meet with an aggressive response from the POA. The POA was also persuaded to accept the new pay reform package known as 'Fair and Sustainable' which as indicated in the paragraph above would create two types of prison officer, both doing the same job, but on very different rates of pay. Unable to leave it there, populist ministers eager to gain brownie points with the *Mail* and the *Telegraph* began cutting paid trade union facility time. Employee representatives have certain legal rights as regards consultation and employees facing disciplinary hearings have the right to be properly represented by officials who have actually had time to read the paperwork and support and advise the employee. Failure to discharge legal obligations towards employees and their lawfully elected representatives only results in the taxpayer picking up the tab at judicial reviews and employment tribunals. The POA has changed its approach in recent years, no thanks to this or the last government. It is a pity that is not recognised and given due credit by politicians.

Where confronting trade unions and privatisation were not seen as the answers both the Conservatives but more particularly New Labour as a consequence of the growth of public 'managerialism', opted for the tried and failed methods of reorganisation and rebranding. I will quote an example. From what appeared to be a minor organisational change implemented in 1992, the replacement of the four regional offices with what became 12 area offices along with the high security directorate, grew empires that resembled medieval fiefdoms. The original area managers were supported by little more than a Governor IV to act as bagman, a personal secretary and a filing clerk. Within a few short years they employed veritable armies of staff as they jockeyed for position and further preferment. All that was missing was the livery although the more sexist incumbents advertised their virility with a bevy of high-heeled pencil skirted retainers walking one pace behind them. Any male area manager with a retinue of less than 40 was considered to have the organisational equivalent of a small penis. There were teams advisors for everything; performance and audit, health and safety, reducing re-offending, security and intelligence, finance, human resources and it goes without saying, diversity. Some even had investigation teams. If they were all that good, why were they not working in prisons? Imagine the cost of 500 plus extra civil servants, some very highly paid, and then imagine this replicated across every government department in the land.

New Labour also cloned failed methods from elsewhere in the public sector. It imported the notion of the internal market from the BBC, later adopted by the Health Service, in which Commissioners theoretically purchased services from providers in a free market place. NOMS vision witters on about being the provider of choice. The facts of the matter are perfectly simple. If a prisoner is sentenced, for example at Norwich Crown Court or Exeter Crown Court, he commences his sentence at Norwich and Exeter prisons respectively. They are the geographical providers and exactly the same happens where the local prison, Birmingham being the obvious example, is in the private sector. It is a complete myth that these services are commissioned just as it is a complete myth that your local A&E is commissioned as a result of a competition within the NHS. Yet people with the job of commissioning services are employed. So where did these people come from? The creation of NOMS in 2004 spawned another layer of bureaucracy, ten Regional Offender Managers (ROMS), who theoretically purchased services but as I have said in practice got what they were given. They were to be the key figures in the latest bureaucratic initiative to reduce re-offending by the criminal classes. They would link together custodial and non-custodial providers, (broadly prisons and probation) and would also link with other government departments, local authorities, charities and other third sector bodies to provide a joined up approach to interventions that would reduce crime. As a grand vision stripped of the market place rhetoric it made sense and deserved to succeed.

However, the new ROMS rapidly embarked on building empires putting together large well-paid teams which co-existed alongside the large well-paid teams that supported prison service area managers. Some demanded the right to set their own targets. Thus a parallel expensive bureaucracy was created and there was an inevitable power struggle. Initially the ROMS appeared to have won the battle when the regional structure formally replaced the area structure and they were graded above the old area managers, now shorn of their empires and renamed Regional Custody Managers, with no function more meaningful than line managing Governors. The victory was short-lived lasting no more than four years before another reorganisation merged the ROMS with the Area Managers. ROMS and their entourage have gone but the Area Managers have survived, rebranded as Deputy Directors of Custody. One hopes in vain that the cost of their entourages has been dramatically slashed to somewhere close to the skeleton staffs they coped perfectly well with back in 1992. Will politicians never learn that when they create a new bureaucracy it grows like bind weed?

Chapter 8
Prison Service Inspectors and Reformers

It surprised me to discover that an independent Inspectorate of Prisons has only existed since 1981 particularly as inspection of police forces dates back to 1856. The creation of HM Inspectorate of Prisons (HMIP) stemmed from a recommendation from the May inquiry into the prison service after a period of industrial unrest from prison officers who felt undervalued and neglected. Its role is to provide independent scrutiny of the conditions for and treatment of prisoners and other detainees promoting the concept of healthy prisons in which staff work effectively to support prisoners and other detainees to reduce reoffending or achieve other agreed outcomes. Put another way HMIP 'guards the guards'. HM Inspectorate of Prisons also inspects Immigration Removal Centres and the Military Corrective Centre at Colchester. The first part of its role derives from the 1982 Criminal Justice Act which formalised the position of the Chief Inspector created the previous year, and the second part as regards healthy prisons derives from HMIP's own interpretation of our international obligations as regards the maintenance of human rights and under the UN Convention regarding torture and degrading and inhuman treatment. The Chief Inspector is a crown appointment, not a civil servant, a status which delineates the constitutional independence. Beneath him or her is a Deputy Chief Inspector, who is a civil servant, and teams of inspectors seconded principally from the prison service, the NHS and schools and colleges seconded usually for periods of three years.

Inspection reports follow a prescribed template marking establishments against four tests of a healthy prison: safety, respect, purposeful activity and resettlement. Prisons are graded as performing well, performing reasonably well, performing insufficiently well and performing poorly against each test. Where the lowest grading is given instant improvement is expected without any delay awaiting publication, which now takes about sixteen weeks. In order to assist establishments prepare, for which notice may or may not be given, HMIP has issued a detailed 'Expectations' document, which when I checked was a staggering 132 pages long. Scotland and Northern Ireland also have their own Inspectorate.

The first Chief Inspector was Philip Barry (1981–82) and he was succeeded by Sir James Hennessey (1982–87). I have to be honest and admit that as serving prison officer during that time I could not have told you who was Chief Inspector of Prisons or told you anything at all about the work of the Inspectorate. Its existence and terms of reference formed no part of our training. I have a recollection that Werrington was inspected once during my service there (1984–90) and believe that it took place in 1987. My only memory of it was that the local paper the Evening Sentinel headlined its coverage of the inspection report by focussing on trainee allegations of bullying which was no great surprise to staff given that the trainees were housed in large ward like dormitories with no privacy and no ability to secure their possessions. This particular inspection predates by a number of years the open availability on line of complete reports. All that I can say that back in those pre-Manchester riot days, inspection reports had only a fraction of the importance they have now where careers are made and broken. In fact no one seemed to get excited at all. There was no staff meeting, no disclosure to staff before publication and certainly no action plan. Things are rather different now and inspections are almost feared in some quarters. In June 2009, Wandsworth and Pentonville swapped a number of difficult prisoners a week prior to an announced inspection of Wandsworth in order to keep those moved from Wandsworth away from the inspection team. Two of the transferees self-harmed after arriving at Pentonville, one of them four times. In October of the same year, the Inspectorate found out about the transfers and the Chief Inspector was quite rightly outraged calling the transfers 'completely pointless, outrageous and potentially dangerous'. This incident is dealt with in more detail in Chapter 10.

The next Chief Inspector, Judge Stephen Tumim (1987–95) was a much higher profile figure with that old-fashioned sense of noblesse oblige. I grew acquainted with him and the work of the Inspectorate via the Accelerated Promotion Scheme. Tumim was appointed by Douglas Hurd and his influence as a reformer was maximised after the Strangeways riot of April 1990. He campaigned vigorously (and successfully) against the degrading practice of slopping out, deplored enforced idleness amongst prisoners, and called for better care of the mentally ill, being a most perceptive observer regarding the effects of Care in the Community on the prison population. He was a thorn in the side of successive Home Secretaries (I prefer to describe him as a nagging conscience) and Michael Howard did not renew his contract in 1995. Subsequently he became the founding President of Unlock, the National Association of ex-offenders. Mr Howard replaced him with General Sir David Ramsbotham (1995–2001), another member of Britain's traditional establishment, believing that a stiff dose of military efficiency and a no nonsense approach in the wake of the Whitemoor and Parkhurst escapes were what the prison service needed.

It was a classic case of beware of what you wish for. Henry the Second chose the worldly Thomas Becket as his Archbishop and Michael Howard chose Rambo, as he rapidly became known. Like Becket, Sir David (since 2005 Lord) Ramsbotham, unexpectedly joined the opposing camp to Mr Howard, preferring to emphasise the rehabilitative aspect of imprisonment rather than the punitive ethos normally associated with his political master. He admitted that he had not expected prisons to be so far behind the curve as regards rehabilitation. However it was with Mr Howard's successor, Jack Straw, that working relationships broke down. Sir David's contract which expired in December 2000 was renewed only for a further six months rather than the expected three years. The cause of the final breakdown was an interview given by Sir David to the left leaning weekly political magazine, *The New Statesman*. Mr Straw was unhappy that the Chief Inspector's criticisms ranged across policy and was particularly irritated when the latter said that there were ten drug dealers in every jail. Most practitioners viewed that as an underestimate. Sir David went further on the subject of drugs in prisons and described random mandatory drug testing (MDT) as 'useless' which gravely upset the Prisons Minister, George Howarth. Random testing is exactly that and an enormous amount of time and money is wasted on testing 5% or 10% of the population of individual prisons, depending on the size of the establishment to massage down headline drug abuse figures in our prisons to politically acceptable levels. One of the best-known scams is to place the known hard core of drug abusers on frequent testing so that they cannot adversely affect random testing figures. This is because a prisoner who tests positive for cannabis cannot be tested again for 30 days, the length of time cannabis remains detectable in the urine, so therefore are eliminated from the pool available for random testing. Sir David further angered ministers with his opposition to mandatory life sentences and infuriated them by saying that Thompson and Venables, the murderers of James Bulger, should be released without transferring from the secure care system to the prison system.

His relations with the Prison Officers Association also went into deep freeze, particularly over Wormwood Scrubs, of which more in the next but one paragraph. Sir David also wanted to end the pay bargaining role of the POA and other trade unions which he believed poisoned industrial relations and hand remuneration over to a pay review body. The government did finally activate this clause in the 1994 Criminal Justice Act seven years later.

Sir David's inspection reports made no concessions to souls of a sensitive nature. In May 2001, I took over as Deputy Governor of HMP Ford. The prison had been inspected the previous year and some of the criticisms were particularly trenchant. I quote at length: Many prisoners reported that some prison staff were unapproachable, unhelpful and unsupportive. Some staff and prisoner relationships were reported to be strained to say the least, up to and including senior management (governor) grades. Prisoners said that staff were rude, ignorant and disrespectful and regularly under the influence of alcohol. Prisoners said that some staff ignored greetings such as 'Good Morning etc...' There were no euphemisms, no flannel and no right of reply. Not for nothing was he nicknamed 'Rambo' though I doubt anyone ever called him that to his face.

An earlier report into Wormwood Scrubs in 1996 spoke of 'rottenness and evil' and echoed the concerns of his predecessor. Two years later a police investigation began into allegations of brutality at the prison, in particular the segregation unit, which Sir David had raised both with Prison Service senior management and the Home Secretary. This was the era when the Prison Service's first, second and third priorities were security, security and security following the escapes from Whitemoor and Parkhurst in 1994 and 1995. Twenty-seven prison officers were initially suspended with six eventually being tried at Crown Court before a judge and jury. All six were initially convicted in 2001 but three were freed on appeal. Despite the scathing criticism of the quality of the evidence against them made by the Court of Appeal, Martin Narey, then head of the Prison Service, refused to reinstate the men, preferring instead to settle the unfair dismissal claims out of court.

I cannot add anything in the way of personal experience as regards Wormwood Scrubs. Stephen Moore, who had been my Governor at Bedford, had been appointed in 1998 to 'clean up the Scrubs'. I can say without fear of contradiction that Stephen Moore is his own man, as well as being a highly personable and humane individual. The local branch of the POA however felt that their members were victims of a witch-hunt by sections of the media, the police and prison service senior management who preferred the word of convicted felons against honest, decent public servants who were only protecting the public in difficult circumstances. At one point mass sick absence was organised and governor grades from all over the country were asked to volunteer to staff the jail until the crisis was resolved. Having just completed 10 consecutive days of duty I declined and took my rest days. A colleague who did go described the atmosphere as both hostile and evil, but then if you are being called a scab it is bound to seem that way. Inevitably as three convictions stood there were civil actions by former prisoners. The service was forced to accept 122 claims of assault between 1995 and 1999 and settled a further 32 cases without admission of liability. Some of the allegations admitted by the service, including mock executions, were horrifying. By the end of 2003, £1.7 million in compensation had been paid out, a figure which obviously excluded legal costs. The service also accepted that it failed to investigate alleged assaults properly. Although no longer Chief Inspector, Sir David's comments were typically trenchant. 'I cannot believe that the senior management of the Prison Service did not know about these assaults. Any responsible management should have done something about it because it was a cancer in their midst.' He went on to say that had repeated warnings about violence at the jail not been ignored, the assaults would not have happened. Nevertheless the government-resisted calls for a public inquiry and in the fullness of time Wormwood Scrubs became yesterday's chip paper, and careers continued uninterrupted. Read on here and in the remaining chapters to understand why this happens.

As with most career soldiers, Sir David had little time for Civil Service obfuscation and prevarication. He believed that the Prison Service was constipated by paper pushing mandarins and over powerful area management. Even Martin Narey, who could never be accused of looking the other way if prisoners were being mistreated, was not immune from criticism. According to Sir David 'the DG looks at compliance with budgets and KPIs... I couldn't give a damn about those.' This was a barely concealed criticism of New Labour 'managerialism'. It was perhaps inevitable that the Chief Inspector also made an enemy of the Home Office Permanent Secretary whom he effectively described as a typical arse-covering bureaucrat preferring to shield his department from criticism rather than take action and deal with the issues highlighted in reports. Unfortunately, when dealing with the senior civil service men of action are frequently outmanoeuvred by the men of words. However he did not go quietly into retirement and continued to be a trenchant critic of government penal policy. In 2010, he lambasted the Labour government for what he saw as its dysfunctional criminal justice policy. He accused the Labour government of making up prison policy on the back of a fag packet, waste of resources and unnecessary crises in services that were crying out for leadership and direction. He criticised the knee jerk approach, the torrent of legislation which had failed to protect the public and again attacked the overcrowding that left many prisoners with nothing to do, with its inevitable effect on re-offending. A National Audit office report in that year found that re-offending by prisoners given sentences of less than 12 months was costing the country up to £10 billion per year. This equated to 2.5p on the rate of income tax. He described NOMS as a monster bureaucracy. Lord Ramsbotham's remarks written before the election were published shortly after in a forward to the Prisons Handbook, produced by the charity, *Unlock*.

Sir David was a hugely popular appointment initially within the service but it is true to say that by the end he was considered to be a dinosaur by those uncomfortable with his military ethos. The word dinosaur is not a term of affection in the service. It is aimed at those perceived as past their sell by, and those not 'on message'. The term is applied to those of unsound views, in other words those capable of independent thought. In the long-run, it does not pay to play the role of turbulent priest, as others less prominent and with more to lose have found to their cost. Almost immediately after his appointment in 1995 he also caused a huge stir within the ranks of prison governors when he withdrew his team from HMP Holloway without completing the inspection. There was no precedent for this spectacular public walkout, and nothing like it has happened since. The inspectors were hugely critical of living conditions inside Europe's largest female establishment. A statement from the team said: "Our early findings identified such shortfalls in the treatment of prisoners and in the conditions of Holloway prison that the proper course was to seek immediate improvements." Sir David advised the Director General and Mr Howard that they would not return to the jail until conditions improved. A huge part of the problem was the massive crackdown in the system that followed the aforementioned escapes from two top security prisons. A climate of fear prevailed amongst Governors, none of whom wanted to be the next John Marriott who had been removed from his post at Parkhurst. Female prisoners found themselves locked up behind their doors for more than 21 hours per day which caused huge tensions. However it should be noted that Holloway's problems were long standing. Judge Tumim in 1992 had described the mother and baby unit as a 'cockroach infested semi basement, looking on to a dirty yard'. Since the loss of the female remand facility at Pucklechurch in 1990 Holloway had become the only female local prison south of Redditch, and remained so until 1996. Thus a woman from Devon remanded in custody would not have found herself in Exeter as a man would. She could well have found herself 200 miles from home in North London despite still being innocent in the eyes of the law. The design of the building was appalling and the lack of natural light oppressive and I shared the views of those who believe that Holloway, despite the very best efforts of staff and Governors, was an affront to decency and should be closed. The overdue closure finally took place in July 2016.

Inevitably there was a scapegoat and the well regarded Governor, Janet King, was removed and sent to the Prison Service equivalent of a Siberian power station, Headquarters, her career ruined and her personal and professional esteem damaged beyond repair. Meanwhile the circus simply moved on. I consider that 1995 was a year that I had a lucky escape. At the time the service was moving from a position where HQ simply posted staff on promotion, to one where qualified staff would compete for jobs at interview. Thus in a typical compromise the HQ grade manager sent me to Holloway for interview. Mercifully Janet King, whom I knew, did not want me, perceiving quite correctly that I was ill suited to working in a female establishment. Also I had no intention of living in North London, or anywhere else in London for that matter.

Sir David and his team also eviscerated one of my former establishments, HMYOI Werrington, in a devastating report subsequent to an inspection in the summer of 1998. I have described in earlier chapters its Nightingale ward like dormitories and also Peter Salter's fight to keep the establishment open. Well, he succeeded and new cellblocks were built and the former dormitories transformed into an education block. The problem was the new cells were for single occupation, as indeed most are, but the cheap populism of politicians whipped up by sections of the press saw a rapid increase in population from 1993 onwards. As ever the solution was to 'double up'. The Chief Inspector said of Werrington, 'To find children no longer eating together, but forced to take their food back to their cells, which are little more than lavatories, to eat, being limited to two evenings of association in a week, on landings where there are no chairs so the time amounts to little more than an hour and a half standing outside rather than inside a cell… I have not come across such totally deliberate and unnecessary impoverishment of children anywhere.' The report had such an impact that Jack Straw was forced to intervene and insist on the single cell occupation originally intended. Even now its overcrowding capacity is 168, only 8 more than its Certified Normal Accommodation of 160. I don't normally like the use of the word children in a criminal justice context as it infantilises young thugs and thieves, but it has to be remembered that these are young people who are still developing morally and emotionally, and thus capable of being influenced positively by appropriate adult role models in a structured setting. In a grossly overcrowded setting, there is more fighting, more bullying, in an environment where more young people are trying to access facilities designed for possibly as little half their number. Prison officers have considerably more people to supervise during out of cell time thus reducing vital individual interaction necessary to influence these young men. The only way to cut fighting and bullying and reduce the numbers needing to be supervised is to reduce the numbers allowed out of cell at any one time. Thus association is restricted and communal dining ceases. There is less opportunity to use the phone and contact relatives. Frustration increases and with it volatile and unpredictable incidents including more assaults on staff who become wary and alienated instead of engaging positively with the young people. This in turn increases sick leave and thus prisoners are banged up even more frequently. As a custodial experience, it is negative and brutalising. For staff and young offenders alike, it is a deadly vicious circle and it is all down to overcrowding created by politicians who then refuse to find the money to fund the extra use of custody brought about by their grandstanding. No wonder the Home Secretary wished to silence the Chief Inspector.

David Ramsbotham's replacement was Anne Owers who remained in office until 2010. Her replacement was Nick Hardwick who had previously headed up the Independent Police Complaints Commission (IPCC). Dame Anne Owers (as she was created in 2009) in turn was appointed to head the IPCC as two of the nation's leading quangocrats swapped jobs. This job swap tells us so much about the how the world has changed since New Labour emerged from 18 years in the electoral wilderness. Dame Anne is a fully paid up member of the new establishment that has ousted the old establishment of family money, public school and the old boy network so memorably described by Anthony Sampson in his Anatomies of Britain. The new establishment are the baby boomers who took full advantage of the brief flowering of grammar schools and much expanded and cheap higher education after 1963 who took the world of the Junior Common Room with them into adult life. While Mrs Thatcher was busy transforming the economic landscape of the country the movers and shakers of My Generation were busy capturing the institutions that would propel them into power. Typically My Generation operated in the trade union movement, the voluntary sector or the professions covering criminal justice and education, or a combination of the three. Not all, (Tony Blair for example) were student activists as university has other distractions, but it was difficult not to subliminally absorb the dominant ideology of our seats of learning. They came fully into their inheritance after New Labour's electoral landslide of 1997. As one who was a politically active student myself and a former President of my own students' union, I can remember the massive importance of issues such as Palestinian and Zimbabwean independence, Gay Rights (not a term used back home in Blackburn) and women's liberation. The most talismanic issue was racism, in those days known as racialism. Since those days Human Rights has been added to the lexicon. Capitalism was the enemy (although the movers and shakers of My Generation have long made their accommodation with it) and the school system was perceived to uphold an unequal and unfair social order with its examinations and discipline enforced by corporal punishment. This was an era of rampant inflation, strikes and inexorably rising unemployment in the traditional manufacturing areas. The executive committee of the National Union of Students, elected by proportional representation, was dominated by the Broad Left Alliance of Labour, Liberal and (Euro) Communist students. This grouping, unlike the majority of the Labour Party of that era in the House of Commons, was most definitely Marxist rather than Methodist in its rhetoric and make up. To the right was the Federation of Conservative Students, only able to be represented at all because the Single Transferable Voting system. To the left of the Broad Left were shifting alliances of political groups who took their cue from the exiled prophet, Leon Trotsky. In those halcyon days, the left and the ultra-left still lionised and deified the working classes. Right across the student political spectrum the independent schools were over represented. Doesn't it all remind you of the modern House of Commons? Provided one remembers that the former Conservative Prime Minister, David Cameron and some of his key acolytes are effectively members of the modern Broad Left you get more than just a glimpse of how the baby boomer generation has moved effortlessly from the student unions to the Houses of Parliament.

Anne Owers' membership of the political class is writ large in her curriculum vitae. Born in 1947 and educated at Washington Grammar School, County Durham and Girton College Oxford, Anne Owers was employed by the Joint Council for the Welfare of Immigrants in 1981 becoming its General Secretary four years later. Before succeeding to the job of Chief Inspector of Prisons she was formerly Director of 'Justice' a human rights and law reform pressure group, and a member of the Home Office task force on the implementation of the Human Rights Act which was the centrepiece of the New Labour project to change the face of our country. Since 2010 she has become Chair of Clinks and a Butler Trust trustee. The Butler Trust is a charity set up in 1985 and named after former Tory Home Secretary R.A. (Rab) Butler. Its function is to recognise and celebrate excellence in prisons. The Prison Service supports the charity by regularly seconding a young upwardly mobile Governor grade to the charity to get actively involved in the awards process. Clinks is a network for the voluntary and community sector working with offenders. An active Christian, Anne Owers is a member of the Race and Community Relations Committee of the Church of England. The retired Archbishop of Canterbury, Rowan Williams, took on her former role as Chair of Christian Aid.

I happen to believe that My Generation has trashed its inheritance and wasted its opportunities in power to transform our society for the better. That is the subject for another book but it does need to be referenced here to put my views on the Inspectorate in context. Socially we have become fragmented, and individual and so-called victim group rights have trumped those of the wider community as evidenced in political class support for the right of Traveller groups to breach planning laws and calls for amnesties for illegal immigrants. The movers and shakers of My Generation have abandoned Marx and with it revolution by a working class they now hold in contempt (but not Lenin with his concept of the elite whose role it is to safeguard the revolution) in favour of new gurus, most notably Gramsci and Marcuse. These post Marxist figures respectively preached revolution through the steady subversion of the great institutions that hold together the state and control of language. It is easy to see how the Church of England, the Universities and criminal justice professions including the police are now dominated at their apex by new establishment figures who seek to control the parameters of debate. Thus those who oppose immigration are racist by definition and those who oppose gay adoptions are homophobic. No ifs, no buts and no job in the public sector for anyone who dares to espouse contrary views. After receiving some justified criticism at Prison Governors Association Conference in 2007 regarding an incident that occurred during an inspection of HMYOI Werrington, a senior member of the inspectorate had the nerve to complain to the General Secretary about a delegate making use of the right of freedom of expression at a trade union conference. He was given short shrift. I am happy to confirm that the criticism was made by me at the conference dinner in my capacity as conference chairman that year. The incident makes my point about the new totalitarianism perfectly. The matter itself concerned use of force on a recalcitrant juvenile. The Inspectors were unhappy about the force used and voiced their unhappiness, which they were perfectly entitled to do. However, despite an investigation conducted by the Governor of Shrewsbury, Gerry Hendry, finding that the use of force was both reasonable and proportionate HMIP repeated the allegation in their published report. In a situation wholly without precedent the Director General, Phil Wheatley, issued a blunt and very public rebuttal which can be found on the internet.

My view is that the Inspectorate has ceased to be independent and is firmly part of the project to create a multi-cultural Britain in which people are defined by their group identity and not their national one, and just as the toleration of sharia law enforces the new Liberal apartheid, the love of all things European further suppresses our democracy. Anne Owers is, therefore, a much more ideological figure than her controversial predecessor. As there is no boundary between what is the prerogative of the political class within parliament and what is the prerogative of the political class outside parliament, Dame Anne was able to publicly support votes for prisoners without her job being at risk and without attracting any significant criticism except from the usual suspects in the *Mail* and *Telegraph*. Less well known is Dame Anne's view that the European Court of Human Rights serves the same function as the US Supreme Court, which can overturn legislation that it views as unconstitutional. This ridiculously compares the constitution of a sovereign nation state with a supra national institution that has aggrandised its powers from the European Convention by aggressive judicial activism that the New Labour government connived in as part of its grand plan to abolish our national independence and change the face of our country beyond recognition. The extent to which the Inspectorate has been politicised can be evidenced from its expectations as regards 'diversity' the all-pervading mantra of the new establishment. I will quote at length from the Expectations document:

"Demonstrates a clear and co-ordinated approach to eliminating discrimination, promoting equitable outcomes and fostering good relations, and ensures that no prisoner is unfairly disadvantaged. This is underpinned by effective processes to identify and resolve any inequality. The distinct needs of each protected characteristic are recognised and addressed: these include race, nationality, religion, disability (including mental, physical, and learning disabilities and difficulties) gender, transgender, sexual orientation and age."

The document also talks about systems, monitoring, reporting, intervention, impact assessments, forums and action plans all of which are part of the managerialist tick-box cultural lexicon. HMIP now seeks to manage prisons rather than inspect them. Their visits have become audits as opposed to inspections. As one would expect from the former General Secretary of the Joint Council for the Welfare of Immigrants, language provision is high on the list. Just as in local government a small fortune is spent on translating huge numbers of documents into a multiplicity of languages, money that could be well spent on English classes for our 11,000 strong foreign national prison population. Diverse ethnicity is to be recognised through events and displays such as Black History month. Gypsies in particular must be consulted. One of my previous Area Managers, Tom Murtagh, when I was Deputy Governor at Dover 2000-01, was clear that though the Inspectorate could recommend, it could not demand. That has changed significantly in the last 18 years. HMIP has its own monitoring unit that demands regular and detailed updates from establishments on the progress of recommendations regardless of the prevailing workloads of those whose job it is to provide the information. Senior management of the service has made no effort to prevent these incursions on to the territory of individual governors of establishments. The beast must be fed.

However these are secondary points compared to the language used by HMIP in its expectations document. The use of the expression 'protected characteristic' is the big give away. It then details who and what they are; ethnic minorities, foreign nationals, minority faith groups, the disabled, the mentally ill, women, gays, older prisoners, and the newest cause, the transgendered. This implies not equality but special treatment. For the politically correct our society is white, paternalistic and heterosexist, all of which of course, are evils that must be purged. Unsurprisingly, equality is not defined as it is an elusive and slippery concept. Do they mean more, greater or absolute equality, or do they mean equality of access, equality of outcomes or equality of opportunity? There are of course no mentions of personal responsibility and what rights should be forfeit as a consequence of imprisonment. One of HMIP's familiar themes in inspections is the risk of alienation of Moslem prisoners. Islamic extremism is not a peculiarly British phenomenon but it is fuelled in the UK by the multiculturalist philosophy which allows minority communities to practice apartheid under the guise of respecting their culture. As a consequence, abuses of women via sharia law, forced marriage and polygamy become institutionalised. We hear very little from feminists and other members of the political class about these abuses at home and the continuing practice of genital mutilation in some Arab states. The multi-cultural ragbag pretty swiftly exposes the highly selective nature of the notion of protected characteristics. The inspectorate has moved far beyond the moral outrage expressed by Stephen Tumim and David Ramsbotham to the adoption of the political programme of the metropolitan elite with all its contradictions and insidious control mechanisms.

I don't believe that I was alone with my growing misgivings about the increased politicisation of HMIP and the ever-spreading tentacles of its bureaucracy. The difficult part was forming a critique. Firstly for anyone still with a career going public with criticism of the inspectorate is a quick way to end it. Secondly most Prison Governors believe that independent inspection is a good thing. Thirdly most right thinking people are instinctively opposed to racism, to persecution of gays, and take a dim view of the myriad indignities suffered by disabled people. Most right thinking people believe that the elderly should be treated with respect and that there should be mutual religious tolerance, not least because of the export of violence from Northern Ireland to the mainland for the last 30 years of the 20th century. These are views that I share. Even those who would lock prisoners up and throw away the key will give a measured view about decency in our prisons if one of their close relatives was incarcerated. The metropolitan elite exploit the inherent decency of most of the population who have long since moved on from Alf Garnett attitudes to ethnic minorities and similar prejudices against gays and the disabled. This allows them to claim popular support. The kind of language that was common and considered perfectly acceptable when I was a young man to describe these groups is now rarely heard outside of a wilfully ignorant small minority. Yet this organic progress fails to satisfy our elite who are intent in putting through a political programme of institutional change that is so ambitious (whilst of course silencing dissent) that it makes the late Baroness Thatcher on the other side of the political spectrum almost appear timid. HMIP is part of that programme, one which has succeeded in making the kind of progress in the UK that long eluded traditional Marxism. As a student of history, I have long subscribed to the view that once something becomes the prevailing orthodoxy, it must be challenged. Those who have travelled on the journey with the vanguard of the political class without paying attention to the destination perhaps need to recover their intellectual compass.

The Prisons Ombudsman (since 2001 the Prisons and Probation Ombudsman) has also participated in the job carousel. Nigel Newcomen previously Deputy Chief Inspector of Prisons, succeeded Stephen Shaw who had held the job for eleven years, in 2011. He stood down in 2017. After an interregnum former prison governor and Head of the Northern Ireland service, Sue McAllister, took up post in October 2018. Unlike the Chief Inspector, the Prisons and Probation Ombudsman is a civil servant. As Ombudsman, Mr Newcomen stood outside the civil service structure, but nevertheless reported directly to the Secretary of State for Justice. The job of the ombudsman's office was originally to be the last line of appeal in respect of prisoner complaints which typically range across the spectrum from adjudication awards to conditions in prison such as the lack of modesty screening for toilets in cells. Following the 2003 Criminal Justice Act the

Ombudsman's office became responsible for investigation deaths in custody and also approved premises used by the Probation Service as bail hostels and halfway houses. This significantly raised the profile of the Ombudsman. Perhaps the most controversial intervention has been attempts to link the self-inflicted death of Christopher Wardally with the notorious prisoner swap that took place between HMP Pentonville and HMP Wandsworth in the Autumn of 2009 in a bid to keep difficult and vexatious prisoners away from HMIP who were due to inspect Wandsworth. The transfer of Mr Wardally was unconnected with the movement of those prisoners, it occurred as a consequence of a court appearance in the Pentonville catchment area. Nevertheless as an issue it rumbled on until 2011 because evidence emerged that activating his request to return to Wandsworth was delayed until the inspection was complete. NOMS closed the matter down by firmly refusing to hold another enquiry.

Prison reform groups are part of what we call the voluntary sector, sometimes known as the third sector to distinguish them from public sector institutions and private sector profit making enterprises. Operating as charities any money they make or raise is spent on the cause of reforming the prison system and assisting offenders. The oldest and best known is the Howard League for Penal Reform, named after John Howard (1726-90) who became Sheriff of Bedfordshire in 1773. John Howard most unusually personally inspected the county's jails and was horrified by the squalor he saw. Howard also toured Europe in 1775–76 and wrote extensively about the state of prisons abroad as well as at home. He campaigned successfully for the abolition of jailor's fees, by which innocent defendants found to have no case to answer faced being returned to prison for debt if they could not pay the jailor. Subsequent Acts of parliament paved the way for prison staff to eventually become civil servants when the Prison Commission was established and local jurisdiction abolished in 1877. In 1963, the Prison Commission was formally merged into the Home Office. That settlement remained undisturbed until 1992 when the first private prison opened and the salaries of staff were met from a source at arm's length from the public purse. The Howard League was founded in 1866 its aim, 'the promotion of the most efficient means of penal treatment and crime prevention and a reformatory and radically preventative treatment of offenders.' In its first annual report published in 1867, the Association stated that its efforts had been focussed on 'the promotion of reformatory and remunerative prison labour and the abolition of capital punishment.' In 1921, it merged with the Penal Reform League to become the Howard League for Penal Reform.

The current director is Frances Crook who was awarded the OBE for services to Youth Justice. The modern Howard League works for less crime, safer communities and less people in prison. The language may be less pompous than that of the Victorian founders but the aims are broadly the same. The League believes that imprisonment should be in proportion to the harm done. Largely it should be restricted to serious and violent offenders and those who are a danger to the public. It believes that solutions to crime lie outside the criminal justice system, and less palatably for *Mail* and *Telegraph* devotees it calls for investment in public services. The Howard League believes in restorative justice whereby offenders make amends to their victims and is critical of the last Labour government for its focus on processes, i.e. being more interested in outputs rather than outcomes, which is the classic failing of public 'managerialism'. It has run high profile campaigns on children and young offenders, women prisoners, self-harmers, community sentences and education. It has student societies in Oxford, Bristol and Brighton universities. Since 2002 it has had its own law department. The Howard League now has a prison law contract with the Legal Services Commission providing the only dedicated legal defence service for young people in custody.

In 2005, the Howard League were invited into HMP Coldingley, by the then Governor, Paul McDowell, and set up a Graphic Design Studio which not only gave prisoners real skills, but almost uniquely within the walls of a closed prison paid them real wages. During my short tenure as Governor of Coldingley in 2006 I had the pleasure of meeting Frances Crook, a passionate and tireless campaigner for initiatives that have the capacity to divert offenders from crime and thus prevent the next victim. The payment of real wages where commercially viable, enables prisoners to support their families (rather than the taxpayer) and also make reparation to victims. Sadly the workshop closed in 2008. Since the 2010 General Election prisoners in open establishments earning real wages working for local firms prior to release as part of their resettlement programme have been subject to a 40% victim surcharge. Rather like the £15 victim surcharge applied to fines in magistrates courts the money goes into the ministry pot and unlike restorative justice, there is no link between the offender and his or her individual victims. As this change has occurred since my retirement, I cannot offer any view as to whether this unnecessary and vindictive measure has impacted adversely on the work ethic of long term prisoners who pose particular problems for effective resettlement as they have been out of community circulation for so long.

The Howard League has a sixteen strong executive team under Frances Crook. Until 2016 the Chair was Sue Wade, former Deputy Chief Probation Officer of Hampshire. Eminent lawyer and former Liberal Democrat MP for Montgomeryshire (1983–97) Lord Carlile, was the organisation's President from 2006 until 2012. In 2006, Lord Carlile published an independent report into physical restraint, solitary confinement and strip-searching (these days known euphemistically as full searching) on young people in prisons. As a follow up to that, he chaired a Commission of Inquiry set up by the House of Lords. More recently the League has set up a commission to research sex in prisons. I have commented on homosexuality in prisons extensively in Chapter 3. Lord Carlile was succeeded as President by Labour peer, Lord Myners. High profile supporters include Cherie Blair, Michael Palin and Sheila Hancock. One of the trustees is former Prison Governor turned Criminology Professor, David Wilson, who is seen frequently on television both as an expert commentator and also as a presenter most recently of a series devoted to serial killers.

The Prison Reform Trust (PRT) was founded in 1981 by Sir Monty Finniston, one time Chairman of British Steel. The organisation split off from the Howard League, ostensibly because the League had moved away from traditional prison reform issues. Its first Director was Stephen Shaw CBE (1981–99) who left that post to become the Prisons Ombudsman, a post he held until 2010. Prior to joining the PRT, Dr Shaw had worked for NACRO, the National Association for the Care and Resettlement of Offenders. A witty and engaging public speaker, I heard Stephen Shaw speak at Prison Governors Association Conference in his capacity as Ombudsman on a number of occasions. He was succeeded at the PRT by Juliet Lyon CBE, who was in turn was succeeded by former Prison Governor, Peter Dawson, in 2016. She was also Secretary General of Penal Reform International. A staunch feminist Juliet Lyon is a member of the Fawcett Society's Gender and Justice Network. Juliet Lyon's influence was also heavily felt on the Detention and Training Orders brought in to replace the sentence of Detention in a Young Offenders Institution for juveniles in 1998. The salient feature was Governors were given no power to award added days to the custodial part of the sentence. Release at the halfway point on licence therefore became a right not a privilege. At the time I did not understand its significance as a part of a political agenda. Four years later we all found out when ECHR ruled that Governor's powers to award added days breached human rights. In order to retain power over time spent in custody by those serving a fixed term sentence where the award of added days was still provided for, David Blunkett was forced to bring District Judges into prisons to hear cases that could merit that punishment. The main objectives of the PRT are to reduce unnecessary imprisonment, promote community solutions to crime and improve the treatment of and conditions for prisoners and their families. The aim is a just, humane and effective penal system. As we have seen, there is no consensus about the makeup of such a system. Former Chairs of the PRT include Edmund Dell, former Labour Trade Secretary under James Callaghan, Broadcaster Jon Snow, Douglas Hurd and Robert Fellows, former Private Secretary to the Queen.

The other traditional offenders' charity is the National Association for the Care and Resettlement of Offenders (NACRO). Historically it focussed on released offenders rather than prison conditions or alternatives to custody. Its current Chief Executive is Jacob Tas. Its origins are in the Central Discharged Prisoners Aid Society founded in 1924, renamed National Association of Discharged Prisoners Aid Societies (NADPAS), before becoming NACRO in 1966. Since 1999 it has styled itself as the Crime Reduction Charity with a vision to reduce crime and change lives. It welcomes putting education at the heart of the custodial experience. Its patron is the Queen. As an organisation, it is large with 2000 staff and volunteers. Although NACRO is active in crime prevention and early intervention its main focus remains the released offender. It has campaigned for changes to the Rehabilitation of Offenders Act (1974) and for changes to the process of carrying out Criminal Records Bureau (CRB) checks which can seriously damage the employment prospects of people with long forgotten, irrelevant minor convictions. The Coalition government eventually made some common-sense changes to a system of CRB check disclosures rooted in the hysteria that followed the conviction of Soham murderer, Ian Huntly, when it emerged that a substantial portfolio of information about potential sexual offences that never reached trial was not available to his employers at the school where he was a caretaker. This was a notable success for NACRO's 'Change the Record' campaign. NACRO works with local and regional partners in carrying out its work.

However it caused a considerable stir in 2008 when NACRO got into bed, as it were, with G4S one of the big three in the private prisons business, to bid for the right to run two new prisons although there was a little less of a stir when NACRO joined a Community Justice Partnership with Essex Probation Trust and Sodexo, another of the private sector's big three 2011, by which time former Prison Governor Paul McDowell had replaced Paul Cavadino as Chief Executive. The G4S bids were unsuccessful but that does not close 'Pandora's box'. NACRO believed that they could get in on the ground floor and help a security company create a regime that focuses on resettlement. I know nothing about Paul Cavadino but I know first-hand how passionately then Chief Executive Paul McDowell espouses successful resettlement of prisoners in the community as a key crime reduction tool, and also knowing his willingness to be bold, innovative and break with tradition, I was briefly stunned but not totally surprised by his adoption of what had previously appeared to be a fundamental taboo amongst generally left leaning penal reform charities. Previously public sector governors had simply defected to the private sector trading job security for a major salary hike and the freedom to manage. Of course if one thinks a little more deeply about this development, experience of Mr Blair's government taught us that My Generation in power had long accepted Thatcherism and made its accommodation with the profit motive as it moved away from industrial socialism to a new agenda based on victim group identity and group and individual rights. This Faustian bargain is far more significant than a new deal for resettlement. Its true significance is that NACRO has fatally compromised its independence. Not surprisingly it was criticised by the Howard League whose spokesman declared that NACRO would have 'blood on its hands'. Juliet Lyon's response on behalf of the PRT was more measured but she questioned the appropriateness of a charity associating itself with a company that by the nature of its business has a vested interest in the use of custody. She also pointed out that there were risks both to the charity's identity and indeed its charitable status from this leap in the dark.

For me, it is rather like a teetotaller joining a brewery and failing to understand that from now on there is a working relationship with alcohol, one that he can never erase it from his c.v. Like the Hotel California you can check out any time, but you can never leave. On a more intellectual note, George Orwell would have recognised that this was NACRO's 'four legs good, two legs better' moment. I am sure that NACRO's Chief Executive is well aware that G4S and other private companies exist to make a profit. Of course they do and I am as capable of getting over that as Mr McDowell, but I am mindful that they make money out of human misery. G4S and similar companies are not noted as employers of choice. As I have said in Chapter 7 they are companies that specialise in low pay and a hire and fire culture. Their presence in what should never have been a custodial marketplace has forced down public sector pay. Subsequently, G4S were also found to be woefully wanting when they failed to deliver on their security contract for the 2012 Olympics and the much-needed leave for a substantial number of troops was cancelled as a consequence. What should particularly have concerned NACRO is that whatever the failings of the public sector, the private sector as a whole has received considerably more criticism for its failings in respect of prisoners than the public sector. The nadir was the disgraceful situation at Ashfield detailed in the previous chapter, a frightening litany of ineptitude, incompetence and ill treatment. It would not and could not have happened under the same Paul McDowell who delivered a brilliant inspection at Coldingley in November 2005.

Anyone who knows anything about prisons knows that security comes first. The Prison Service imposes significant restrictions on access to IT and in particular the Internet, for reasons that are well understood; preventing cybercrime, preventing the harassment of victims, preventing sex offenders from accessing hard core pornography are obvious examples. Temporary release for resettlement purposes is hedged in by strict qualifications and in depth risk assessments. The private sector may be able to allow telephones in cells, but it is just as bound by security and safety of the community rules as the public sector. NACRO is delusional if it believes it will have more power to affect this from within rather than without. Indeed almost as surprising as taking a private sector partner is the implied accommodation it has made with prison service bureaucracy. This also raises the issue of whether it would retain the trust of prisoners. The privatisation programme in the Prison Service may have been suspended, but the privatisation of probation service work in the community continued apace. Another former prison governor, Kevin Lockyer, also worked for NACRO as Services Director and both he and Roger Hill, former public sector South Regional Offender Manager (ROM) who was Director of Community and Partnerships at Sodexo, were key players in securing the Essex partnership.

Of the other charitable players the best known is Unlock. This was founded by ex-offender Mark Leech who quickly established a rapport with Martin Narey, Head of the Prison Service 1998–2005. Unlock styles itself as the national charity for people with convictions. "We are here for law abiding people with convictions." Mr Leech is the editor of the Prisons Handbook, an invaluable guide to the regimes in English prisons and also editor of *Converse*, which rivals *Inside Time*, published by the New Bridge Foundation, as the most widely read paper in our prisons, not surprising as most of the contributions are from serving prisoners. Mark Leech is also a restaurant proprietor, helicopter pilot and fellow of the RSA. However Mark Leech's rapport with Martin Narey did provoke suggestions from opponents, perhaps jealous of the access he enjoyed, that the perceived cosiness of his relationship with the Director General amounted to going native. Another player is Inquest founded in 1981 that focuses on deaths in police, prison or immigration custody. It offers a free service to bereaved relatives. It has particular concerns about the deaths of women, black people, young people and those with mental health problems. This reflects the charity's commitment to challenging discrimination among what it perceives as victim groups. By implication, police and prison officers are cast in the role of villain. Historically charities have existed to fill in the gaps not covered by the state or local authorities. They exist also to prick the conscience of both our rulers and the individual citizen going about his private business. The medieval monasteries which gave alms to the poor were amongst the first official charities. The genesis of public education is also in charitable provision.

I readily accept that most of the Chief Executives, Trustees and prominent supporters of charities would bridle at any suggestion that they were not independent, not in the face of government when necessary and not critical of selfishness and corruption wherever they may find it. Paul McDowell I know loathed prison service bureaucracy with a passion. Anne Owers regularly jousted with Jack Straw over immigration issues before being appointed HMCIP. Penal reform charities have not been slow to criticise cheap and sometimes hypocritical populism from government ministers stirring Jack Straw into attacking the charities for their concerns for offenders rather than victims. The charities would themselves argue that their programme would reduce the number of victims of crime and as such shows proper respect for the law-abiding community. Quite properly the charities pointed out that such groups prevent the state from neglecting and abusing criminals. For all my criticisms of the Inspectorate and what I see as its politicisation, I readily accept that they carry out the same essential function.

Chapter 9
Prison Service Employment Practices and the Headquarters Culture

At various points in this book I have mentioned Prison Service Headquarters and rarely have the references been complimentary. Although I am not familiar with other civil service departments it is unlikely that my experience of Home Office bureaucracy and since 2007, Ministry of Justice bureaucracy is markedly different from that of former civil servants in any other government department. In the private sector, large companies routinely cull their bureaucrats when they become too expensive, and particularly when the company starts to serve the bureaucracy rather than its customers. In the Civil Service, this does not happen and no one should be misled about the nature of the significant cuts in the size of the prison service that have taken place since 2013. The bulk of cuts are always to front line services. Between March 2010 and June 2017, when front line staffing fell to its lowest, the number of operational staff fell by 31.5%. The fall in Headquarters staff using the same dates was 14%. One can be sure that departments which monitor performance measures and issue directives about the latest priority as regards equality and diversity or green energy initiatives will survive relatively unscathed. The Civil Service continues to serve itself as it always has done. In order to keep this chapter moderately tight and disciplined, I have chosen to focus in particular on the employment practices of the Prison Service up until my retirement in 2010 to help the reader understand how the modern day Civil Service functions. As I have said, I have no reason to believe that the Prison Service is untypical of the Civil Service and indeed the rest of the public sector. I refer to the Prison Service rather than NOMS as a whole, as those who worked for the now defunct Probation Trusts, were never made civil servants.

As a civil servant, your expected loyalty is to the crown not the public. The problem is that bureaucrats have long since usurped crown prerogatives. It is important to remember that the function of the civil service is administration which simply means the execution of rules governing public affairs. Management is about procuring the compliance of those affected internally and externally by the rules, and also the compliance of staff engaged in administering those rules. In this context, management and administration are largely indistinguishable as concepts, but are very distinct from leadership, where the ability to motivate, to inspire, and to use initiative and look beyond the status quo for alternatives that keep an organisation fresh and vibrant are key components. This is why the Civil Service can be an uncomfortable place for Prison Governors who have been recruited to lead. In the Civil Service, leadership has a different function which is at odds with the normal features of leadership of which I have given examples above. It is essentially about establishing and then preserving a broad status quo which defines and limits the boundaries in which change takes place. Change therefore is slow and organic, reactive rather than proactive, and part of a continuum rather than a radical departure. Only cataclysmic events or ultra-determined ministers alter the pace of change. The Civil Service loves to make rules and better still to gold plate those emanating from the EU, which is probably the ultimate in unaccountable bureaucracy, and doesn't even bother to pay as much as lip service to democracy. The mandarin class at the head of the Civil Service regard themselves as the real rulers; the professionals fending off amateur politicians and their ill-conceived notions. Civil Services whether here or abroad are 'top down' organisations. Mrs Thatcher, that most radical of Prime Ministers, and Mr Blair, who had no hesitation in by-passing the mandarins, were both highly critical of what they saw as civil service inertia, obscurantism, and despite a glittering array of Oxbridge degrees, incompetence.

One thing the Civil Service is superb at is absorption. Senior Prison Governors making it to the Senior Civil Service (SCS) can be relied on to go native. The same phenomenon is readily observed amongst the ranks of the less exalted exiled from prisons into obscure lower level HQ roles that usually mean pestering the life out of those trying to run prisons with petty diktats and requests for information. Unlike Treasury Grades who have spent their entire lives in HQ, they have no cultural excuse. The Civil Service is also exceptionally good at double speak. It is perfectly capable of executing policy in a wholly perverse manner while at the same time pretending that it is administering the rules fairly and impartially. Making employment and promotion practices the main theme of this chapter allows me to illustrate this perfectly.

I was interviewed for the Prison Service three days before Christmas in December 1983. I can recall sitting in a waiting room in Norwich prison awaiting my turn. At one point (I can't recall whether it was a Principal or Senior Officer) someone with rank came in to say a few brief words about training and proceeded to tell us that he was hard but fair, repeating it several times. If I am honest, my silent thoughts were 'what a dickhead'. This view was reinforced when he handed out the expenses in cash which had already been pre-calculated on the mileage between home and HMP Norwich. Unfortunately, I had moved home between sitting the qualifying test at Leicester in early October and being called for interview at Norwich in deep and dark December, something the bureaucracy had not caught up with. Thus I was paid only mileage between Kings Lynn and Norwich rather than rail fare from Stoke-On-Trent and an overnight hotel bill and he was either unable or unwilling to rectify the matter. I mentioned it later to one of the ex-servicemen on my course who simply smiled and said that he had been fucked around by professionals; the clear implication being that I should get used to it. Like most people encountering this sort of bureaucracy for the first time I protested not too strongly being concerned that it might affect my employment prospects. The interview in front of a three-man panel was exceptionally hostile and at times I felt it necessary to give as good as I got. At the time I wondered if it was the right thing to do, but again I learned later that hostile interviews were the norm and it was part of testing how you coped in a hostile environment, which looking back seems entirely reasonable, although it didn't appear to test anything else. As for the expenses, I put it down to experience but did get my own back some months later. During the four-week induction at Stafford the Training Principal Officer made us come in the Spring Bank Holiday which was not the norm when under training. Therefore it should have been paid at double time. After some wrangling and support from the Prison Officers Association, I eventually got the further eight hours pay that I was owed.

Thirty-five years ago Principal Officers in charge of training were exceptionally powerful. Although I did not know it at the time without their say-so you would not progress to Officer Training School (OTS), or once there to your establishment. A colleague of mine at Werrington House had been sacked at Stafford by the Principal Officer before completing the four weeks training at the joining establishment that preceded the eight-week residential course at either Wakefield or Leyhill. After some months, he was reinstated and commenced training at Shrewsbury, completed all stages successfully, and arrived at Werrington House three weeks after me as a fellow probationer, where he continued as a valued and loyal member of staff until he retired. Similarly a small minority of New Entrant Prison Officers (NEPOs) as we were called, (the name had been changed from the less user friendly POUTs, which stood for Prison Officers under Training) disappeared from the residential course at the half way stage, which was when the letters notifying you of your posting were given out. Those considered not to be up to standard were quietly escorted from the premises never to be seen again before the ritual opening of the letters began.

Thanks to another bovine piece of bureaucracy the posting process for my course was extremely fraught. On joining in May 1984, we were simply told that the rules had changed and no longer would the posting to our first establishment be classed as a transfer at public expense. This was a consequence of an efficiency report by Lord Raynor, who I believe was a former Chairman of Marks and Spencer's. The previous practice had enabled the postings board to send newly trained officers anywhere in the country safe in the knowledge that the service would pick up the tab. It was a good way of manning the landings of London local prisons with young single men who could hardly complain about the posting if their expenses were paid, and also of ensuring that prisons in remote locations occasionally got some new blood. Also most prisons had quarters, although not always enough to go round, and officers could be required to occupy them as part of their terms and conditions. Indeed I had to seek formal permission from the Governor of Werrington House to live in my own home, which was a formality given that there were no spare quarters available. For ex-servicemen, the move from military quarters to prison service quarters was familiar territory and if they had to live in a cheap hotel or lodgings until one became available, expenses could be claimed. The new regime caused consternation particularly among those who had been unemployed and long exhausted their savings. It was no consolation that the four weeks spent at the establishment were now classed as detached duty and therefore travel and subsistence could be claimed. The hard faced view from government was that most recruits would not turn down what was a well-paid and secure job, but would bite the bullet and somehow fund their own transfer. For me, it would have been back to classroom making a living as a supply teacher until a permanent teaching post came up.

As it turned out the new regime was not fully tested at this stage. Whether or not it was the fear of losing recruits I do not know. Whether someone stepped in to ensure that the posting process for once paid any heed to requests from recruits (we were asked to give three preferences in descending order) again I do not know. The posting process in those days was conducted in an office in HQ in London and led by someone no more senior than a Higher Executive Officer. I believe the Prison Officers Association had the right to observe the process. However, the majority of my class were happy with their postings and comparatively few people had the worry and distraction of submitting an appeal. Single men and married men with no children (my status at the time) did not necessarily get sent to London. I imagine smaller establishments like Werrington House which would have been low priority for filling vacancies were happy as they got new staff straight from training out of the process. I should add that in those days established staff could apply for own expense transfers and join a waiting list. Typically staff did this to get back to their home area. Establishments had no power to refuse them on the basis of poor sick or disciplinary records so it was often the case that 'popular' establishments had more than their fair share of dysfunctional staff. In the end, the Home Office accepted that making the change without notice was unfair and retrospectively paid expenses to those affected from courses 270W and 271L. In my case, I was the beneficiary of the law of unintended consequences and got the closest posting possible to home which was a relief given that persuading my wife to move from Staffordshire a second time would have been fraught with considerable divorce potential.

Part of our terms and conditions was the mobility clause, the one in which the service asserted its right to post you to any establishment in England and Wales. (Scotland and Northern Ireland are separate jurisdictions) In practice, unless your establishment closed or you were given a disciplinary transfer, a prison officer who was content to stay at that level could serve out their entire career at one establishment. Promotion theoretically demanded a move as like the Police in 1984 in situ promotions were frowned upon, particularly for the first promotion on to management ladder. In practice, persistence paid and those prepared to wait two or even three years would eventually get an in situ posting or other posting of their choice. There were some expert players of the system… and there were also freemasons who could lean on HQ for a fellow member of the fraternity. It was once seen as undesirable and indeed unfair to the officer to put them in a position of being permanently in charge of those with whom the previous week they were serving at the same level. The women's service was rather different. Filling senior and principal officer vacancies from outside London was exceptionally difficult, so in situ and double in situ promotions were the norm. Male staff in London taking promotion(s) would simply go on a magical mystery tour of the big London local prisons, although for others it was the opportunity to get out of the capital if they had the patience to wait.

Governor grades did not have the option of remaining in one location. Even though it was possible never to be promoted from the rank of Assistant Governor, AGs were given development moves at roughly three-year intervals. They simply received a letter informing them bluntly of the next posting and the date and time they were expected to report. According to old hands, the service seemed to have a sixth sense when an AG had formed a relationship with a colleague and duly transferred one or both to locations so far apart that maintaining a relationship was a significant challenge. Protesting against postings on family grounds often cut no ice, the service taking a view that it employed you, not your family. Given that most recruits were male this was the patriarchal society at its most explicit. Female recruits as officers or assistant governors were disproportionately single, which was probably just as well in terms of avoiding wastage. The message was clear; you fitted in with the needs of the service and not vice-versa. Even the military for all its rigidity and its infinite capacity to mess its personnel around did not treat families with this kind of contempt.

The same attitude prevailed at work and caused problems for primary carers (mainly female) or those who simply were not streetwise when time in lieu replaced overtime after 1987. Cross sex postings made only the most basic concessions to female staff now working in male prisons such as the provision of female toilets, and if they were lucky, a solitary grubby shower. At Ford that was still the provision almost two decades after cross sex postings for officers were initiated. One of the problems of working in an organisation where there is a round the clock commitment is covering unexpected emergencies, such as a prisoner needing to be escorted to casualty at evening lock-up. It was fairly easy when there was overtime; someone would always volunteer. When time off in lieu (T.O.I.L) replaced overtime, there were often no volunteers and those who owed the most or more likely were owed the least hours could simply be instructed to carry out the duty. Many of those going home simply shrugged and said it was not their problem. Overtime was inefficient, expensive and bad for the health of staff but its availability (indeed at one time it had been compulsory) ensured that loyalty was very securely bought. The trick as the wise heads soon learned, was always to keep a stock of hours owed to you by the establishment so that you would rarely be in line for inconvenient emergencies. Small victories over the system were much prized. Sadly, sometimes, small victories over colleagues were also prized, especially in the early days of women working in male establishments.

As I have said in Chapters 4 and 5, recruitment was largely class based and the rank structure based on the military model of mess apartheid. Theoretically prison officers could become governor grades and a handful each year would do so until the Assistant Governor scheme was abolished in 1987. I was actually a candidate in what I believe was the last closed competition (i.e. restricted to prison officer grades only). The three-day assessment centre was modelled on that used for recruiting civil servants direct to the old administrative class. My recollection is that for the oral sessions candidates were divided into groups of six, apart from your individual interview where you could select some of the subjects for discussion. Exercises included free debate in which if you were speaking the act of drawing breath was taken as a cue for someone to interrupt. There was also a project exercise in which the trick seemed to be to argue to a consensus. Despite Mrs Thatcher being Prime Minister, finding yourself in a minority of one was not a good place to be. There were also written exercises which tested your facility on paper. I think there were also further tests of non-verbal reasoning and arithmetical skills. We were told that in theory everyone could be selected or no one at all. However, the prevailing view amongst candidates was that the limited competition was just tokenism, the organisation paying lip service to the concept of equal opportunity and the chance of finding pearls amongst swine. The AG board was referred to as the 'Country House' test and although the days had gone when someone watched whether you could hold a knife and fork properly and be trusted not to pass out at the bar, the overwhelming feeling was that we were being judged ultimately on subjective criteria that formed part of an unwritten code that could be trusted to eliminate those who 'were not the right sort of chap' which as prison officers was most of us. I should add that those recruited externally as assistant governors whose careers did not prosper also felt the same way. In an anonymous satirical article published in the Prison Governors Association magazine *The Key* in October 1990, the author wrote ... 'It is not of course possible to give objective standards of assessing such qualities, but the department does have other tried and tested and proven ways and long experience of doing so. The first of them is the gradual and adventitious building up of an accepted profile of the officer, (then a collective term for civil servants generally) and since we are dealing with perceptions and extempore judgements, such an explanation is not possible. The correct repository of such information is in the minds and consciousness of those who jealously guard the reputation of the service...' I think this captured it perfectly.

Promotion was also dealt with centrally when I joined the service and with the exception of some regional competitions in London and the South East, continued to be so until the mid-90s. Unlike initial recruitment interviews promotion boards were always held in London and each year hundreds of staff would trek to London for a forty-five minute interview (and not always that long) that would determine their suitability for the next grade. The composition of three-person panel could change on a daily basis and interviews were not always conducted professionally. The graveyard slot was first interview after lunch, particularly if board members had dined well, or worse still drank well. The system applied to treasury grades as well as to prison officer and governor grades. It must have cost a fortune in rail fares particularly in the case of those forced travel at peak times. Governor grades were entitled to first class travel. Promotion boards ran for weeks on end. Just to give the reader an idea of the timescale I was interviewed for my Governor V (junior governor grade) board in July 1994. The results were published in December 1994. I took up my new post in May 1995. Compared to those people determined to secure a post without moving home, this was quick. Qualifying for a promotion interview was via the Annual Staff Report (ASR). Until around the time I joined staff did not even see these reports, they were confidential. Whether open reporting influenced grade inflation I cannot say, but in order to secure a promotion interview for Senior or Principal Officer, it would be necessary to have a sequence of usually three consecutive 'fitted' markings in order to qualify for a board. Often the standard was higher, requiring 'well fitted' markings. As well as the promotion appraisal it was often necessary to have a sequence of 'Box 2' performance markings, i.e. above average performance of duties. In practice, long serving staff expected these markings as of right, regardless of whether or not they had passed the promotion examination. You can readily see the attractions of freemasonry to ambitious officers. It was observed that at HMP Leeds after a particularly bad year for suicides that 70% of prison officer grades had achieved above average performance markings. This was not untypical no matter how squalid the establishment, no matter how poor the treatment of prisoners, no matter how disengaged the staff.

Eligibility for the Prison Officers Promotion Examination (POPE) was based on length of service. Four years had to be completed before it could be sat. Examinations were held locally on the first Friday of every May, so someone who joined in June could wait almost five years before being allowed to compete. Back in the 1960s before the senior officer grade was introduced the qualifying period was nine years. The examination was divided into two papers, a prison paper and an English paper, one sat in the morning, the second in the afternoon, usually at a local technical college. The prison paper carried a slightly higher weight. Until the mid-90s when the system was changed it was possible to pass despite scoring less than 50% in one part of the exam. It explained the significant presence of knowledgeable semi-literates at middle management levels. Although partially immersed in the drinking culture it still surprised me that some colleagues knocked back a swift half gallon in the lunch break between the two papers. For some, it was a day out. Until 'Fresh Start' was introduced in 1987 others expected to go back to their prison and work an evening duty as overtime. The prison paper was about the regurgitation of knowledge of standing orders and procedures. The availability of promotion classes varied immensely. It was an advantage to work in a large prison with a full time training principal officer who would set up classes, have a stock of past papers and perhaps even some knowledge of exam technique that could be passed on to candidates. For most uniformed staff, seeking promotion that was the one and only qualifying examination in what was a service stratified by class and education. As can readily be seen, the pursuit of promotion was a long haul. In the north, it could take 10 years to reach Senior Officer and 17 years to reach Principal Officer. Promotion for Assistant Governors was also painfully slow.

As a system, it was inefficient and archaic but eventually the service would both throw out the baby with the bathwater and introduce promotion and selection systems that would prove when taken in the round, as or even more flawed than the old and out-dated system, setting new standards for nepotism and corruption. The basic rule of thumb in the modern prison service is the more senior the position advertised, the less transparent and more corrupt the process is likely to be. The reality is that people are competing for the patronage that leads to promotion. Beginning in the mid-1990s the service made a series of changes to recruitment, promotion and selection procedures, some of which it has to be said were very welcome as part of the devolution of HQ functions to establishments. This relinquishing of control should not be overstated as HQ produced Prison Service Order (PSO) 8010, entitled 'Filling Vacancies' a bloated bureaucratic tome the thickness of an encyclopaedia. Recruitment of prison officers and promotions to senior and principal officer were among the functions devolved. Part of the thinking behind local recruitment as well as increasing efficiency and reducing costs was that new recruits would have complete predictability about their place of work on completion of the training course. This was a welcome move away from the military model and paved the way for the significant recruitment of women with young children, both married and single mothers. It did much to redress gender imbalances amongst the prison officer workforce and brought in a whole cadre of mature streetwise women who had often underachieved at school but were now ready for a career, women like Claire Leask and Karen Thorpe at Woodhill.

Existing staff could still apply for sideways moves, but other than for compassionate transfers, establishments could now reject staff with poor disciplinary records and those whose sick records needed a Pickford's truck to transport them. The change did not solve staff shortages in unpopular and expensive locations but combined with local promotions establishments could and did hothouse their own talent. Woodhill where I worked from 1995 to 1998 was a particular example, and indeed I was a beneficiary myself. The prison opened in 1992 and the main prison officer grade was a mixture of new recruits and established staff attracted by a public expense move to a brand new establishment. In 1997 when Woodhill joined the High Security Estate and simultaneously opened its special unit for the most disruptive prisoners in the system, most of them Category A, the prison had an on-site plethora of talent ready and able to take up the much expanded opportunities for promotion to senior and principal officer. However rapidly rising house prices combined with falling unemployment was making initial recruitment much more difficult. Seventy new officer posts were created as a consequence of the plans for the special unit alone, and this was without the extra staff needed for the rest of the gaol as it entered the High Security Estate. The bean counters intervened and a decision was taken not to offer public expense sideways transfers for experienced staff, and to rely entirely on recruits from off the street. It had the inevitable effect of diluting the experience profile of the staff, reducing the availability of experienced mentors and reducing the quality of recruits. The prison became more difficult to manage as a consequence with increased incidents and sick leave as nerves became strained. The reports from HMIP dispensed much less praise. From being an outstanding flagship establishment in its early years that made people burst with pride at working there, it became just another place of work.

HQ in its infinite wisdom put up another recruitment barrier in this era. It decided that new recruits should have five GCSE ordinary level passes at grade C or better, or their equivalent, before they could be considered for interview. The effect of this shortsighted and mercifully short-lived policy was catastrophic for establishments with recruiting difficulties. It ruled out older recruits who had attended Secondary Modern Schools and left school at 15, (the school leaving age was not raised to 16 until 1972). It ruled out many typical ex-armed services recruits who frequently did not have a single school exam pass to their name. It ruled out those solid citizens who had been troubled adolescents and as a consequence also had few exam passes to their name. It made no allowance for those unfortunate enough to have attended the crappiest comprehensives, nor did it allow for the fact that CSE passes at grade two and three were often every bit as good as Grade C at the new GCSE. I should explain for those who have never heard of the Certificate in Secondary Education (CSE). It was introduced in the mid-1960s as an exam qualification for the minority in Secondary Modern Schools who remained until they were sixteen. As comprehensive schools replaced the old grammar and secondary modern schools and the school leaving age was raised, it became the exam sat by the majority of pupils until both it and the GCE designed for the more academic pupils, were merged as the GCSE (General Certificate of Secondary Education) in 1985. A CSE grade one was considered the equivalent of a GCE Ordinary Level pass. The problem of course is that by no stretch of the imagination is a GCSE pass the genuine academic equivalent of a pass in the former GCE. Some Area Managers granted a dispensation. Other establishments replaced the former entry test with that given to prospective administrative officers, which was reputedly of an equivalent standard to an ordinary level pass. This ludicrous policy was swiftly buried, but from time to time its devotees raise their heads above the parapet. The Howard League has called for prison officers to have degrees, oblivious of the fate of the nursing profession.

Until 1998 prison officer recruitment was still conducted by formal interview. The format, depth and quality varied from establishment to establishment, as did the marking schemes and selection criteria. Training Services eventually put on a Board Members course which I attended, but inevitably it reached only a fraction of those interviewing actively. Sometimes decisions were made on gut instinct. I can remember one interview to this day of a female candidate at Woodhill one hot summer day. Those who remember the late Kenny Everett will remember his comedy character Cupid Stunt, who at regular intervals ostentatiously crossed and uncrossed her legs saying at the same time, 'All in the best possible taste.' Along with a female interviewing colleague I was treated to regular flashes of her bright orange knickers as she crossed and uncrossed her bare legs on numerous occasions during the interview. We put it down to nerves and offered her a job. A genuine eccentric she acquired the nickname 'Mystic Meg' who I believe was a raven-haired female character on the National Lottery programme. On another occasion, I was interviewing with David Wilson, now a Professor of Criminology and regular TV contributor regarding high profile murder cases, and he insisted that we take a candidate about whom I had considerable doubt. David was right and the candidate became a good solid prison officer. At Woodhill we combined opinion questions on such issues as the death penalty or the issue of condoms in prisons, with situational questions for example asking how they would handle pressure to bring prohibited items into a jail. It was probably as good a method as any but whether it was any better at eliminating the small minority of staff unable to relate normally to their fellow human beings as well as those who were simply cynical or dysfunctional is unproven. Psychometric testing is not a solution as smart candidates can soon work out the preferred answers. In 1998, the service introduced the Job Simulation Assessment Centre (JSAC) for recruiting and in fairly short order introduced it further up the service. The aim was to confront candidates with live practical scenarios, which for all recruits had no connection with the prison service, and aimed to test what were called core competencies, designed and defined by our good friends, the psychologists.

The number of disciplinary issues which I encountered as a governor grade, suggest that the new method is no more successful than the old. However, part of the problem lies in training with the modern assumption that all recruits are expected to pass the course on the basis that they have passed the assessment centre. Although the course is now only partially residential, people cannot help but reveal themselves during substantial periods of residential training, thrown together with a random group of people with whom they have to bond. I quote just one example, again from my days at Woodhill where one recruit on his first day at the Wakefield Officer Training School (OTS) thought it was acceptable to put a female colleague across the snooker table in the local pub, pin her down and simulate sex with her. The student concerned was brave enough to complain the following morning being wholly clear that she had not invited this behaviour which was straight out of Life on Mars. Instead of being required to hand over his uniform and take a taxi to the station for the train home, he escaped with a warning. Before completing his probation this individual was dismissed by the Governor for a further act of blatant sexual harassment that went far beyond tearoom banter. A quick look at the personnel files of prison officers who get into disciplinary problems often shows that issues have arisen in training and have not been seriously challenged. Generally speaking such officers were not only allowed to complete their training, but also their probationary period, thus acquiring employment rights. There has to be due process but those who are clearly in the wrong job, when they can be bothered to turn up, should be invited to choose another career. Of course some do sort themselves out and deal with their issues, but most in this category are permanently dysfunctional and cause problems up to their retirement, typically spending their last six months on the sick, just before half pay kicks in. The other paralysing fear is political correctness. As far back as 1993 when I worked at Bedford, there was great reluctance to challenge a member of staff suspected of a corrupt relationship with a prisoner, simply because he was black and more pertinently the establishment's only black officer at the time. In the end, it was a prisoner who went to the police regarding items of his property being held at the officer's home. He was allowed to resign quietly as was the norm in those days.

Recruiting for prison officers is now probably the least corrupt process as it largely involves people from off the streets, not usually known to prison management, and if they are, they are unable to affect the process. Indeed I have to be fair and accept that the process of initial recruitment is as fair as it could be, although this does not necessarily give the assessment centre system a clean bill of health. The entry test which determines who goes forward to the assessment centre, has also been updated. Recruitment in my time was largely controlled by Chief Officers and it would not be surprising if at the very least sub-consciously they had a profile in their minds of the ideal recruit. Back in 1984 virtually every Chief Officer sitting on a recruitment panel would have been a former serviceman simply because their generation was subject to national service. A number would have seen action in places like Korea and Cyprus. It should not surprise us that the ranks of the military were providing the bulk of recruits nor should it surprise us that those with family members already in the prison service had an advantage. These advantages continued when local recruitment was devolved to establishment interview panels. Where prison auxiliaries were concerned they were of course already known to local management. It could be a considerable advantage if the answers to significant parts of the entry test were made known in advance to a candidate and this certainly happened. Equally skulduggery could work the other way if a powerful local senior manager was determined to veto a candidate. One former colleague whose line manager I had been suffered in this way and had to wait a further three years to become a prison officer. As it turned out on this occasion, I interviewed her myself along with the Deputy Head of Personnel and it was a straightforward decision. She went on to have a successful career and had been promoted when I last heard from her in 2010. This particular senior manager, who had once been my immediate boss, was hugely influential on interview panels. If he said a confident candidate was cocky, that an assertive candidate had an attitude problem, or that a nervous candidate was weak, it was amazing how often his view prevailed. The assessment centre put an end to this sort of occurrence, but only for recruits.

On another occasion, I had to step in to prevent an abuse of the vetting process. All establishments have a police liaison officer (PLO), and in the High Security Estate at the time, the post was a full time secondment. Typical post-holders were veteran Detective Constables for whom this nine to five role was a reward for long service and good conduct. On this particular occasion the PLO, whose job was to run all successful candidates through the Police National Computer (PNC), had found that a particular candidate who had worked as a security guard had once been arrested after a robbery which was believed to be an 'inside job' but subsequently cleared without going to trial. As a consequence, junior staff in the security department were about to advise the personnel clerk that the candidate was unsuitable. Fortunately, I got wind of this and stepped in. I should be clear that PNC checking by the PLO was perfectly legitimate and a vital part of his role. Although prison officers who have criminal convictions are sometimes employed, there are obviously certain offences which are incompatible with a career as a prison officer. Equally it is necessary to discover those who have not disclosed convictions as deceit of this nature is frequently worse than the offence. What was not legitimate was to base employment policies on wholly unfounded allegations and I spelt this out in big letters. However, since the notorious Soham murders of 2002 by school caretaker Ian Huntley there has been a backlash and the Vetting and Barring regulations now not only prevent persons who are the subject of unproven allegations and may even have been cleared by a jury, from being employed, they also permit the dismissal of existing staff who then have no recourse to an employment tribunal as the legislation automatically deems such a sacking as 'fair'.

The Job Simulation Assessment Centre (JSAC) rapidly became the system of choice for both recruitment and promotion, with eventually only the Accelerated Promotion Scheme continuing to recruit via its own exacting qualifying tests and the traditional three-day residential civil service competition. The service refined the system so that there were JSACs for initial recruitment, for promotion to senior officer, for promotion to operational manager (to use the preferred terminology of our leaders) and for promotion to senior operational manager (again for convenience at this stage I am using HQ terminology as this is what would confront potential applicants). Like all parts of the public sector, the top of the prison service is never happier than when reorganising its management structure. To explain the former governor grades 4 and 5, which previously held separate promotion boards were amalgamated to form the operational manager grade, which had two pay bands labelled E and F. Although the service maintained a fiction that an upward move from F to E was not technically a promotion it was regarded as such at establishment level and treated as such for eligibility for a public interest (expense) transfer. The former Governor grades of 1, 2 and 3 all of which previously had separate boards were amalgamated to form the senior operational manager grade. To refresh if you're not keeping up, Governor 3's were Deputy Governors in large establishments an in-charge Governors in the very smallest. Governors 1 and 2 governed the largest and medium sized establishments respectively. Initially senior operational manager had four pay bands, A to D, but in 2008 the small number of D grade in-charge Governors were all upgraded to pay band C, just like that! In a further reorganisation since my retirement, the number of pay bands for in-charge Governors was reduced further to two. In theory, these arrangements refined a clumsy and bureaucratic system that had required someone who joined as a prison officer after 1987 to get through seven promotion boards to reach Governor 1 down to just four visits to an assessment centre. The requirement for multiple 'fitted' markings on the annual appraisal was also removed allowing people with ability and genuine potential to be promoted speedily even without the benefits of accelerated promotion. All that was required was the support of the Governor, and for the senior operational manager (SOM) JSAC, the support of the Area Manager, which would often be given just to keep people onside, trusting the process to find them out. The qualifying period for taking the promotion examination was reduced to two years thus removing another barrier. However, promotion to Principal Officer remained by interview only, an anomaly that remained until the abolition of the grade in

2009, only for it to be reinstated and renamed Custodial Manager with the same uniform and similar insignia a couple of years later. Had the service listened to practitioners earlier on this issue rather than management consultants, much unnecessary pain may have been spared.

On the face of it, these changes should have produced a system that is fair and non-discriminatory. After all the JSAC process has undergone an Equality Impact Assessment. Candidates either pass or fail, there is none of the nonsense of being marked as qualified but not included on the promotion list which clogged up the system with appeals. It is virtually impossible to successfully appeal against a JSAC failure as the candidate can only contest the outcome on procedural grounds. I only have personal experience of the JSAC at the highest level; the qualification to govern. I have to admit that it took me four attempts to pass, although when I did get through I passed with flying colours. There are two earlier stages which involve respectively written exercises and commanding a serious incident, both of which I passed first time. Technique matters and I eventually learned that the key to success at stage three was to treat it like an oral version of the old Maths O Level and show all the working out. Candidates like myself used to dealing with business at speed and rapidly sifting out what we knew to be irrelevant back at the ranch on the basis of long experience, were being penalised for leaving out detail and what the assessors were seeking to test, the development of your thinking. I'm rarely grateful to psychologists, but thanks to Val (surname escapes) for sorting this one out. Nevertheless it is significant that the process favoured less experienced candidates and figures I saw prior to 2006 when Age Discrimination legislation kicked in, showed a dramatic fall in the pass rate for over 45's. I was 52 when I passed in 2005, and I believe I was the oldest successful candidate on the list. The JSAC also reflects the public sector obsession with the Diversity agenda. The pass mark for respect for diversity is higher than for any other core competence. The big weakness is that the right way to handle scenarios where role players are disabled, use homophobic language or behave in a manner that could be perceived to be racist, can be taught to those prepared to listen. There have also been issues about how well exercises have been devised. It is not uncommon for candidates who have been Diversity managers to fail to reach the required pass mark in the respect for diversity category!

However, the reality of the supposedly equality proofed procedure is very different, the crucial difference being that other than for prison officer recruits, passing the JSAC is only a qualifying hurdle. The old system had its weaknesses but if you had passed the board you were guaranteed promotion, and a HQ based grade manager would in the fullness of time issue a posting notice. You may not have been posted where you wished, you may have had a long wait, but it would happen and the service would fund the transfer without argument when a move of home was involved. Similarly with an own request sideways move, there might be a long wait, but it would be granted albeit at own expense except for a move to a Dispersal (now known as High Security) jail. As a system, it was faceless and anonymous at lower and middle levels. It was not family friendly but neither was it discriminatory. Within the governor grades there was more than lip service paid to career development and moves were designed to add experience to potential. Indeed there was once a staff college also at Wakefield the main purpose of which was the development of future leaders. The closure of the staff college can only be described as an act of cultural vandalism. It is akin to a company like ICI closing its research and development (R&D) department.

Instead of being posted qualified candidates now compete for posts. It is called Equality of Opportunity and was embraced by the Prison Service along with many other public sector employers in the late 1990s. As one would expect, there is an Equal

Opportunities Statement which appears at the top of every advert telling candidates that there is no discrimination on irrelevant grounds such as race, gender, sexual orientation, and since 2006, age. The reality is that the Prison Service is an unequal opportunities employer that practices corruption and nepotism on an industrial scale. Were it possible to persuade a high street bookmaker to take bets on the outcome of competitions for in-charge and deputy Governor posts, they would be bankrupted in a month. As I said at the 2008 PGA Conference, prison service promotion procedures would be recognised as good practice only in failed state such as Equatorial Guinea. Sometimes the process is insidious, on other occasions downright crude. A few examples will illustrate my points.

On one occasion, I believe back in 2001, I applied for the Deputy Governor position at a Yorkshire Young Offender Institution. In the waiting room, I met another candidate with whom I was acquainted. He said we had no chance today as Phil Wheatley's staff officer was up for the job, Phil Wheatley being Deputy Director General at the time. Staff Officer postings in the office of the DG and his deputy were much prized and went to those marked out for great things. The most prestigious secondment of all was to the Minister's office. These jobs were virtually never advertised and equal opportunities never got a look in. When one of these tours of duty was complete, the incumbent could expect to be posted to a senior operational role with just the minor inconvenience of applying for an advertised post that was already in the bag. Other candidates would waste hours on application and preparation, and travelling to and from interview. The service would waste money on their expenses. How does this happen? Well it is very simple and an example will suffice. About 18 months before I retired the in-charge post at Dover became vacant. I had no intention of applying for a post in an Immigration Removal Centre in any case, but discovered that the Area Manager's ear had been bent, it being suggested to him that someone more than competent to be Deputy Governor of Belmarsh, the country's most complex prison, could not really be turned down for the job at Dover. And so it transpired. The individual concerned is in fact very able. My problem is that the service was unable to be honest and simply move him into the job. Martin Narey when Director General of the Prison Service, reserved the right to override promotion procedures and post where he thought appropriate, a power he exercised occasionally and transparently. Most of us could accept that certain moves were necessary for the good of the organisation; all we asked for was honesty.

What has happened is that agendas are clumsily concealed and that Area Managers have appropriated for themselves the powers we hoped would be reserved for the Director General. A typical situation occurs when the Area Manager wishes to move someone out of an establishment, sometimes at the instigation of the Governor. Since the abolition of central postings in-charge Governors have increasingly assumed that they have a divine right to a deputy of their choice, (and sometimes a whole new senior management team), while the rest of us are simply expected to lead, manage and motivate those we inherit. However, I would stress that sometimes moves of this nature are very necessary. Some partnerships never work, and sometimes, working relationships break down. There has to be a procedure whereby people can be moved swiftly to similar jobs elsewhere in the service regardless of who else may have coveted the job. Sometimes people need a break from the front line. Sadly some people also need to be hidden where they can do no damage, as it is virtually impossible to sack or demote someone for poor performance. Indeed some of them are recommended for promotion and pass the JSAC. Amazingly having got this far these people are not left to rot on the list, as incompetence does not have the same power to disqualify as not being on message or holding politically incorrect views. So yes, some of them actually govern prisons and prosper on the backs of able subordinates as opposed to being given a desk job where they can be quietly forgotten and in theory do no damage. However in fairness it must be said that non-operational jobs in HQ, Area Office or Home Office (now MOJ) Controllers Offices can be bona fide development roles.

However on three occasions when I applied for jobs as Deputy Controller in private sector establishments (Home Office Controllers monitor compliance with the contracts and have the power to levy fines for contractual failings) there was a clearly an agenda. At Buckley Hall, then in the private sector, there was only one other candidate. The Controller, my prospective boss, had clearly been leaned on to take the man from Manchester so that he could be taken painlessly out of the front line. At the interview I was asked an outrageous and wholly irrelevant question about why I wanted a public expense transfer. I objected vociferously to the question, partly because it was irrelevant but also because I hadn't raised it at interview, and you know the outcome. I did have the pleasure of embarrassing the Controller in a debate about promotion procedures at PGA Conference the following year and when he challenged me at the tea break, (he didn't have the bottle to speak at the rostrum) I told him to fuck off. To remind the uninitiated public expense transfers were not granted automatically for voluntary sideways moves, only for those initiated by the service. It would have been much simpler for him to have asked the Area Manager not to approve a PIT (Public Interest Transfer is the correct but rather less transparent term) if I was genuinely the best candidate, but of course this ran the (very small) risk of me accepting. I have seen this trick pulled by one my former Governors for a senior officer position. As a board, we both surprised and upset him by recommending an applicant on level transfer from another prison. The Governor wanted the internal candidate and secured him by the crafty move of asking the Area Manager, a man of noted frugality, not to approve a PIT. The stratagem worked perfectly as she turned the job down on that basis. The other Deputy Controller's job was at Forest Bank, Salford, which was about to open at the time. On this occasion, the pre-board visit to my prospective new boss had gone very well but the job still went to someone who was being pulled out of Manchester. In fact, if I remember rightly the interviews were simply cancelled. Yet again the taxpayers' money was wasted and yet again we are back to the basic lack of honesty and openness. On a further occasion, I was turned down for the Deputy Controller's job at HMP Dovegate on the basis that I was too well qualified and should be governing!

No doubt someone can trump this story but easily the most suspect competition I was ever involved in resulted in what I believed was a sexually transmitted promotion. Again I had a brief chat with another candidate whose line manager I had once been. After going upstairs, I was informed that the board chair had been changed at the last minute. It was widely reputed that my former subordinate and the new (female) board chair had previously enjoyed a sexual relationship when they had worked together at a large northern prison. I am sure you have worked out already that he got the job. One of the most basic integrity rules is that you do not sit as a board member where there is a candidate with whom you are having or have had a relationship of that nature. Sadly casting couch promotions are not an unusual method of career progression. Proving it in specific cases is another matter and I decided that there was little point in complaining.

The upshot of the so-called equal opportunities policy is that qualified and experienced candidates remained on the list, un-promoted. In the spring of 2010, three successful candidates from the 2005 SOM JSAC and one from the 2004 competition, still remained on the list. Three of us were members of the National Executive Committee of the Prison Governors Association. What a coincidence that was! The remaining individual, a black man who had joined the service in the same year as me took NOMS to an employment tribunal. As the settlement was made confidentially, I am not aware of its terms. One of my fellow NEC members did achieve promotion before I retired, but not into an in-charge post. Despite his undoubted ability and Balliol honed intellect, he never governed and retired in 2018. The problem for Area Managers who controlled Governor and deputy appointments within their fiefdoms, and HQ movers and shakers with their own agendas was that people they did not necessarily want were getting through the process, and conversely members of the golden generation earmarked for stardom were sometimes failing the process. Area Managers had found the answer to this problem before the JSAC system replaced national boards; they used the device of temporary promotion. The earliest JSACs had a three-year limit on the validity of the qualification. Just think if your university degree expired after three years. Inexplicably the prison service missed a trick and removed the time limit. It was later reinstated and the PGA had to thwart a plan to apply it retrospectively which would have neatly got rid of the four of us referred to in the previous paragraph. To get round the problem they came up with another wheeze and created a group within a group of people deemed to have exceptional potential. They were selected by HQ, and did not include anyone inclined to intellectual rumination about the direction of travel, and certainly no troublesome trade union officials. I did not bother to apply.

This particular wheeze came about in two ways. Firstly the almost all-powerful Area Manager group had been baulked in a bid to include an interview as part of the process, which would have allowed an apparently legitimate weeding out of the wrong sort of chap regardless of performance in the JSAC exercises. They wanted a process by which they were no longer forced to shortlist people they had no intention of employing. The creation of the elite group solved the problem. Secondly NOMS had over-recruited in its direct entry scheme at SOM grade D level. It had far more people than there were posts with the result that a significant number of these individuals were overbearing, or in plain man's language being paid a higher salary for a lower grade job than their peers in those lower grade roles. We asked the Director General to justify the continued recruitment. His response was that the scheme helped the service hit its ethnic minority recruitment targets. This sort of tokenism sickens ethnic minority recruits who have made their own way in the job and find themselves tarred with the failings of those recruited and promoted for political reasons rather than their ability. Political correctness therefore dictated that there must be room at the top for these recruits, a number of whom struggled because they had no means of relating to ground floor staff having never got their hands dirty, and duly found their way into well paid Monday to Friday HQ roles without any of the pressures they would have been used to in the private sector. Others are simply carried by immediate subordinates. The other very important effect of elitist policies and recruitment gimmicks is that promotion opportunities for those joining as prison officers are being steadily restricted. It is now much more difficult for them to reach senior rank. The service is regressing towards where it was in 1987 when it was class-based service. Once again senior rank will become the preserve of those with university education but with one crucial difference. The right sort of person will not be an independent thinker, he or she will be recruited for their perceived diversity but will be expected to be a fully paid up corporate clone signed up to the mantras of political correctness that happen to be in fashion.

I can make reference only to the prison service, but I can see that this kind of expensive and wasteful social engineering goes on right across the public sector, the police being the most obvious example. The Home Secretary and the Chief Inspector of Constabulary are very much enamoured of a similar plan to admit entrants to the police directly at Superintendent level, somehow believing that the skills needed to run a supermarket will translate to managing major incidents in which lives are at risk.

Employment practices are not just about recruitment, promotion and selection. They are about staff engagement, discipline (covered in the next chapter) and in the public sector about dealing with trade unions. Readers will no doubt have mixed views about trade unions. I am happy to declare my interest, I am a trade unionist of long standing and for my last three years was a member of the National Executive Committee of the Prison Governors Association. All prison service staff with the powers of a constable which are Prison Governors, Prison Officers and their private sector equivalents, are forbidden by law both to strike and/or take other forms of industrial action. The Prison Governors Association, like the Royal College of Nursing, does not believe that it is acceptable for its members to take industrial action and had taken this position before a 1994 legal judgement declared industrial action then being taken by the Prison Officers Association to be unlawful. I am not going to pretend that there have never been times when trade unionists have behaved badly, nor am I going to deny that there has also always been a small hard core of elected officials more interested in revolution than the pay and conditions of their members, but broadly trade unions are a force for good. They police the boundaries of capitalism, the frontiers of which at times can be like the 'wild west'. White-collar trade unions such as the PGA also bring the collective voice of skilled professionals to the table. Trade Unions hold both employers and governments to account and non-trade unionists benefit from the existence of such bodies without paying any subscriptions. Without trade unions ceaselessly lobbying government, employees in the private sector, parts of which are a trade union desert, would not have the benefit of the minimum wage (ungenerous as it is), nor would they have four weeks paid holiday per year. Trade Union membership has declined from its peak of 13 million in 1979, (the year Mrs Thatcher came to power) to 7 million or so today. The unfortunate thing is that although something like two-thirds of public sector workers are members of trade unions, only one in eight private sector workers enjoy the privilege of membership, and those are concentrated largely in former nationalised industries. As a consequence of social change and de-industrialisation, trade unionism has become a largely public sector preserve. I do not dispute that in the public sector we enjoy better pay, holidays and pensions, but they do not on their own make a good employer.

As a Prison Governor, there were occasions when I found individual local officials of the Prison Officers Association to be exasperating. Nationally I despaired of the lack of trust, the crude rhetoric and public antipathy to my own trade union. In reality at local level industrial relations are largely good and local officials very dedicated, giving time to members far in excess of their allocated facility time. I have good memories of branch officials at Dover and Lewes in particular. Local officials do have the problem of members who talk a good fight at branch meetings, but would never consider joining the committee. I realised a long time ago that some of the more militant language occasionally spoken or written by local branch officials is for show and designed to convince this kind of member that their committee takes no crap from management. It is part of the game and it is best to let it pass over your head rather than rise to the bait. So what did being a national official teach me? Well I learned why it was that the POA did not trust the senior management of the service. I also discovered that whereas NOMS as by this time it was, had no problem accepting the PGA's role as the voice of professionals on criminal justice matters, they did not accept the legitimacy of our trade union role, at least not during my time as an NEC member, which was dominated by management proposals for Workforce Modernisation, known by the acronym WFM.

I wrote about the trust issue and my experiences as a trade union negotiator in my editorial for issue No 76 of *The Key* the magazine of our Association. In it I quoted Jan

Berry, former leader of the Police Federation which represents officers up to the rank of Chief Inspector, speaking about her experiences.

'I have really tried to work with different government departments… but it is as if they don't want you until they have made up their minds. You are there to legitimise the process.'

'… It just felt like the word negotiation was superfluous. There was no negotiation. They want to dictate the whole time. They don't want to work in partnership.'

I described the Home Office (later MOJ) understanding of partnership as being like a 1950s marriage, where one partner exists only to be shafted. For me, it felt like we being treated as a company union. That was on a good day. On a bad day, it felt like we were expected to carry out the rubber-stamping function of a trade union in the old Soviet bloc. Because we were a professional association for some reason we were expected to be an arm of government rather than an independent trade union trying to represent the legitimate aspirations of our members. Of course where our interests coincided or where proposals were well thought out, we would do that. Those of us with folk memories of the 'Pay and Grading' negotiations a decade earlier were wary. Back in 2000, the NEC had been dominated by in-charge Governors more willing to trust the organisation and had seen that trust betrayed. We warned NOMS negotiators that they would not be able to go over the heads of the NEC again by taking advantage of superior communications facilities. Service wide E-mail would allow us to instantly rebut any propaganda or attempts to divide the members. We also made it clear that we would be balloting our members on the offer rather than NOMS hustling people to sign up for a small taxable consideration, as had happened in 2000. NOMS simply didn't get it. They believed until the bitter end that we were unrepresentative, and that they could rely on in-charge Governors to deliver the company message to our members in establishments, and they would fall tamely into line. Our employer only got the message when two-thirds of our members rejected the offer in a secret ballot, which was a staggering snub. 90% of members of the Prison Officers Association rejected the offer, despite it being tailored to main grade prison officers who comprised the great majority of their members. Phil Wheatley, then Director General of NOMS reacted with predictable sourness, saying crudely that we would get WFM 'without the Vaseline'. The Vaseline was a £50 million sweetener, which was withdrawn when WFM was rejected. It sounds like a lot of money but in government spending terms it is insignificant. All it would have given members was a few hundred pounds to accept new terms and conditions, which would have been subject to tax and national insurance. In 2000 that figure had been a mere £200. As most of our members are higher rate taxpayers (40% plus 2% additional national insurance) in the pocket this was worth the princely sum of £116, which wouldn't cover a family meal at a middling restaurant.

I won't bore the reader with all the gory details of WFM, just the principal issues. Suffice it to say it was just another proposed reorganisation put together by another set of expensive management consultants. There were no pay rises in it, indeed quite the reverse. The biggest initial sticking point was the proposal to reduce the top of scale pay for our Governor V (operational manager pay band F in NOMS speak) members. We managed to get over that one but NOMS negotiators had a wheeze up their sleeves to negate that. We accepted that a Job Evaluation Study was needed to grade jobs properly as the Pay and Grading structure was accepted by NOMS as no longer fit for purpose. Our view was that it never had been. We could understand that some jobs may be downgraded. The problem was that NOMS negotiators would not guarantee that all of our existing members would map across and therefore not be faced with a very lengthy period on mark time pay if their posts were evaluated as being in a lower grade. Imprinted in every public sector trade union negotiator's DNA is what happened to the nurses in 1986, when very many of them found that instead of a deserved pay rise the job evaluation scheme was skewed so that jobs were graded lower than expected. Basically the nurses were cheated and we were determined that our members would not suffer the same fate. Needless to say prison officers were given the guarantee that all their jobs would map across and therefore their members would continue to have access to their existing pay scale! All we wanted was the same treatment for a mere 600 junior governor grades that was being given to 30,000 prison officers. It was obvious to me why NOMS were digging in; they expected a particular result from the job evaluation process and saw us as thwarting the process of reducing the pay of what is the workhorse grade. As a strategy, it was brainless. More than half of our members were F grades. It was like asking turkeys to vote for Christmas. We were being asked to sell out more than half the membership. As an NEC had we been stupid enough to trust the organisation and the process and recommend acceptance, we would have faced a vote of no confidence. Amongst our bosses I am sure that some of them fervently hoped that the PGA would fall apart over WFM. Didn't they realise that most of our F grade members would simply have joined the Prison Officers Association, which shared with us joint negotiating rights for E and F grades even though very few eligible governor grades remained as members of that association? It defies belief that NOMS would actually want to see large numbers of governor grades join a trade union that campaigns for the right to take industrial action to be reinstated. Yet the POA with all its traditional militancy was courted, while we were castigated.

NOMS were determined to concede nothing. We even had to fight off plans that would have allowed treasury grades to undertake governor grade duties such as adjudications and the duty governor role without being accredited. NOMS also had another crude tactic based on a perception that as a small trade union we could not afford to fight them in court. Terms and conditions of employment are negotiable rather than consultative but NOMS frequently indicated that it would only negotiate on matters that it believed were terms and conditions rather than what was laid down in the civil service code. Our members unanimously voted for an increase in subscriptions to provide a fighting fund. NOMS got the message. No doubt Treasury Solicitors had told them they would lose in court, but the organisation had a history of not listening to its in house legal advisors and fighting cases it was bound to lose. The case of Carol Lingard, a senior officer at Wakefield prison who sued the prison service for constructive dismissal and received a record award of just under £480,000 in 2005, is a classic example of huge cost to the taxpayer and public reputational damage suffered as a consequence of poor judgement and unjustifiable obduracy at senior levels in the organisation. Industrial relations did start to recover from their nadir, assisted by a change at the top of the organisation and I believe have improved further since my retirement. The service has begun to remember that it needs to have its senior managers onside, not alienated from the organisation. A prison service at war with its governors is on very shaky ground and risking its credibility with the public, more sensible politicians and less partisan media commentators. It makes sense to have governors on board in a time of austerity, further organisational change, and when prisoner privileges are about to be reduced with the concomitant risk of an adverse prisoner reaction.

Chapter 10
Prison Service Staff Corruption and Discipline

Back in 1999 I attended a presentation at the Prison Service College on the subject of staff corruption delivered by a (then) upwardly mobile member of the accelerated promotion scheme. It is probably unfair to blame her for the quality of the brief and it certainly wasn't a factor in a less than stellar career. The most charitable thing that could be said about the presentation is that it was a start. A more accurate description would be that it was simplistic claptrap. The basic thesis was that corruption was linked to debt and therefore by gathering financial information on staff, the service could compile a list of vulnerable staff and perhaps even prevent those with debts from entering the service. As a thesis, not only did it make huge unproven assertions about human nature but failed to take into account social changes such as the huge expansion of credit and the proliferation of divorce, the latter being a prime cause of debt which was only worsened by the creation of the child support agency in 1993. In addition, high interest rates were government policy which pushed up the cost of mortgages to eye watering levels at a time when house price increases were massively exceeding the rate of inflation. I can remember myself paying 12.35% interest on a mortgage in 1991. As I said in the earlier chapter on prison officers, prior to 1987 relatively few staff owned their own homes as prison service were quarters were available and rents were low. All this was to change with Fresh Start and the discount sale of quarters. In short, prison officers along with all other public servants and private sector workers took on levels of debt that had been inconceivable to their parents' generation, and all as a consequence of government policy. Nor was corruption new. There has always been another motive; greed, and there have always been people who have either believed they are too clever to be caught or have simply been reckless as to the consequences.

At this stage it would be useful to define corruption. My Collins dictionary defines it as that which is 'morally debased'. The Latin word 'corruptus' is the past participle of the Latin verb 'corrumpere', literally meaning to break. Thus that which is corrupt is utterly broken. PSO (Prison Service Order) 1215 which is publicly available on the internet says regarding corruption '(staff)... must not solicit or accept any advantage, reward or preferential treatment for themselves or others by abusing or misusing their power and authority' in other words not break the trust that the public expects of them. In the section on relationships with prisoners, it states these must not be open to misinterpretation and it applies not just to dealings with prisoners, but also their relatives and friends and also former prisoners. The watchword is professionalism and there are proscriptions against passing personal information to prisoners, unauthorised contact outside the workplace with prisoners and ex-prisoners, and accepting approaches for favours. As one would expect, sexual involvement is also specifically forbidden. All of this derives from prison rules. Prison rule 62(1), the General Duty of Officers, requires them to support the governor and obey his or her lawful instructions, the very foundation of a disciplined service. Prison rule 63 requires that no officer (the word is used to describe all employees, not just uniformed prison officers) shall receive any unauthorised fee, gratuity or other consideration in connection with his office. Prison rule 65 forbids pecuniary transactions with prisoners, Prison rule 65 (2) forbids trafficking, i.e. bringing in through the gate unauthorised items intended to come into the possession of prisoners and Prison rule 66 forbids contact with former prisoners without the knowledge of the governor. Prison rules and PSO 1215 therefore cover the principal forms or sources of corruption although in practice the term is often applied narrowly to dealings with prisoners whereby the staff member receives some form of pecuniary reward for supplying prisoners with prohibited items, (usually junior staff) or alternatively it is applied to situations where staff accept rewards to enable private companies to circumvent to competition rules in order to gain a slice of often lucrative prison service business,(usually more senior staff). It is not applied to receiving a bottle of wine or lunch in return for a speech. This is common sense and you simply declare it to avoid any misunderstanding. Expenses fiddles are usually described as fraud since it involves only the individual and his or her employer. However, one other form of pecuniary advantage now being defined as corruption by the police and CPS is the sale of information to the press by employees.

Sexual involvement is frequently described as an improper relationship but in reality it fits easily within the definition of corruption as there is both preferential treatment and the abuse of authority. Close emotional relationships between staff and prisoners that have not crossed a sexual boundary can also be perceived as bordering on the corrupt as it puts a prisoner in a special position that he or she can exploit, just as if intercourse had taken place. It also follows that close relationships between staff members which may or may not be sexual, have potential for corruption. This applies almost entirely to situations where promotions and other attractive postings are available and one individual by virtue of the power associated with their office can clandestinely ensure that a favoured individual gains preferment. This kind of corruption over jobs is now endemic at senior levels in establishments and the former Area Offices, now known as Deputy Directorates of Custody (DDC). Sexually transmitted promotion is merely the most extreme form of this type of abuse of office. Needless to say the service remains in hypocritical denial over the cancerous abuses that make the once problematic influence of freemasonry seem very small potatoes. The honesty and integrity required of staff is traduced on a regular basis and I refer you back to the previous chapter.

In the professional standards statement prison service employees are required to be loyal, conscientious, courteous, reasonable and fair. As has been said above, they must act with honesty and integrity. There must be no unlawful discrimination, harassment, bullying or victimisation. Staff must avoid conflicts of interest, not engage in criminal activity and must conduct their financial affairs responsibly. They must act with discretion in matters of public and political controversy and protect official information. Lastly they must not bring discredit on the service, a useful catch-all clause to deal with less specifiable misconduct. Thus if a member of staff is bound over to keep the peace or is in receipt of anti-social behaviour order, the service could take disciplinary action up to and including dismissal even though no criminal offence has been committed. Most of these areas of potential disciplinary infractions whereby staff fall short of the standards required do not involve corrupt behaviour. The other fruitful area for disciplinary action is the failure by staff to obey rules and by doing so put the public or the reputation of the service at risk. An obvious example would be the failure to secure handcuffs properly. As can be seen, most of these examples of areas where staff can transgress do not involve corruption. They involve stupidity, negligence, and sadly sometimes they involve sociopathic behaviour. However similarly to corruption there are often the assumptions by individuals either that the rules don't apply to them, their Governor will take no action, or that no one will dare complain.

Most staff will have had limited or no known contact with colleagues corrupted by prisoners during their career. This is because unlike the police where corruption has affected entire squads whose activities often continued unchecked for years, prison service corruption tends more to be the work of individuals, some of whom have long been considered suspect by colleagues, but others of whom it comes as a shock when they are suspended from duty, sacked, and more recently, imprisoned. On the other hand, all of us will have had colleagues who have been disciplined mainly for low level misconduct, and some for more serious disciplinary infractions where jobs or rank were on the line. People like me who ascended to a management role will have also led disciplinary investigations that take place prior to disciplinary hearings, at establishment level in front of an in-charge Governor, at HQ in front of a senior civil servant. Those who like me who have been trade union officials will have also represented those being investigated, and beyond that at disciplinary hearings if the individual was charged with a disciplinary offence. A select few who have combined being an in-charge Governor with a trade union role will have experienced all aspects of the process. My own personal experience of corrupt or potentially corrupt colleagues is likewise limited. Prison officers despise corrupt staff and this cultural attitude I believe is a significant deterrent. Those who do not conform to cultural norms suffer a form of isolation that is unique to uniformed services. I do not believe that it is endemic nor do I believe that historically it has always been condoned. This view is not shared by some senior police officers who work on the iceberg theory. The increased number of court cases tells us not that there is more corruption or other serious misconduct, it tells us that there is greater openness in that these matters are being brought before the courts rather than allowing individuals to resign quietly . Prisoners also disagree and periodically angry letters appear in *Converse* or *Inside Time* making allegations that staff are on the take across the service. They are confusing often arbitrary and sometimes unfair decisions about transfers, about jobs within the prison, or privileges such as temporary release with corruption. Stories have occasionally circulated that allocation departments in local prisons are corrupt in that they accept payments in return for transfers to open prisons or other favoured establishments. There is no corroborated evidence to support this contention.

Nevertheless fourteen prison officers from HMP Pentonville were suspended in 2006 and subsequently charged with accepting bribes to smuggle in drugs and mobile phones, the most common forms of contraband, as well as weapons that could assist escape. Drugs and mobile phones allow criminality to continue unchecked in jail. The case collapsed in 2009, and the two prison officers who had been convicted on the evidence of colleagues had their convictions overturned on appeal. The outcomes were hugely embarrassing for the prison service, but it is important to remember that the verdicts of the courts must be respected. If professionals do not respect the verdict of a court, at least in public, then we undermine a system that protects us against the arbitrary power of the state. Inevitably there was renewed debate about the extent of corruption amongst staff in English prisons. Some estimates I have seen talk of 1300 corrupt staff operating at any one time in the system. This works at around 9 members of staff per establishment. Based on around 34,000 operational staff including governors and support grades at the time of my retirement, this is a corruption rate of under 4%, which in anyone's language is disturbing, but would not suggest the problem is endemic. It is important to remember that on the basis of these figures, over 96% of staff are honest and operate with integrity. However, the view of the Metropolitan Police quoted in the *Daily Telegraph* in 2008 was that around 10% of prison officers (thus excluding governors and others with prisoner contact) were corrupt, which would have translated to 1000 prison officers in the London area alone. In the same year, a former head of drug treatment at NOMS, Hussain Dejemil, asserted that the bulk of what he estimated to be £100 million worth of illegal drugs smuggled into prisons on annually, were brought in by corrupt prison officers. The Chairman of the Independent Monitoring Board at Wandsworth supported him. Tory MP Henry Bellingham went further and said 80% of drugs in prisons were down to corrupt staff. In 2007, the IMB at HMP Wandsworth had drawn attention to the fact that 250 mobile phones had been found in the jail in the first five months of the year alone. A corruption rate of 10%, if correct, is massively more worrying. However it is important to remember that these allegations are unsubstantiated.

So what is the response of the prison service? I mentioned earlier the presentation given at Training Services in 1999. Three years later the service set up its Professional Standards Unit in rural Worcestershire. Its main job is to receive and pass on intelligence. Its existence is publicised via PSO 1215, first published in 2003. The Prison Service order is essentially about process and has nothing to say about the root causes of corruption. The Metropolitan Police employs a similar number of staff to the prison service, but boasts around 2,000 staff in its Department of Professional Standards. It makes us sound incredibly amateur, but it has to be said that the record of the Met in fighting corruption does not bear scrutiny. Twenty-five years on the smell of corruption hanging over the investigation into the murder of Stephen Lawrence has not gone away and this is merely the best-known skeleton still rattling around in their cupboard. However a report delivered by Met Commissioner Ian Blair, to Martin Narey, the NOMS Director General in 2005 had six key findings. These were disclosed under Freedom of Information to the BBC. In summary these were: significant problems with respect to drugs, racism and corruption; a lack of appropriate intelligence systems; ineffective professional standards arrangements; a prison service structure that undermines the ability to tackle corruption and criminality; insufficient investment in investigating corruption; and finally the need for greater police involvement and independent oversight. The initial response of the service was the equivalent of drawing the wagons into a circle. The Met were forced to withdraw its most senior advisor to the service, Commander Gary Copson, and the size of Police Advisors Section, based in NOMS HQ and consisting entirely of serving police officers whose role it was to support the prison service with regard to crime in the nation's prisons, was reduced. However the prison service could not withstand media attention focussing on prisons allegedly awash with drugs and this time a review was to some extent acted upon. The Professional Standards Unit was renamed the Corruption Prevention Unit. In the capital, the London Prisons Anti-Corruption Unit was set up. According to John Podmore who headed up the CPU 2008–10, he inherited precisely ten staff, six of whom were administrators. There were no full time workers in the areas and regions outside London. In August 2010, he found himself surplus to requirements and his unit subsumed into the intelligence unit. According to Mr Podmore who retired in 2011, the merged unit contained less staff and none who had ever run a prison.

Answers to parliamentary questions provided by NOMS officials are no more illuminating. In 2010, John McDonnell MP attempted to find out how many illicit phones were found in prisons and how many had been found on staff, on prisoners and in communal areas. The response of the service was that such information was not held centrally. It was also revealed that no research was under way to find out how mobile phones came into prisons. Anecdotally it is not difficult; over the wall and/or through visits then up the arse, or via staff simply walking in with them. What we don't know are the percentages and clearly this was not being pursued with any urgency. Philip Davies MP asked for a breakdown of seizures attributable to a) sniffer dogs, b) closed circuit TV, c) strip searches, d) intimate searches, e) cell searches and f) police intelligence in each of the last five years. He was told that the cost of collating such information would be disproportionate. Information requesting a breakdown of visitors, staff and prisoners attempting to smuggle illegal drugs into prisons was simply not available. So we are no closer. Some senior and serious people have made some dramatic assertions about the extent of the problem but there seems no willingness to prove them right or wrong. As a consequence, I have some sympathy for POA officials tired of unsubstantiated attacks on their membership. Instead the service relies on its random MDT positive test figures for a positive spin on drug problems in prison. As I have said earlier in the book, random testing is deeply flawed and easy to manipulate.

I still prefer to believe that staff corruption is not endemic. However, it does feel anecdotally that corruption is a greater problem than when I joined in 1984 and that it grew in that time. I believe it is a complex interplay of social change and bureaucratic practice. As I wrote earlier, debt is an issue brought about by government policies that pushed up house prices, increased the supply of credit, and unloosed the Child Support Agency. It cannot always be blamed on loose living. After 1987 with the abolition of overtime, there was limited scope to earn one's way out of trouble. In the south of England, a prison officer's pay is a fairly ordinary salary compared to say somewhere like Stoke-On-Trent where a long serving prison officer's salary is not far off twice that of local industrial workers in an area where the minimum wage is the going rate. Although it is only a small part of the jigsaw the absence of overtime brought about a proliferation of second jobs. Staff could be found as semi-professional footballers, taxi drivers, and even on the books of escort agencies. At one establishment I worked with a divorced senior officer who basically ran a company that supplied stewards. It is one thing to provide staff to work as stewards at Silverstone or Charlton Athletic, but it is another matter entirely when serving prison officers are employed at clubs where stewards will forever be referred to as 'bouncers' and can be frequented and sometimes owned by local gangsters. One prison officer of my acquaintance endured a lengthy suspension before being cleared as a consequence of working as a bouncer in a dubious establishment patronised by career criminals. The service has tried unsuccessfully to clamp down on unsuitable second jobs and staff are supposed to seek permission. In practice, it is difficult to police as many staff now live significant distances from their establishment and hardly ever bump into colleagues outside work, let alone socialise with them.

The partial demilitarisation of the service that began after 1987 was in many respects a good thing. The downsides of the military mentality translated to civilian life are swiftly rehearsed; insularity, rigidity and resistance to change. Yet we have lost its virtues; loyalty, duty and community. When quarters were sold after 1987, prison service communities were gradually broken up. They may have been claustrophobic but in those communities everyone knew about their neighbours' life styles and any unexpected windfalls that manifested themselves in new cars or other forms of conspicuous consumption would swiftly have been noted. Although current service job adverts indicate that a military background is now back in favour, recruitment policies have themselves created problems via our old friend, the law of unintended consequences. As I have said in an earlier chapter, local recruitment was in principal a good thing and helped particularly in recruiting more women and ethnic minorities with family ties previously discouraged from joining a service that reserved the right to dump them at the other end of the country after training. However recruitment policies combined with shortsighted policies to reduce the pay of new starters had a very significant downside. Reduced starting pay drove down the average age of recruits thereby driving down the relative maturity of new starters. This phenomenon was readily observable when the new accommodation opened at Lewes in 2008 and we recruited a large contingent of new officers to make up our staffing complement, including two 18-year-old recruits. For the most part, I think it is too young although just to show that the exception proves the rule, one turned out to be absolutely superb but the other one had to resign some months later after admitting visiting a serving prisoner in another jail. Fortunately, her sexual relationship with this man predated his incarceration and was therefore not a potentially criminal matter, but her position was untenable as a consequence of her not breaking off the contact which not surprisingly filtered back to prisoners in Lewes. Local POA officials helpfully pointed that out to her and saved the necessity of a messy sacking. Lack of maturity is something that prisoners can and do exploit and this was a classic example. Recruitment policy also means that unless young recruits live with their parents in middle class districts, there is a greatly increased risk of them living cheek by jowl with the offending classes, often people whom they knew at school. It is perfectly logical that the less rent you can afford, the further down market you go. Young prison officers can find themselves alone in the community and surrounded in the workplace. Ethnic minorities can have a similar problem if they cannot escape from an environment where the neighbours do not aspire to work in law enforcement and indeed actively resent it. The salary structure which now caps new prison officer pay at 5k per annum less than colleagues recruited under old terms and conditions will only help to drive down standards towards those of the private sector. I would not argue that low pay is a direct cause of corrupt behaviour, but it is one of a basket of factors that can render individuals vulnerable. Low pay causes resentment, leads to demoralisation and adversely affects professionalism.

Finally I think the decline of deference must be weighed into the mix. The Inspectorate and the Director General both pushed very hard for the end of the traditional practice of addressing male prisoners by surname alone. Adults were to be addressed as 'Mr' and young offenders by fore name or other preferred name. In practice, implementation has been patchy. Equality of address amongst adults and greater informality generally are long term social changes. My generation as children would never have addressed an adult neighbour by Christian name. My neighbour's now teenage boy has used my first name from the day we moved in eight years ago. It is perfectly normal and it doesn't bother me at all. However in the context of a prison informality is a symbol of dumbed down authority and more importantly it also dumbs down offending behaviour. The removal of those natural almost invisible barriers that governed the relationships between the staff and those they incarcerate comes with risk. Distance helps protect staff from financial blandishments and equally it reminds staff that sexual relationships with prisoners are out of bounds. As a policy, it risks losing respect rather than gaining it. I stress it is a generalisation and just one of a cocktail of ingredients that make the professional lives of staff just that bit harder and leave them just that bit more vulnerable. It does surprise me that an organisation that employs so many psychologists has never bothered to consider and examine the potential negative effects of significant social and organisational change on the behaviour of staff.

I am certainly not pretending that all was well back in the mists of time. I actually worked for six years with a prison officer who was convicted of murder after his retirement. He survived to be released but committed suicide shortly after. The trial took place over 20 years ago and the case attracted little publicity outside the home area. Even though he has passed away, I will not name the individual as I have some moral reservations about the newspaper practice of rooting out lifers who have reached open conditions and looking forward to a quiet anonymous release having served their time even though I acknowledge that there is a legitimate public interest. Thus the individual will be recognisable only to those of us who worked with him as colleagues and those who have had closest contact during his sentence as his jailers. What I can say is that this individual was disciplined for taking a discharged young offender into his home. The Police found out and reported the matter to the Governor. He did not have permission and it is inconceivable that it would have been granted. At the time the in-charge Governor was not empowered to deal with serious disciplinary cases and the matter was referred to the Home Secretary. As I recall, he was not suspended. The disciplinary penalty imposed was not dismissal. His long service increment was delayed by 12 months, the equivalent of a stiff fine. The main mitigation was his staunch Christian faith and status as a lay preacher which also saved him from ostracism from colleagues. The incident was swiftly forgotten until many years later, soon after his retirement, he murdered the self-same former prisoner with whom it turned out he had been having a gay relationship. It was a tragic case. A life was needlessly cut short, families destroyed, and what should have been a well-earned comfortable retirement exchanged for a prison cell from which he would emerge only as an old man with no future. Life for former prison officers serving sentences is every bit as uncomfortable as it is for former police officers.

The action of this officer of taking a former prisoner into his own home was not corrupt in itself, but its potential for corruption was significant. Unlike police officers who can retain considerable residual power after being corrupted particularly when it is a group activity, prison officers are at an instant disadvantage and vulnerable to exposure from the minute they cross the line. There is no corporate culture that protects them, although this has not historically applied to other forms of wrongdoing. The risk reward ratio is massively skewed against corrupt prison officers. Indeed they may be the ones paying out, if not in cash in useful information, which is quite simply blackmail. It was drummed into us in training that once you crossed that line there was no way back as prisoners would never permit it. We were told very firmly that the corrupt officer gets up every morning wondering if today is the day that he is thrown to the wolves by the prisoners to whom he is no longer useful and can no longer be bothered to keep their mouths shut. The officer I referred to was probably lucky not to have been revealed as having homosexual leanings whilst still an employee of the service. Like the armed forces it was not tolerated amongst male uniformed staff, although the female service, separate until 1989, had a different culture. The real risk for his colleagues was not his sexuality, but the possibility that he may have been forced to reveal information about home addresses or the peccadilloes of colleagues in relation to the familiar vices of strong drink, slow horses and fast women. All of this information is immensely useful to the criminal classes. For example if you know that a prison officer is single and you know details of his shift pattern, and you also know that he has neither a dog nor a burglar alarm in his home then his property becomes a prime target for an offender who acquires this information. In a prison situation, a compromised officer may reveal details of impending cell searches thus allowing favoured forms of contraband such as drugs or mobile phones to be moved. If the contraband includes weapons, there is the obvious potential for serious injury to colleagues. Facilitating escapes by leaving potential escape equipment insecure or simply leaving gates unlocked is now more difficult as better procedural security means that individuals at fault, (and usually it is simple negligence) can be identified and disciplined. Nevertheless before we got better at procedural security in the mid-1990s there were instances of compromised teachers driving or attempting to drive prisoners out through the front gate.

As motives I understand greed and arrogance. They are unpleasant characteristics found in people of all walks of life. It is almost a pre-requisite for investment banking. However I struggle to understand sexual involvement with prisoners. During my short stint at Wakefield, prisoners on my wing included a life sentence prisoner who had been having a sexual relationship with a long serving female officer at Liverpool and two convicted rapists who had been serviced on a regular basis by a female officer at HMP Woodhill before they were transferred. This happened only a few months before I moved to that particular establishment. I accept that unless you are Ann Widdecombe or the Pope unwise liaisons are part of most people's sexual history at some point in their lives, but I cannot for the life of me grasp how any woman let alone someone who claims to be a professional can seriously enter a cell alone and have sex with a convicted rapist. Yet this was happening when the prison was in patrol state, i.e. all prisoners behind their doors and just wing patrols on duty to answer bells and deal with emergencies, only the most extreme of which would justify opening a cell alone, and only then after radioing for assistance. Secondly as the majority of prisoners are drug abusers often with very colourful sexual back catalogues, the risk of sexually transmitted diseases, most notably HIV, is particularly heightened. A prisoner's medical history is confidential to medical staff. Unless they choose to tell their landing officer they are HIV positive, an unlikely event, those staff working on the wings with prisoners will have no knowledge of the state of a prisoner's sexual health. To engage in sexual relations with a prisoner is career suicide. To engage in unprotected sexual activity with prisoners is pure madness. I can think of only one venue more squalid than a graffiti ridden cell on a mattress that hundreds of prisoners may have slept on and that is a squat. In fact that may be unfair to squatters who I am sure do not have sexual intercourse in a toilet. It leaves me truly baffled and yet it happens.

Of course if the prisoner is in open conditions it is easier. The privilege of town visits is available. In Bognor Regis hotels rent rooms by the afternoon. If the prisoner or staff member lives locally, it cuts out the middleman, yet some sexually incontinent staff will even compromise the security of their home address. Those who believe they are shrewder and cleverer than those who screw on the premises wait until the object of desire is transferred to open conditions, or until he is released on licence. One former officer I know did effectively get away with it. Her liaisons were taking place when the prisoner was on temporary release from open conditions. Her good fortune was that unknown to the Governor, she had been the mistress of the person commissioned to carry out the disciplinary investigation. It goes without saying that the investigation, which took place before I arrived at that establishment, was a whitewash and she escaped with a warning. My own view is that the investigating officer knew full well that the illicit affair had gone to fourth base, but chose to leave that bit out and save her neck. It is a speculation but had she been dismissed she would have nothing to lose by letting his wife into their secret. This is a classic example of sexual corruption. It would have been much better had the matter been prosecuted in the courts rather than referred back to the Governor. Leaving matters to the disciplinary process avoids public reputational damage, but as in this case there can be unexpected outcomes. As it turned out the female officer in question did eventually resign as nothing could quell the suspicion of colleagues that she was culpable of far more than minor professional misjudgement. To finish the story she had the nerve some months later to seek reinstatement. I can claim some of the credit along with the Head of Security, for presenting irrefutable evidence to the Governor that reinstatement was a very bad idea.

The prison service is not the direct employer of a substantial number of staff employed to work in prisons. Other branches of the public sector such as Further Education Colleges, Libraries and Probation have long seconded staff to penal establishments. Until cross sex postings came in, unless the prisoner had a plum job making tea for admin staff, (no longer permitted) this would be the only opportunity to see the female form in the flesh. Of course the same also applied to prison officers, which is why so many found every excuse in the book to visit administration and glimpse a well-turned ankle. The advent of female prison officers on the landings simply added to the lust potential, despite the unflattering uniforms. More recently the NHS has established itself as a significant employer in prisons as a consequence of NHS trusts taking over prison healthcare. Nurses are predominantly female as are their managers. It does not help when the Head of Healthcare is the one engaged in an affair with a prisoner on licence in the community as happened at one of my former establishments. In cases like this where the prisoner has completed the custodial part of the sentence and can only be sent back to prison for re-offending or otherwise being in breach of his licence conditions, it is extremely unlikely that the criteria for a prosecution for misconduct in public office are likely to be met. One would expect it to be different if the ex-prisoner had resumed re-offending and this was being concealed. At the time this matter came to light, there was no evidence of a return to crime. In these situations, the Governor has no disciplinary power, which is a matter for the contractor, in this case the NHS, but does have the power to exclude from the establishment. It baffles me how she hoped to get away with it as the local probation service supervising the released prisoner rapidly became aware of the affair, not least because he had moved in with her! Unprofessional behaviour of this nature has professional consequences and events duly took their course. The man concerned re-offended in the fullness of time. How much of her money along with her dignity, status and trust he finally stripped away from her I do not know. What I do know is that even the most apparently successful people can be lonely, suffer from low self-esteem and therefore be readily susceptible to flattery, and as a consequence become vulnerable to the blandishments of alcoholic, gold digging scumbags for whom the bedroom is merely a short cut to getting at more material assets. I know of no anti-corruption programme that can detect the potential for this kind of outcome.

Sexual relationships that cross professional lines are not just confined to the lower grades in the prison service or to contracted professionals for whom the wiles of offenders are a closed book. Sadly it sometimes happens amongst governor grades and above. The best-known recent case concluded with Russell Thorne, an acting junior governor grade at Downview women's prison, but nevertheless one with the power to approve temporary release according to the prosecution, being sentenced to five years imprisonment for misconduct in public office in the summer of 2011. Thorne was suspended along with two prison officer colleagues in January 2010 as police investigated alleged sexual activity with female prisoners going back to 2006. All pleaded not guilty. The lurid allegations included repeated sexual intercourse, threesomes including Thorne and two women, and lesbian sex shows put on by vulnerable prisoners for the entertainment of the defendants. The prosecutor said that if matters were not so serious it would sound like a 'Carry On' farce with Sid James and Barbara Windsor playing the lead roles. A second defendant whose partner was a prison officer committed suicide on the first day of the trial by throwing himself from a tower block in Sutton, Surrey, a fact which of necessity was kept from the jury and forbidden to be published until after the trial. A third defendant went through the ordeal of two trials where the jury could not agree verdicts at which point the judge ordered that not guilty verdicts be returned, the prosecution having accepted that a third trial would appear like a witch hunt. I should add that he was acquitted of three of the slew of charges at the first trial. Whether he has been able to resume his career I do not know. I was slightly acquainted with Russell Thorne from my stint at Surrey and Sussex Area Office 2005–07, but can't honestly say that I had formed any sort of view of him. In many respects, this was a brave decision by the prison service to have this case pursued through the criminal courts, as it relied heavily on the word of convicted criminals who had to face the ordeal of giving evidence before a jury under fierce questioning by defence counsel. In the end, there was only the one conviction, but there will have been quiet satisfaction at nailing the main man.

The most recent development in terms of corruption has been the use of the common law offence of misconduct in public office against staff alleged to have sold information to the media. This has come in the wake of the Leveson inquiry into media standards which followed the revelations about phone hacking by the now defunct News of the World. The most high profile case occurred in February 2013 in respect of the Metropolitan Police where Detective Chief Inspector April Casburn was convicted of misconduct in public office and sentenced to 15 months imprisonment after allegedly asking a newspaper for money in return for information that would embarrass her employers. It was a strange case not least because she was convicted on the uncorroborated word of a journalist. As regards the prison service an Officer Support Grade, (OSG, the grade below prison officer that replaced the prison auxiliary 20 years ago) Richard Trunkfield, from HMP Woodhill was convicted of misconduct in public office in March 2013 and sentenced to 16 months imprisonment after being paid £3,500 by a newspaper for information regarding Jon Venables, one of the murderers of James Bulger, whose whereabouts and identity at any given time are protected by a lifelong injunction. This case was more straightforward as Trunkfield pleaded guilty, although taking the matter to court had the effect of admitting that Venables, under whatever name he is known by now, had been at HMP Woodhill. Nevertheless this successful prosecution should act as a significant deterrent. Even if Trunkfield had taken no payment, this would have been a very serious matter as by no stretch of the imagination can this be termed as 'whistleblowing'.

Some establishments have had serious problems with constant leaks to the press of information which is potentially of great interest to readers, but sometimes of dubious morality and legality. In 1994, someone at Wakefield prison decided to let the press know that a paedophile prisoner suffering from terminal cancer was a patient in the local hospital. Lower down the scale were a later generation of revelations from HMP Woodhill. At one point in the late 90s the local paper carried stories on an almost weekly basis about one of Britain's most notorious lifers, Charles Bronson, who it should be added in the spirit of fairness has not killed anyone nor committed any sexual offences. It is his penchant for hostage taking that has added to the legend. The probable source of the stories was a local POA official who was known to have a weekly drink with a local reporter who no doubt got his story via the traditional method of alcohol loosening the tongue. For the most part, the stories were harmless rubbish although whether Bronson shared that view is not known to me. However, HMP Ford where I was Deputy Governor 2001–05 has been a serial sufferer from internally inspired negative publicity. Back in 2002 it was reported to me that a female officer had been identified when visiting a prisoner at an establishment in the East Midlands. A member of staff who was a former colleague had recognised her. It is virtually impossible to keep this kind of thing quiet even if the staff member resigns before a formal investigation can begin. As a governor, I would never have disclosed to the press that an officer had resigned in these circumstances, let alone give out the name, although I readily accept that it is a matter of legitimate public interest. Ford's phantom leaker ensured it reached the newspapers. Whether the individual was paid I do not know. There is an argument that this was 'whistle blowing', and therefore not a criminal matter as long as no money changed hands. However what was utterly despicable was that our leaker gave the press her home address where she and her young children were duly badgered by door stepping journalists. For obvious reasons, giving out the home address of colleague is a sacking offence. Mercifully colleagues at Lewes had higher moral standards when the very similar case referred to earlier occurred in 2009.

Other leaks included a story sold on to national newspaper by a local journalist regarding a family day at HMP Ford in 2004 where there was a steel band playing and a buffet served to prisoners and their families which reflected the ethnic mix. The aim of the day was to get fathers involved with their children and strengthen family ties. The involvement of fathers not merely impacts positively on re-offending by those fathers, but also impacts positively on sons for whom the presence of a father who has abandoned crime and accepted his responsibilities is a key barrier to preventing juvenile offending. The Area Manager was supportive, not the experience of every Governor subject to a media firestorm, and fortunately, I was not misquoted when the story was sold on to the *Daily Express*, it falling to me to deal with as the Governor, Fiona Radford, was on leave when the story broke. It helped also that the local MP at the time, Howard Flight, was not ill-disposed to the establishment. Fiona Radford would have a harder time from the press over absconding foreign national prisoners, the Area Manager again being supportive, but at least she was spared the intrusions into her personal life that were inflicted on her successor subsequent to the New Year's Day riot in the early hours of 1 January 2011. There can be no legitimate interest in the sexuality of a public official unless it is linked to unlawful or corrupt activity. Where sexual orientation was of legitimate public interest was when serious allegations of lesbian bullying were made at HMP Pentonville some years ago. There can be no argument about the right to know in that situation. My successor as Deputy Governor also found himself pilloried in the press, not so much for an ongoing disciplinary matter which resulted in his dismissal, but for his alleged support for the release of Learco Chindamo, convicted as a 15-year-old boy of the murder of Headmaster, Philip Lawrence. I have no idea of his professional view on Chindamo's release, what I do know is this was a calculated smear which had to come from an insider aimed at his integrity to which the affected individual had no right of reply.

One of the most sensational leaks from HMP Ford occurred in December 2005, less than a year after I had moved on, regarding a life sentence prisoner sentenced as long ago as 1973 for an utterly horrendous offence involving the murder of three young children when babysitting at their West Midlands home. The *Daily Mirror* had published an article about this individual in 1996 but since then he had been under the radar and worked his way back to open conditions. *The Sun* newspaper published an exclusive splashing his long forgotten offences (apart from where they took place) across its pages rendering his situation in open conditions untenable. At the time the offender was on the verge of release to a hostel in Liverpool. He was returned to closed conditions and eventually released on life licence in 2019. Indeed between 2009 and May 2013 it would have been unlawful to publish his name as he launched an unsuccessful legal action to be returned to open conditions. I don't propose to do so now even though his anonymity was removed in 2013 by order of a judge.

He would no doubt argue that the press is preventing his release. Newspapers would argue that the public has a legitimate right to know when a notorious malefactor is close to release or being put in an open establishment from where he would have privileges that would include going out into the local community. This situation can be fairly compared to examples of violent schizophrenic patients released from mental health establishments on the basis that they are either cured or that their condition has been stabilised by medication, assuming they take it, who then go on to commit horrendous offences. No one has the right to know because of medical confidentiality and no one is held accountable. My own considered view is that the right to know should normally trump the right to anonymity in a situation where there is a legitimate public anxiety, but at the same time I accept there have to be exceptions if only to prevent vigilante justice . However I am absolutely clear that I don't believe that the Ford leaker acted out of altruism. The individual or individuals who have drip fed the press down the years do it because they get a kick out of it and continue to do it because he, she or they continue to get away with it. The only motive is their own perverse amusement.

*****

When I joined the prison service in 1984, a very different staff disciplinary system existed. The Governor had no power to dismiss and serious cases were referred to the Home Secretary, although whether he ever dealt with them personally is another matter. Prison officers also did not have access to employment tribunals, the court of appeal against dismissal or other serious penalty being the recently abolished Civil Service Appeals Tribunal (CSAB) whose findings were binding on all sides. However on the other side of the coin, like the police, the standard of proof for disciplinary matters was the criminal standard of beyond reasonable doubt. Minor matters were dealt with by the Governor who could caution, admonish or give a formal written warning. Management grades from first line supervisors upwards could formally charge a junior colleague with a minor disciplinary offence to be heard locally by the Governor. This was sometimes referred to as getting a docket or more familiarly a 'half sheet' as the size of the paper was A5, which is half of the normal A4 size of a page. Veteran officers told me that there was a time these were issued frequently and for matters as trivial as not wearing a cap. By my time, they were issued much more rarely and certainly not for drunkenness which appeared to be condoned. At Werrington I can recall only one being issued and that was for insubordination. I only ever issued one myself to an officer who had failed to carry out a lawful instruction. I think it was in 1993 or 1994 when the system changed. The 'half sheet' was abolished, the Governor was given powers to dismiss or demote, and the standard of proof reduced to the civil standard of the balance of probabilities with the rider that Halsbury's law applied in that the more severe the potential penalty the greater the probability required although short of the criminal standard. On the plus side, staff gained access to employment tribunals as well as access to the CSAB which was retained until abolished by the Coalition government. The job of the CSAB was to review the process for fairness, not re-hear the case. Before the CSAB got involved the appeal against a Governor's finding was usually to the Area Manager, now renamed Deputy Director of Custody, or another senior civil servant. This step has caused some issues as some of these individuals have done little to diminish the view that they are there simply to rubber stamp the original decision. In fairness, others have acted with great integrity particularly when there must have been a degree of pressure further up the food chain. However, the CSAB was genuinely independent and as such was trusted by the Prison Governors Association even if we didn't get the decision on the day.

Possibly the worst example of blinkered partisanship in a disciplinary case in this instance liberally laced with political correctness, occurred in the case of Colin Rose, a prison officer at HMP Blundeston who was dismissed for an alleged racist remark in

2003. This case made me ashamed to be a Prison Governor, as by implication as a cadre we were associated with the decision to hound Colin Rose out of the service. The incident itself was trivial. Officer Rose slammed his keys down the key shute and made a comment about Osama Bin Laden. Within sight but not hearing were female Muslim visitors waiting to visit a prisoner. Other than gate staff the only person who heard the remark was the Deputy Governor. Instead of issuing a swift verbal reprimand for a minor piece of unprofessional behaviour, the Deputy Governor chose to report the matter to his immediate superior, the Governor, a man named Jerry Knight who later decamped to the private sector. Mr Rose was dismissed and his appeal failed. At the subsequent employment tribunal, the Prison Service was absolutely lambasted by the Tribunal judge. Jerry Knight was labelled 'vindictive' and the appeal authority condemned as 'lazy and incompetent'. The Deputy Governor, Andy Rogers, had persisted with the party line at the tribunal and with no sense of irony told the panel he was 'offended' by Mr Rose's remarks. Presumably he had forgotten Bin Laden's role in what forever will be known as '9/11'. The settlement was not disclosed and Mr Rose was reinstated.

After the tribunal, the Director General of the Prison Service, Martin Narey, condemned the tribunal decision in a statement and went on to defend the indefensible on David Frost's Sunday morning programme. Mr Narey truly believed that this case was about fighting racism and in doing so forgot that justice to an individual must always come first. It is scarcely believable that a senior civil servant was permitted to go on television and attack the verdict of an Employment Tribunal, particularly one that the condemned the behaviour of Prison Service managers unequivocally. Moreover, it is totally unacceptable for the head of a law enforcement agency to be seen publicly to dispute the verdict of a duly constituted court of law. This is the sort of behaviour one would expect in Zimbabwe. There has to be respect for due process and that sometimes involves gritting one's teeth and swallowing the unpalatable rather than attacking the integrity of a system that you may yourself seek to rely on one day. I would hope that Sir Martin would remember the fate of one his predecessors, Derek Lewis, who was the victim of arbitrary, unfair and wrongful dismissal in a case where a minister assumed he had dictatorial powers.

I recall one case in particular where I was forced to swallow the unpalatable and in this case there was a genuine moral dilemma, not one manufactured from a desire to burnish impeccable anti-racist credentials in public. This particular case was one of ongoing sexual harassment, and one in which others would come forward. Yet my own Governor not only refused to suspend the individual but also refused to place the staff member on detached duty where he would have no contact with the complainant. Conduct and Performance section in HQ were appalled. As a decision it stank. I commissioned the investigation and in due course it reached a disciplinary hearing. By the time this took place, I was Acting Governor, but not having passed the Assessment Centre was not qualified to conduct the disciplinary hearing so it was necessary for me to obtain the services of a substantive colleague in the area. To cut a long story short a known sex pest was not sacked and escaped with a final written warning. How did this happen? The likeliest explanation (as with the non-suspension) is freemasonry, although it is impossible to prove. It may be that the Hearing Authority was genuinely sympathetic to the mitigation. However the fact that it would wreck his marriage if his wife found out is not most people's idea of mitigating circumstances. It could simply be a bad decision, but nothing will ever dispel the suspicion that other forces were at work. Some years later a source gave me a list of freemasons still working at HMP Ford. I also know from another good source that his national union representative told him in no uncertain manner that he had got a real result.

There is no happy ending to this story. The principal complainant in due course spent so much time on sick leave that the service was forced to dismiss her on the grounds of medical inefficiency. Emotionally and mentally she was wrecked by the outcome and was simply unable to accept that her tormentor was still at work. This case did not ultimately become as notorious as that of Senior Officer Carol Lingard, who was bullied and harassed at Wakefield at around the same time and won record damages after being forced out of the service, but it had all the potential. Of course not everyone can face the stress of prolonged litigation. I still have difficulty reconciling the moral dilemmas this case causes me but I hold firmly to the view that it is not possible for a judicial or quasi-judicial system that allows what are effectively prosecution appeals, to operate with integrity. As I have argued vigorously that it is not right for Martin Narey to play God, then equally it would not have been right for me to have attempted to have the matter re-opened on suspicions I had no ability to substantiate. The Prison Service claims to be tough on sexual harassment, but this is not the only example of selectivity at work. Some years ago a very senior gay sex pest was paid off, a decision made at board level, and more recently an in-charge Governor was allowed to resign prior to a disciplinary hearing rather than be dismissed in the face of what I am told was overwhelming evidence.

Returning to race and there is no subject more sensitive in the public sector, one of our own members was on the receiving end of a decision that did not attract any publicity, but still fell under the heading of political correctness gone mad. It was not a case in which I acted as a union representative. It involved a governor grade working as a Deputy Controller in a private prison and concerned an adjudication in which a black prisoner was facing a disciplinary hearing for using the word 'nigger'. At the time private sector managers were not permitted to carry out adjudications, so these were always carried out by the Controller or Deputy Controller. I had dealt with a similar case myself at Dover where two black prisoners were placed on a disciplinary charge for referring to each other as 'niggers'. I found them guilty and they readily admitted when asked that they would not accept the use of the word by white people even if they had difficulty grasping their own hypocrisy. Only recently I discovered that for some unaccountable reason it is considered acceptable in some black circles for the word to be used amongst black people and is seen as reclaiming the word from whites, when a public row broke out over a black comedian using the word repeatedly at the annual dinner of the Professional Footballers Association. The union's former Chairman, Clark Carlisle, who himself is black, does not share this view and was thoroughly appalled. I agree with Mr Carlisle and with our former colleague who is also now retired. What was her crime? She asked the prisoner how he would feel if she called him a nigger, and someone (not the prisoner) reported it as a racist incident. As Richard Littlejohn would say in his twice-weekly column in the *Daily Mail* regarding what happened next, you couldn't make it up. Not only did an investigation recommend a disciplinary hearing, the senior manager who carried out the disciplinary hearing demoted her two grades, although the penalty was never carried out. Has he never heard of context? The whole point was to make the point that no one whatever the colour of their skin has the right to call someone a nigger. If it is OK for black people to direct the word at other black people, how can you hope to get across the message to would be white racists that they cannot use that word to or about members of the black community?

Most cases in which members of staff use the kind of language that may be perceived to be racist are dealt with proportionately. There is a significant difference between being insensitive or stuck in a time warp about what is acceptable in conversation and being a dyed in the wool racist. Bad jokes and banter that staff may have not realised are hurtful are best dealt with by advice and guidance, and on occasions where it is merited the 'fast track' disciplinary procedure whereby staff are given the opportunity to admit misconduct at an early stage and in return receive a maximum penalty of a final written warning. Looking back to when I was a prison officer myself I can recall a colleague who would say with a glint in his eye, 'come here, brown boy' and get the response 'what you want, honky?' We no longer consider that acceptable, but the right approach now would be advice and guidance as this officer was known by all not to be a racist. It is a matter of education. On the other hand, I can recall another officer going back to a similar time, mid-80s, calling a prisoner a 'horrible coffee coloured convict'. There was no context and no mitigation. This was a crude racist remark which in those days prisoners were forced to tolerate and these days would quite rightly merit the sack. As I recall, the prisoner did not wish to complain nor did he wish anyone to complain on his behalf, telling me that there was no point which in those days was true. However for some years now since Martin Narey's time as Director General, managers who did not report such an incident or if of the appropriate grade failed to commission an investigation would potentially face disciplinary action and/or adverse comments on their annual appraisal. We have come a long way since the time when casual racism was seen as the black man's burden, indeed to a point where nothing makes our leaders twitch more than race. Sadly with the appalling revelations about police conduct in the Stephen Lawrence case common sense is unlikely to break out soon. The risk is that that more disproportionate and heavy handed treatment will be visited on unsuspecting individuals who suddenly find that they are, like Colin Rose, to be made an example of not on the merits of the case, but so that the service and ambitious individuals within it can demonstrate their anti-racist credentials. There is nothing like a bit of white guilt.

However, that aside my experience is that colleagues find trouble rather than trouble find them. I represented one individual faced with a gross misconduct charge for allegedly doctoring an E-mail from a senior colleague and then sending it to other members of her team. Unfortunately, she had given two colleagues her password. That was only her first mistake. Her second mistake was to attend the interview with the investigator without the support of a colleague, something to which she was legally entitled. Without realising the significance and seriousness she basically accepted that she must have sent it. Although it is not gross misconduct to share your password it is extremely unwise. It is gross misconduct to tamper with or doctor E-mails. I can remember trying very hard at the hearing to suggest that the investigator had failed in his job by not exploring the alternative explanations, i.e. that one of those colleagues, one of whom could have had a motive, was just as likely to be responsible and therefore the standard of proof was not met. It was like pissing in the wind as the senior civil servant hearing the case kept pointing out that she had admitted the offence. As a union rep, you do your best to maintain morale, but you also have to be realistic. It came as both a relief and a surprise when she escaped with a final written warning. There was not a happy ending as one previously very committed but now thoroughly disillusioned prison governor decided to resign and left the service a few weeks before me. For the record, I think the individual referred to above, the one with a motive, tampered with the E-mail in question. Although it would never be admitted I also think that deep down that was the view of the senior civil servant carrying out the disciplinary hearing, but of course there was no evidence produced and it would be difficult to reject the work of a Senior Investigating Officer (SIO) where an admission, even on the basis of 'well, I suppose it has to be me' has been procured. Normally in these situations a member of staff would be sacked as no ifs no buts, it is an irreparable breach of trust. Her survival was in my view a political (with a small 'p') decision.

One long serving governor, however, probably owes his career to politics with a large P. On 5 May 2000, Eoin McLennan-Murray who would be my boss at HMP Lewes 2007–09 and my colleague on the PGA NEC when he was elected President in 2009, was removed from his first in-charge post at HMP Blantyre House, a resettlement prison deep in rural Kent. Later that day which was a Friday and continuing into Saturday, the prison was locked down and subjected to an in depth search, on the orders of the Area Manager, Tom Murtagh, acting with the full knowledge and authority of Director General, Martin Narey. Only those who needed to know were in the know, which included my Governor, (I was then at nearby Dover) but quite rightly did not include me. In brief, the senior civil servants believed that the governor was running a regime that was not merely too liberal, but one that was in contravention of prison service orders and instructions given by Mr Murtagh, thus raising disciplinary issues which would be investigated, as well as questions about judgement. He believed that key staff had been conditioned and that widespread and co-ordinated criminality was being conducted by influential and well-connected prisoners who had no intention of going straight and who should not have been trusted in that environment. Indeed Martin Narey felt so strongly about the affair that he penned the forward to Tom Murtagh's book, *The Blantyre House Prisons Affair: Lessons from a Modern Day Witch Hunt*. On the dust jacket Martin Narey is quoted as follows: "Tom Murtagh's actions in managing Blantyre House not only preserved all that was good about the Blantyre regime... but may also have saved my then job and perhaps that of the Home Secretary." The book was published in 2007, more than four years after Mr Murtagh retired, and two years after Martin Narey left for the voluntary sector, freed from the constraints of being a senior civil servant. On the other side was Eoin McLennan-Murray, an independent thinker and possessor of one of the most powerful intellects I have ever encountered and also a passionate penal reformer with a powerful belief that not only can bad people change, but also that they should be given the opportunity and the measure of trust that goes with it. In a different context, the clash came only eight years after the Area Manager grade was created and was now fully professionalised in that incumbents were all former prison governors rather than the mix of those promoted from the governor ranks and generalist civil servants from other departments of state. This new cadre took seriously their responsibility to line manage governors and therefore challenge the powers once enjoyed by the latter. Although Tom Murtagh was significantly the older man, it was he who represented the new breed of hardnosed demanding bosses who focussed on performance and reined in the mavericks. As a consequence of the raid, some contraband (although it has to be said significantly less than expected) was found and Eoin McLennan-Murray faced disciplinary action.

How then did he survive? Well he would find that far being isolated he had powerful friends. The inspectorate and the powerful Home Affairs Select Committee (HAC) in the House of Commons were his principal allies. Indeed at times it seemed like Tom Murtagh's career was under greater threat when the HAC published its report. He retired in 2002, his anger still evident in his book. Eoin McLennan-Murray got his career back on track and was promoted to in-charge Governor at HMP Lewes in 2003. He retired from the service in 2015 and it remains to be seen if Tom Murtagh is allowed the last word. Martin Narey's career also prospered and he was upgraded to Second Permanent Secretary. He departed to take over as Chief Executive of Dr Barnados in 2005.

Less lucky was Stephen Honey, Deputy Governor of Coldingley who found himself not just at the centre of a media firestorm when a prisoner he had temporarily released was murdered, but also jobless. On appeal, he was reinstated at a lower grade. I believe that the reinstatement was a principled call by Colin McConnell that few other senior civil servants would have made. Until the appeal hearing it seemed that no one cared about the mental anguish Stephen had gone through, not just about how he was going to pay his mortgage, but about the guilt anyone would feel, about a decision taken in good faith but outside the rules, that set off a chain of events which led to a man's brutal murder. When it comes to interpreting rules creatively, let he who is without sin cast the first stone.

In 2009, I found myself involved in a disciplinary case as a representative where politics with a very large P threatened to intrude and not to the benefit of our members. This was the notorious case where it was alleged that governor grades up to an including the in-charge Governors at two establishments, HMP Wandsworth and HMP Pentonville colluded to ensure that vulnerable and self-harming prisoners who might adversely affect the inspection at Wandsworth were transferred to Pentonville in exchange for some of their difficult customers. It is a sad state of affairs when the pressure of inspections, audits and performance league tables burrows so far into the psyche of establishment senior management teams, that something as ill-judged as this can actually happen. This is the toxic legacy of the managerialist culture. The transfers took place in May 2009, and the firestorm broke in October the same year when Anne Owers, the Chief Inspector of Prisons, went public with the allegations, after one of the prisoners who had been transferred wrote to the Chief Inspector. The Secretary of State, Jack Straw, instructed Phil Wheatley, then Director General of the Service, to commission an internal inquiry. The investigating officer was Peter Dawson, Governor of High Down, who also held senior civil servant status, which allowed him to investigate other in-charge Governors. The Disciplinary Hearing was conducted by Michael Spurr, then Phil Wheatley's number two and eventual successor. The outcomes are a matter of public record. The instigator, a Functional Head at Wandsworth who was third in charge and a residential governor grade at Pentonville who agreed the deal both received final written warnings after admitting gross misconduct. As their names were not in the public domain, I will preserve their anonymity. The two in-charge Governors, Ian Mulholland at Wandsworth and Nick Leader at Pentonville, whose names were in the public domain were cleared of the disciplinary charges against them, i.e. that their conduct was disreputable in that they knew about and colluded with junior colleagues who arranged the exchanges. The Deputy Governor of Wandsworth, whose name was also not in the public domain, was given advice and guidance, a non-disciplinary finding. By the time the storm broke, Mr Mulholland had been promoted to senior civil service status within the organisation. Mr Leader had been moved to the even more challenging job of Governor of HMP Whitemoor, a top security establishment. The story was front-page news in all the main newspapers but the disciplinary findings attracted fairly muted criticism from a strangely incurious press.

My role was to represent the Wandsworth third in charge, who took full responsibility for the idea to exchange prisoners. I am sure that his honesty and openness had more impact on him retaining his job (he retired shortly after) than the quality of my advocacy. However when I eventually had time to reflect on events I came to the conclusion that the outcomes were actually a very clever piece of politics. Having resisted the call for a public inquiry, the last thing the minister needed was a messy and very high profile employment tribunal involving dismissed staff. Indeed it would have resembled ferrets fighting in a sack. At the time, October 2009, a General Election was only a few months away. Although a tribunal would probably not have sat before the election, its findings were potentially explosive for the Minister concerned, Jack Straw, particularly if the Labour Party remained in office, either as a minority government or in a coalition. Even had the election been lost, which as we know is what happened, there would have been reputational damage. For those who don't quite follow disciplinary proceedings are held behind closed doors away from the prying eyes of the press, and unless someone leaks there is much potentially juicy material that stays secret, which should not happen as investigation reports are confidential documents. Unauthorised leaks although much loved by the press can affect the integrity of the proceedings and damage individuals as well as having political 'fall out'. For this reason, the PGA did not leak and neither did the NOMS Board. It is a game with rules understood by both sides and this author, although not precluded from expressing an opinion on the outcomes, will stick to those rules. However in employment tribunals the press and public are admitted and evidence is given and challenged in open court. Peter Dawson's report would have become a public document with the findings, the recommendations for disciplinary hearings, and potentially incriminating E-mail trails being picked over in court. It would have been dynamite. For this reason, the two more junior grades could not be sacrificed, which is what one might have expected given their admitted culpability. The two most senior staff who as I should reiterate were cleared of any misconduct, were very highly regarded and seen as prisons board material, although Nick Leader has since departed for the private sector, angry at having his integrity impugned. Ian Mulholland retains the confidence of HMPPS and continues to operate in a high-profile senior role. The Deputy Governor of Wandsworth was one of the HR Directorate's 'Golden Generation' of mainly London based, mainly female fast tracked early thirty some-things earmarked at that time for in-charge roles in the not too distant future. Notwithstanding the receipt of 'Advice and Guidance' this individual was in fact promoted to an in-charge role two pay grades higher barely three months later. At the very least it begs the question as to how someone could be suitable for promotion to a higher grade so soon after receiving advice and guidance regarding the performance of their duties in a lower one. One thing is certain; the secretive modus operandi of our senior civil service masters will never willingly change.

Almost as a footnote HMP Blantyre House was not so lucky. It closed in January 2016, ostensibly for refurbishment. Although the MOJ denied it was a permanent closure planning permission was sought in 2017 to use the establishment as a staff-training centre for the next five years. So much for the commitment to resettlement.

One thing is certain; the modus operandi of our senior civil service masters will never change.

Chapter 11
Postscript: A Prison System in Crisis

Since I completed the original manuscript in the summer of 2013, the prison system in England and Wales has lurched into a crisis brought about principally by austerity, by a government that appears not to give a damn about conditions in Britain's prisons, not that the other main political parties appear any more interested. It is, therefore, necessary to add a significant postscript so that chapters two and three are seen in the context of my time in the service, a time since overtaken by events.

The reader will be very well aware of the low opinion I have of some of the service's leaders who have done little to alleviate the bureaucratic burdens imposed on hard pressed prison governors, but this crisis was caused by a deliberate decision to impose austerity on a service unable to cope with the consequences. Let me be clear, I am not one of these people whose knee-jerk response is to call for more spending without first considering the means to pay for it. The period of austerity inaugurated by the banking crisis had already started to bite by the time I retired in 2010. I was very glad to have old terms and conditions which allowed me to take my pension at any time between my fifty-fifth and sixtieth birthdays. A voluntary redundancy process began the following year and it was soon oversubscribed, a ready indicator of the discontent that already existed.

Other public services and their spokesmen have also beat the drum for more resources. The police have not been exempt from drastic cuts, but those cuts have come against a backdrop of falling crime, at least until the most recent figures, where the chickens may have finally come home to roost. Cuts to the Fire Service have come against a backdrop of a much-reduced number of fires. Cuts to the Armed Services have come against a backdrop of British withdrawal from Afghanistan and Iraq, and the success of the peace process in Northern Ireland. All those cuts had their critics who rightly pointed out the risks, but they came in services where on the face of it, there was some wiggle room. Even hard-pressed councils have more room to manoeuvre as they have the ability to raise revenue. The NHS can charge foreign nationals for some of its services, if it could be bothered, but sadly the Prison Service cannot bill other EU countries for the cost of keeping their citizens in custody. According to figures published in April 2016, there are around 4,600 EU nationals residing in our prisons at a cost of £150 million per annum, plus another 6,000 foreign nationals from all over the world, many from countries which are recipients of overseas aid from the UK, yet between 2010 and 2015 over the lifetime of the Coalition government, the annual prisons' budget was slashed by a quarter, £900 million in round figures.

This brings me to the fundamental point. You can have deep cuts in the prisons' budget any time you like, but at the same time you need to cut the number of people we incarcerate. To do that you need to both drastically reduce the use of short prison terms for petty offences and reverse the trend of longer prison sentences at the heavy end of the market. If governments wish to continue with their addiction to imprisonment, they must be prepared to pay for it and squeeze taxpayers accordingly, at which point they may be rather less keen. According to the prison population figures for 21 July 2017, there were 86,168 people in custody in England and Wales, 1,016 more than the corresponding week twelve months earlier. Back in July 2010, when I actually worked at Population Management, there were 85,200 people in custody. This is the nub of the problem. The prison population has actually risen since 2010, but the number of staff and governor grades available to look after them has been slashed by 30%. The population problem has been around for a long time, ever since hard-line Home Secretary, Michael Howard, declared that 'prison works'. I have described in chapter two the extent to which sentence lengths have increased. I add another statistic: since 2005, the number of sentences of ten years imprisonment or more imposed by the courts has tripled. Mr Howard's Labour and Coalition successors remained in thrall to the same mantra. Any hint of a deliberate policy to significantly reduce the prison population is immediately challenged by Tory backbencher Philip Davies and the Daily Mail. It almost seems at times that one daily newspaper and one otherwise obscure backbencher have the right of veto over penal policy. It's hard to believe that when Ken Clarke handed over stewardship of the Home Office to Michael Howard in May 1993, the prison population was little more than half of the current figure. I don't recall the streets being significantly less safe as a consequence.

The outcome is that we have a prison system that shames us as a nation. Two thirds of our prisons are overcrowded in that the operational capacity exceeds the certified normal accommodation. Translated into the prisoner experience around 20,000 prisoners share a cell that was designed for one person. Some cells are so small that there is no room for a second chair. One prisoner must either sit on his bed or sit on the toilet. There is obviously no privacy when using the toilet. In establishments where there is no facility or insufficient staff to supervise dining out of cell, prisoners are forced to take their meal in the same room as the toilet. Overcrowding means competition for scarce facilities. Assuming prisoners are actually unlocked, the queue for the phone is longer, the queue for the showers is longer, the queue for the pool table is longer, the waiting lists for classes and offending behaviour programmes are longer, there are less opportunities to use the gymnasium and library. These are treatable symptoms of an impoverished regime. Prisons are emphatically not holiday camps.

Most of all prisoners are denied access to staff. Individual staff may be disliked by prisoners, but there is no substitute for prisoners seeing the same old faces of the staff who know them. It's called continuity and it works. A cohesive team of staff who know their prisoners makes for a generally orderly environment. We used to call it dynamic security. It is vital that there is enough staff to watch, listen and make relationships.

Under the whip of ministerial discipline in 2013 NOMS, as it was still then called, implemented new staffing levels for governor grades and uniformed staff under the title, 'Fair and Sustainable'. Unfair and unsustainable would be more accurate. I have described earlier in the book how prison officer's pay for new joiners was forced down. The effect on recruitment has been disastrous particularly in London and the South East, the two regions where public sector pay lags behind private sector pay. Thus, prisons that have already lost 30% of their staff actually run far below their new authorised staffing level with an obvious impact on the regime. Elsewhere in the country, the prison service is no longer seen as a career by a significant number of new recruits. Instead, it is something that looks good on the curriculum vitae three years down the line. This assumes they stay that long. In areas where employment is buoyant, new recruits can just walk away rather than take the abuse, the squalor and the casual attitude of an uncaring employer. Needless to say, staff sickness levels are way above target and there is insufficient resilience in staff profiles to cope. The result is even more 'bang up' and an even more impoverished regime. It is obvious to any half-wit that the situation is not merely unsustainable but actually in meltdown. It's hard to believe that back in the mid-90s, we had something called the Better Jobs Initiative. Like a number of headquarters initiatives it never really took off, but it did at least demonstrate a desire to invest in staff.

In 2013, Public Sector workers had just emerged from a two-year pay freeze for those at the top of their scale. Indeed, Phil Wheatley attempted to anticipate the freeze shortly before his retirement in 2010 as Director General of NOMS by recommending a zero pay rise for prison staff to the independent pay review body. From 2013 to 2017 pay rises were limited to 1% and staff have also been faced with increases in pension contributions as a consequence of pension reform. For those staff who remain on pre-2013 terms and conditions, government policy has been to freeze their pay until the new recruits catch up. With rises capped at 1%, hell will freeze over first. The Prime Minister may have declared an end to austerity but it was her government that in 2018 overturned the 2.75% pay award from the independent pay review body, substituting a 2% award with the remaining 0.75% given as a non-consolidated payment. Staff will rightly ask whether there is any point having an independent pay review body when modest recommendations that were broadly in line with other pay review bodies can be overturned on a whim.

As I said in Chapter 2, control of prisons by staff and managers has always depended on the acquiescence, if not the active co-operation of the prison population. Over the last four years, that tacit consent has largely been withdrawn, part of the toxic mix that has seen our prisons spiral out of control. The Chief Inspector of Prisons, Peter Clarke, warned ministers privately in February 2017 that not a single young offender establishment or secure training centre, that had been inspected, was safe to hold children and young people. This is a staggering conclusion. Mr Clarke's annual report launched publicly on 18 July 2017 stated, "The current situation is dangerous, counterproductive and will inevitably end in tragedy unless urgent corrective action is taken." Peter Clarke is not a man to shroud wave and it is not difficult to interpret the meaning of his words. Mr Clarke also said that there was no credible plan to break the cycle of violence. I fear it will take an incident of the magnitude of Strangeways or the murder of a prison officer before ministers actually get the message. It needs to be remembered that because prisons are awash with mobile phones, it is actually possible to co-ordinate rioting across the prison estate. If this ever happens, the system will collapse in days, and it may need troops to restore order, a horrendous prospect. The response thus far has been to shuffle the deckchairs on the Titanic.

An MOJ spokesman boasted of creating a new youth custody arm of the service, headed for the first time by its own executive director. The same spokesman boasted of increasing front line prison staff by 20%. This will require money to pay these staff and a dramatic increase in the facilities to train them. The public may not be aware that it takes around a year from the filling in of the application form to get a recruit on to a prison landing. Even if the target of 2,500 recruits proves to be attainable, and the service claims it has recruited 650 in 2017, it is still barely a third of the 7,000 who were granted redundancy. The loss of vital experience remains total. The same MOJ spokesman said that "the safety and welfare of every young person in our custody was their absolute priority". As ever words, not deeds. Young Offender institutions have always been more difficult to manage. The immaturity, impulsiveness and poor decision-making of young offenders is well documented. They lack subtlety in their dealings with authority figures and are more prone to confrontation. Good prison officers make good role models, which only serves to emphasise the importance of the continuity I mentioned earlier. With the exponential growth of the gang culture, young offender centres have realised their potential to become lawless jungles. It has taken government neglect to bring that to pass.

In Chapter 2, I wrote about the progress made in the prison system to make it more humane and more responsive to the needs of prisoners. I wrote about the decency agenda launched by former Director General, Martin Narey, and continued by his successor Phil Wheatley. When he retired in 2010, not every prison in the system would have passed Phil Wheatley's test of being decent enough for a member of your family to be incarcerated in, but the direction of travel was emphatically clear. However, in the last few years, the direction of travel has been firmly backwards. Prisons are now terrifying places with violence and drug abuse endemic. John Attard, PGA National Officer speaking at the Prison Governors Association conference in autumn 2016, told delegates that since 2012 violent assaults on staff had increased by 146%, self-inflicted deaths had doubled, and instances of serious self-harm had risen by 10,000. The trend is still upwards. *The Sun* reported that in a five month period from the beginning of April 2016 to the end of August 2016, there were 2,959 assaults on staff, which equates to around 19 per day, and 8,065 prisoner on prisoner assaults of which 109 were sexual assaults. As far as prisoner on prisoner assaults are concerned, these are only the recorded figures. Since that headline in *The Sun*, after initially complaining it did not comment on leaks, the prison service has been forced to confirm its accuracy. In the financial year 2016-17, there were 7,159 attacks on staff, an enormous 32% increase on the previous year, which rounded up is 20 assaults per day.

The most recent figures were released in October 2018. They make terrifying reading. The total of assaults on staff and prisoners came to 32,559 in the year ending June 2018. That equates to an assault taking place every 16 minutes somewhere in our prison system; 9,485 of those assaults were on staff, another increase of 32% compared to figure for the financial year 2016-17. Serious violence, defined as that which sees staff taken to hospital increased by 19%. The number of prisoners dying in custody was 325, the highest figure ever, and twice that of six years ago. There were 5 homicides and 87 suicides, up from 78 the previous year. The figures speak for themselves and are utterly unacceptable in a civilised society.

In another unfortunate social development, female staff are no longer off limits for gross personal violence. A female officer at Brinsford was brutally assaulted in the autumn of 2016. Neither it seems is the in-charge Governor. In August 2016, the Governor of Wayland prison, Paul Cawkwell, was so badly assaulted that he needed facial reconstruction. I cannot think of a precedent for this incident. Serious assaults on staff are now so commonplace that they struggle even to make a regional news bulletin. When staff protest by refusing to unlock prisoners, as prison officers did at HMP Lindholme in October 2018, the first response of the MOJ is to seek an injunction ordering staff back into the prison. There are very compelling reasons why prison officers are not permitted to strike, but the inability of prison officers to take legal industrial action is ruthlessly exploited by an unsympathetic employer.

In the first edition of this book, the drug, 'spice', a synthetic cannabinoid, barely rated a passing mention. Indeed, it was legal to purchase it in the community until May 2016. Like all un-prescribed narcotics, it has always been prohibited in prison. The system is currently awash with spice. A peer survey by prisoners suggests that the use of spice is triple that reported by the Chief Inspector of Prisons for 2014-15, with around a third of those surveyed having used spice in the last month. Emergency ambulance callouts to prisons increased by 52% between 2011 and 2015. Every trip to hospital takes two officers off the landings and results in regime closures. In a very short period, it has become the drug of choice and its effect on the user is far more dramatic than cannabis or cocaine. The user can be reduced to a zombie like state, sweating and palpitating. It can also make the user horrendously violent, fighting with the strength of several men. In situations like this staff get seriously hurt. Unlike cocaine or cannabis secondary inhalation of fumes by staff causes very considerable harm. The Prison Officers Association reported that in one week in 2017 at HMP Holme House in the north-east of England twenty staff had to go off duty, including twelve in one day because of the effects of inhaling spice. Symptoms included headaches, dizziness, hallucinations, racing heartbeat and anxiety. One officer's partner reported that her spouse was short tempered and aggressive for several days after.

Holme House staff did have one success, a find of 5.6kg of spice, the largest ever package found in a British jail, worth around £200,000. Police are reported to be investigating how spice came to be concealed in containers of coffee, packets of cereal and bars of soap. If the setup is the same in the north-east as it is in the south-east then I may have the answer. Coffee, cereal and soap are available for prisoners to purchase. The traditional system was that prisoner canteen orders were dealt with internally. Operational support grades would go and purchase the goods at a local cash and carry, with the money deducted from prisoner spends accounts in order to pay the invoice. The staff would then bag up the orders and take them to the wings for delivery. The only way to beat that system would be to corrupt the staff involved. Then some bright spark came up with the idea of regional centralising of canteen provision. It would achieve economies of scale and provide work for prisoners. Thus, HMP Ford became a depot and prisoners were given the job of bagging up the orders for delivery. These are then delivered unopened to the recipients in neighbouring closed establishments. They are delivered with the seals intact to prevent recipients from claiming that goods have been stolen in transit. You can almost guess the rest. An open establishment where supervision is minimal, hiding places are numerous, and staffing levels are wafer thin is perfect for exploitation by criminal gangs.

MPs and members of the public often express their profound disbelief that the authorities seem to be able to do very little about the industrial nature of drug smuggling into our prisons. I have covered this issue in detail in Chapter 2, and the conclusion remains unchanged: major investment in staff, drug dogs and technology. You will never have entirely drug free prisons without ending open visits, but you can get a long way on the road. You just need a government with the will, and the willingness to find the money. There is the technology to make mobile phones useless in prisons which would destroy overnight much of the crime organised from behind the bars. Drones present a different problem but actually using staff to patrol the prison grounds would make this method of delivering contraband far more risky. Of course it would help if security equipment that is available, was actually repaired. According to whistle-blower, Kim Lennon, speaking in August 2014, the security cameras in the visits room at HMP Lewes were not working and had not been for some time. My most recent information, June 2017, is that the cameras have still not been repaired because the service will not cover the £16,000 cost. It's small change in terms of the national budget and you would have thought cameras were essential in a Category B establishment. I call it deliberate neglect.

Until the advent of spice the Prison Officers Association concentrated its fire on tobacco smoking and the dangers that posed to its members and has not changed its position that prisons should be smoke free. Nevertheless, prison cells were exempted from the national crackdown on smoking in 2006. I speculated in the first edition of this book that the exemption of prison cells would be challenged again in the fullness of time. After legal challenges to the exemption failed, a 2015 report on second-hand smoke in prisons left the MOJ with little choice but to retrieve the smoking ban from the long grass.

In 2016, a rolling program began in Wales, and just two years later English and Welsh prisons became officially smoke-free when the last two establishments implemented the ban on 30 April 2018. Her Majesty's Prison and Probation Service (HMPPS) has been claiming success for the scheme. The official rather complacent line was that prisoners would accept the ban, something which failed to acknowledge just how deeply rooted tobacco is in British prison culture, where 80% of prisoners smoked. However, an independent report into the smoking ban at HMP Cardiff found a sharp rise in vandalism and violence due to withdrawal symptoms. Channings Wood has had similar problems to Cardiff. A riot at Erlestoke in May 2016 has been linked to the smoking ban as have significant disturbances at Haverigg, Liverpool and Drake Hall women's prison in Staffordshire. A spike in violence at HMP Leicester found the smoking ban to be a salient factor. In December 2016, HMP Birmingham suffered the worst riot in a British prison since Strangeways in 1990, but it still implemented the smoking ban the following July. Predictably, there was a further, less serious disturbance within weeks. These are only examples of outbreaks of disorder. Many smaller incidents do not reach the press. From the vantage point of retirement it's hard to know just how close the prison system came to meltdown as a result of adding the smoking ban to the toxic mix, but experience tells me that the service was much closer to disaster than will ever be publicly admitted.

The health arguments need no rehearsal from me. They are incontrovertible. The timing, however, could hardly have been worse given the temperature in the prison system, and has been very costly in terms of property repairs and staff sick leave taken as assaults rocketed. It has been a pyrrhic victory. I should add that there is a difference between banning and eliminating tobacco, which has always been a currency. It is now part of the illegal black market and is smuggled into prisons in the way as narcotics and mobile phones. A small pouch of tobacco costs between £150 and £200, and a skinny roll up can command up to £10. Consequently, there is an upsurge in prisoner debt and the violence used to extort payment.

Moreover, after initially rejecting the provision of E-cigarettes as a legitimate smoking cessation tool, HMPPS backtracked and made vaping devices available for prisoner purchase. It is tempting to conclude that at least some of the havoc that the prison system endured could have been avoided had vaping been part of the initial strategy. Stable doors and bolting horses come to mind. Giving up smoking is hugely difficult. Expecting people to pack up smoking on a given date with just nicotine patches for company was never going to be the answer. How much was official complacency and how much was ministerial interference and the institutionalised Tory Party contempt for prisoners, we shall never know, unless Michael Spurr writes his memoirs. It is worth noting that the Scottish prison service, which implements its ban in December 2018, already has vaping equipment for sale in prison canteens. Scotland is rather more fortunate in that the Minister works with the Chief Executive rather than around him.

I am concerned that a government that affects to be as tough on 'hate crime' as the Labour opposition is content to treat prisoners as a lesser breed and do nothing to discourage those whose prejudices would disappear overnight if one of their family were to end up in prison. It is important that there are people to speak up for prisoners and to challenge the norm that terms of imprisonment, long and short, are the panacea for tackling criminality. It is always worth remembering that apart from a small number of people serving whole life tariffs, serving prisoners will eventually return to a society that seems happy to mock them. The legal system is long winded, complaints procedures are bureaucratic; thus, it is inevitable that prisoners will articulate their concerns in a violent and destructive fashion if the authorities take them for granted or treat them with contempt. Everyone remembers Strangeways in 1990 but there was a major riot in Hull back in 1976. It is often forgotten that the majority of our prisoners actually return to society very quickly and indeed that is one of the prison system's perennial problems.

Defenders of short terms of imprisonment happily point out that those serving 12 months or less represent no more than 8% of the population, and that those serving six months or less represent just 4%. This is one of the most misleading statistics peddled by any government department in Whitehall. The important figure is the churn. The Prison Reform Trust found that 47% of the 68,000 offenders sentenced to a term of imprisonment in 2016 were sentenced to six months or less. With 50% remission, they will serve no more than thirteen weeks in jail. Those eligible for home detention curfew will serve even less. The system can do nothing with these prisoners other than warehouse them in local prisons or fill up spaces in open prisons. There is no time for any offending behaviour work and often it is as much as staff can do to prevent them from being homeless on release. Invariably, those who had jobs will lose them. It will come as no surprise that the reoffending rate is at its highest amongst those serving the shortest sentences.

As I mentioned earlier in the book, the Prison Governors Association has previously called for the abolition of custodial terms of less than twelve months. There has to be a better way to deal with serial petty offenders. Also clogging up the system are those returned to prison for breaching licence conditions. The law of unintended consequences has reared its head and affected what was a well-meaning reform to the system. In May 2013, the Secretary of State for Justice, Chris Grayling, announced that as part of a reform programme to be rolled out in 2015, that offenders serving 12 months or less who were previously exempt from licence conditions when released at the midpoint of their sentence, would now come under supervision. These are often the very people who lead the most disorderly lives and find themselves recalled to prison.

In a disturbing development, there is evidence emerging that short sentence prisoners on licence are deliberately breaching their licence conditions in order to be recalled to prison and operate as a drug mule, something which can pay handsomely, or alternatively discharge pre-existing debts. Once safely on the wing, the drug packages can be safely recovered from their backsides. Whatever the answer is, it does not lie in using short periods of custody except to deal with those who refuse to pay fines, breach non-custodial penalties, or defy civil court orders. The Government should be seeking to build confidence in community disposals which are proven to be cheaper and more effective in reducing reoffending. There is something very wrong when prisoners tell you that the only place where they can get effective drug treatment, assuming they are serving long enough, is in prison. As a form of punishment, prison is just about the most expensive we could devise at £35,182 per prisoner place per annum in 2015-16. The average community disposal costs less than 10% of that and the reoffending rate is much lower than that of short periods of imprisonment for petty offenders. Drug treatment is much more effective when administered in the community and technological advances make surveillance of offenders in the locality much easier than it was two decades ago. According to the National Audit Office dealing with petty offenders by imprisonment costs the country around £10 billion per year.

At the other end of the spectrum the shocking revelations about the predatory behaviour of former Disc Jockey Jimmy Savile after his death in 2011 have been followed by a moral panic that has brought about a massive spike in elderly men being given lengthy prison sentences as a result of being convicted of historic sex offences.

This development goes much of the way to explaining the huge increase in deaths in custody from natural causes and is another topic that is difficult to discuss without being howled down or trolled online as heat displaces light. The willingness of victims, sadly not all genuine, to come forward, has been assisted by two significant developments in the legal system, plus a greater openness about an evil previously suppressed. In 2002, Parliament abolished the requirement for corroboration of an allegation in English (but not Scottish) law. This is hugely significant where there are no witnesses, no surviving forensic evidence, and the accused is a person of good character. The effect of this change is seen at its most dramatic where there is only one complainant against the accused, as it can boil down simply to who has the best barrister, and a non-legally aided defendant, which is most of them in cases of this nature, may not be able to afford a barrister who specialises in this field of law.

Secondly, the Crown Prosecution Service has significantly lowered the bar for what is considered to be a 50% chance of conviction. Like the 2002 change in the law, it means the cases which would never have been prosecuted 15-20 years ago, now reach the courts. It gives victims a chance of justice that they would never previously had, indeed some defendants actually do the decent thing and plead guilty, but it is also a charter for gold diggers and attention seekers. However, the bar has been set so low that at times it appears that CPS is either blinded by political correctness, or simply dumping the responsibility on a jury rather than risk criticism for dropping a case they cannot hope to prove beyond reasonable doubt. Fortunately, British juries take the burden of proof seriously, but the sheer volume of cases means that wrongful convictions are inevitable in a system that has been totally rebalanced against defendants. We should never forget that it was a similar moral panic that produced the wrongful convictions of The Birmingham Six, The Guildford Four, The Maguire Seven and Judith Ward, in the wake of IRA atrocities in the 1970s.

The explosion in historic allegations being pursued in court has inevitably been felt in the prison system. The number of offenders over the age of sixty was already increasing exponentially before the Savile scandal broke in 2011. Between 2004 and 2014 the number of over 60s in jail in England and Wales increased by 130%. At the time of writing, there are over 4,000 elderly offenders in custody. Compare this to just 442 in 1992. Some 100 offenders are over the age of 80. In December 2016, a 101-year-old man received a staggering thirteen-year sentence, effectively a death sentence, for historic sex offences, becoming the first centenarian ever given a custodial sentence. As has been said, the trend was upwards before the Savile scandal broke. It is not just about more prosecutions, but also very much about significantly more severe sentencing, sparked not by the judiciary, but by government guidelines to the courts which have encouraged longer prison terms. One example will suffice. In 2000, former professional footballer, 44-year-old Graham Rix, received a twelve-month custodial sentence for unlawful sexual intercourse with a 15-year-old girl, pretty much the standard penalty for the offence at the time. Fast forward to 2016, 28-year-old footballer, Adam Johnson, received a six year sentence for the sexual grooming and sexual assault (until 2002 known as indecent assault) of a 15-year-old girl. The difference in the two sentences is jaw dropping, particularly as it could be argued that Rix committed the greater offence, sexual intercourse not having taken place in the case of Johnson.

For the avoidance of doubt, I am clear that the government and its law officers are perfectly entitled to pursue historic sexual offences against elderly and not so elderly people on our behalf. There is no statute of limitations on offences in this country, and no serious public campaign for one. They are also entitled to reflect public opinion, provided they do so accurately, in ensuring that fairly convicted offenders receive substantial jail terms where that is necessary in order to protect the public. The question in terms of sentencing is whether they should reflect public opinion, which is typically anti-offender, or whether they should seek to lead it. The prison system is in crisis and elderly offenders are the fastest growing group inside of it. The plain fact is that prisons are ill equipped to deal with large numbers of elderly prisoners. Prisons are not suitable places to cope with people with mobility problems, poor eyesight or poor hearing. They are not suitable places for people who have suffered strokes, are susceptible to falls, and they are most certainly not the places for sufferers of senile dementia. They are not suitable for those needing palliative end of life care. If as Chief Inspector Peter Clarke says, our young offender establishments are not safe for young people, then our adult prisons are certainly not a safe environment for the old. No government has ever thought to make contingency plans for the outcomes, intended and unintended, of criminal justice policy with respect to historic sexual offending.

It may be that what can only be described as secure old people's homes are the answer as the risk of using open prisons is likely to be too great. The environment can be specifically tailored to the needs of older and infirm people. The Chief Inspector of Prisons has voiced his support for this imaginative approach. A more radical approach would be the imposition of suspended sentences for those elderly historic abusers who admit their guilt, where the risk of reoffending is judged to be low. I have no doubt that some victims of abuse would be unable to see the merits of this proposal and that is understandable given what they have suffered. Nevertheless, I submit that for a victim, an admission of abuse has much more to commend it than a conviction from a contested case where the defendant denies his guilt from the outset and continues to do so in prison.

Under successive governments, the number of children in prison has been systematically reduced, and by 40% in the last decade. Despite the public outcry, the 10-year-old murderers of James Bulger served all their time in secure care, rather than be transferred to a Young Offender Institution when they reached the age of fifteen. This was a compassionate approach that reflected the fact that they were children. There was also the practical point that it prevented them from being torn apart. Although I had considerable reservations about them avoiding prison, I am always mindful of the lynch mob that attempted to storm the transport carrying the boys as it arrived at the Magistrates court for their first appearance. My real point is: if government can run ahead of public opinion in terms of dealing with juvenile offenders, then it can do the same with respect to elderly historic sex offenders.

Custodial sentences are normally expected to serve four purposes: protecting society by removing the offender from circulation, retribution, deterrence and reform, the last of these more typically described as reducing reoffending. Prison is spectacularly bad at reducing reoffending and hopeless as far as sex offenders are concerned, particularly now that the Sex Offender Treatment Programme is discredited. Long sentences for elderly prisoners do take them out of circulation, but they are also in many cases a death sentence, which is wholly unacceptable in a society where capital punishment has been abolished. Under our laws, only the very small number of prisoners convicted of the most heinous murders are supposed to die in prison. This is very little evidence that prison is an effective deterrent. This leaves only retribution and it seems to me that at the moment that is all prison achieves, particularly when dealing with older offenders

Newspapers and MPs pursuing their own agenda do not make it easy for the general public to evaluate the prison system objectively. HMPPS, however, continues to shoot itself in the foot by its lack of transparency. There has always been a culture of secrecy in Whitehall; therefore, the prison service was hardly unique. Until 1989, it would not have been possible to publish this book under the 'catch all' section two of the 1911

Official Secrets Act, without the permission of the Home Office; therefore, potentially committing a criminal offence. Even if permission had been granted, the manuscript would have been so severely censored as to make publication totally pointless. Although criminal sanction is no longer available, the publication of criticism of the service is safe only from the vantage point of retirement and even then according to the staff handbook technically permission is still supposed to be sought. Fortunately, unlike former employees of the EU, the payment of a civil service pension is not tied to a gagging clause. Far higher profile former prison service staff than me have ignored this unenforceable prohibition, but for those still in employment, the Code of Discipline applies and only elected trade union representatives speaking in a strictly trade union capacity enjoy any immunity from the ultimate sanction of dismissal for "bringing the service into disrepute". Even then you should not expect your career to prosper. Banishment to an MOJ equivalent of a Siberian power station is a familiar sanction for prison governors with too much to say about departmental policy.

For those without the protection of elected office in a recognised trade union, there is no protection from draconian sanctions as Lewes prison officer, Kim Lennon, found out. Back in August 2014 in despair at the effect of staffing cuts at her establishment and the failure of management to arrange for the repair or replacement of the security cameras in the visits room. Ms Lennon went public both in her local newspaper and regional television station. The inevitable lengthy suspension followed culminating in dismissal in November 2015. Her appeal was turned down in January 2016. Kim Lennon has been unable to find employment since and any new job is likely to be on a much-reduced salary. The total financial hit she will take in terms of lost pay and pension over the rest of her lifetime is likely to be around £250,000 before inflation. For someone both younger and more senior, the financial penalty will be even more draconian. Whistle-blowers in the NHS in particular have told how the mental stress of being hunted down relentlessly by a vengeful employer determined to enforce the code of silence isolates them, destroying their mental equilibrium and their relationships, as well as taking a wrecking ball to their finances.

In former Officer Lennon's case everything she disclosed was in the public domain apart from the unrepaired security camera. It could be argued that this disclosure was at the very least unwise on the basis that this information would be gold dust to serving prisoners and their criminal associates. However, anyone who believes that the prison population were not fully aware of this security failing is living in cloud cuckoo land. Ms Lennon lost her case at tribunal but despite the adverse ruling, I believe that a public interest defence should apply when exposing a systematic, deliberate and ongoing breach of security in the same way as the NHS has been forced to see disclosures of scandals that have led to patient deaths as being of legitimate public interest. In the NHS it has often proved to be the only way to get meaningful change. HMPPS, however, remains firmly wedded to secrecy and is not opposed to dirty tricks to enforce it.

Without a proper investigation which the Governor of Lewes and his line manager, the Deputy Director of Custody for the region, both blocked, the truth will never be known, but the likelihood is that Kim Lennon was the victim of one of these dirty tricks. During her suspension, Ms Lennon had the misfortune to appear in the local magistrate's course on a charge arising out of an altercation with an influential local landowner and former racehorse trainer over her dog. She was duly acquitted of the charge but during cross-examination by the CPS solicitor, it was put to her that she was suspended from duty pending investigation of an improper relationship between herself and a prisoner. This was simply not true, then or at any point in her career. Nevertheless, it could have influenced the outcome of the trial and I have no doubt that this was the intent as a criminal conviction would have made success at an Employment Tribunal impossible, and crucially would have allowed HMPPS to use the summary dismissal procedure.

The question obviously is how did the CPS solicitor come into possession of this false information. The defendant's antecedents are normally provided to the court by the police. Previous convictions will be available on the Police National Computer, but employment details can only come from the employer. In a prison the obvious conduit is the police liaison officer. Every prison has one, usually an experienced detective constable, for whom it may form a small or large part of his or her work. This officer will routinely speak to the staff in the Security department, but will also come into contact with staff as senior as the Deputy Governor. There is no way of proving it, but the probability is that the unwitting conduit was the police liaison officer, who almost certainly passed it on in good faith, having no reason to disbelieve what he or she had been told, whether or not it came from someone senior or junior in the hierarchy.

However, whoever gave that little snippet to his criminal justice colleague on behalf of the prison, almost certainly did not act in good faith. Attempting to influence a court in this way is an utterly disgraceful breach of professional ethics. There was a clear prima facie case for a gross misconduct investigation, but Ms Lennon's perfectly reasonable demand for a full disciplinary enquiry was rejected by the Governor, who in turn was supported by the Deputy Director of Custody when Ms Lennon appealed. Whether an investigation would have revealed a culprit is another matter but we shall never know because HMPPS covered up, just as it did over the prisoner swap between Wandsworth and Pentonville prisons in 2009 that was exposed by the Inspectorate. It refused to even consider that there might be an email audit trail. Having exhausted the grievance procedure, Kim Lennon had no other internal route open to her and there the matter rested. Sussex police were no more cooperative when rejecting a request under the Freedom of Information Act (FOI).

It remains to be seen whether the impending change in leadership at the top of HM Prisons and Probation Service (HMPPS), as it was renamed in 2017 after thirteen years as the National Offender Management Service (NOMS), will make any difference to the secretive bureaucratic culture that is part of the problem rather than part of the solution. In September 2018, the Permanent Secretary of the MOJ announced that Michael Spurr, Chief Executive of HMPPS would be stepping down in the spring of 2019 as part of a change of direction. Although the Secretary of State has no power to dismiss a senior civil servant, as Michael Howard found out more than two decades previously, it is difficult to believe that the Permanent Secretary did not act without prompting from David Gauke. Michael Spurr will no doubt receive a generous early retirement package, but I doubt it will do much to assuage the feeling that he has been hung out to dry for the repeated failings of government policy since 2013. It was not Michael Spurr's fault that an idiotic and scarcely believable ministerial directive to prevent books being posted into prisoners was ruled to be unlawful in 2014. It was not Michael Spurr's fault that a perfectly sound system of incentives and privileges was wrecked same Secretary of State, Chris Grayling, and duly contributed to the ongoing unrest in prisons. It was not Michael Spurr's fault that the so-called 'rehabilitation revolution' crashed and burned, taking with it whole chunks of the Probation Service as it did so. Ministers wrecked two proud services that once commanded public confidence, not Michael Spurr. His successor will be taking on a poison chalice. Where I take issue with Mr Spurr is not over policy which is a matter for government, but the organisational culture over which he and his two immediate predecessors, Phil Wheatley and Sir Martin Narey, presided, about which I have written at great length in this book.

It is a very sad note on which to end a book. I have been taken to task for lack of idealism, disloyalty and the strength of my language after the first edition of this book was self-published. I stand by every word. Let's deal with the thinly disguised charge of disloyalty first. There are those who honestly believe that as a someone in receipt of an enviable pension should not bite the hand that feeds them. Then there are those who see me as not quite a gentleman, someone who should never have been admitted to the gubernatorial club, someone who should never have been allowed to progress from the corporals' mess. For them I am simply not the right sort of chap. Were I applying for membership of their golf club or their Masonic Lodge, I would be blackballed. I refer these people to Groucho Marx. For others the problem is that despite being a graduate, I refuse to subscribe to the mantras of the liberal metropolitan elite. Again I make no apologies for exposing the contradictions at the heart of post-modernism, and for gleefully pointing out the occasions when the Emperor is clearly naked. This is what my critics really mean by disloyalty. I am happy to be an iconoclast. As a History graduate, one of the lessons I learned from the discipline is that when something becomes the prevailing intellectual orthodoxy, it must be challenged. How can the frontiers of human knowledge be advanced otherwise?

As for idealism, it should be obvious to any reader that I stand firmly in the reforming camp when it comes to treatment of offenders within the criminal justice system. Those whose idealism has been compromised are actually those who have substituted the creed of public managerialism, with its targets, its league tables and its crippling bureaucracy for the leadership that HMPPS sorely needs. It has not got better since I retired. The service has flirted with the dangerous idiocy of 'payment by results', as regards the re-offending rates of individual prisons. No doubt some mathematician somewhere can produce a highly complex system for evaluating which prisons have the best re-offending rates, but the cocktail that produces those statistics will always be volatile, unreliable and flawed, and just like the other major so-called performance measures, it will encourage staff to tell lies and to move difficult prisoners, just as senior managers at Wandsworth and Pentonville were caught doing in 2009 to keep them away from members of the inspectorate. The service seems incapable of initiatives that do not involve increased bureaucracy and actually disempowering in-charge Governors on the ground. A recent initiative to devolve power back to Governors was duly scuppered at Board level by senior civil servants who would have found a comfortable niche in Lilliput. Equally the service appears to have learned nothing as regards its employment practices from the Carol Lingard case as it contemplates the financial and reputational consequences of the Employment Tribunal's judgement in the case of former Woodhill prison officer, Ben Plaistow, in February 2019. The full judgement, available on the internet makes horrifying reading. The new Chief Executive, Dr Jo Farrar, needs to start by dismantling the secretive and defensive culture that has defined HMPPS for so long.

Einstein is reputed to have defined insanity as doing the same thing over and over again and expecting different results. As a scientist, Einstein would also have been familiar with the manipulation of performance data, the manifestation of a phenomenon first observed as long ago as Roman times when Emperor Caligula claimed to have invaded Britain. I make no apologies for occasionally dipping my pen in acid as I cannot and will not disguise my anger at the wilful destruction of a public service in which I was once proud to work.